THE
1867
NEGRO
BASEBALL
1955
LEAGUES

A Photographic History

D   McNAIR · JOSEPH MORRIS O.JOHNSON ROGAN ALLEN   MENPEZ MOORE W.BELL   HAWKINS

THE NEGRO BASEBALL LEAGUES

1867

1955

DUNCAN   C. BELL   MOTHELL   McCALL   DRAKE   SWEATT   WILKINSON   DR. SMITH   SPEDDEN   POMPEZ

A Photographic History

By Phil Dixon with Patrick J. Hannigan

Amereon House
Mattituck

FIRST COLORED WORLD SERIES.
OCT. 11, 1924.   KANSAS CITY, MO.

BOLDEN   SANTOP   WINTERS   CURRIE   LEE   CARR   C. JOHNSON   J. JOHNSON   RYAN

To order contact
Amereon Ltd.
Post Office Box 1200
Mattituck, New York 11952-9500

ISBN 0-8488-0425-2

Manufactured in the United States of America

CKEY ALLEN   CAMPBELL   LEWIS   THOMAS COCKRELL   BRIGGS   WARFIELD STEVENS   LAMBERT

To Kerry, Joseph and Erika
and all of God's children

P. D.

In Memory of Anthony R. Fava
and Michael (Bumpa) Chandler

P. J. H.

Acknowledgements

Four individuals warrant special mention for their unique contributions to this work: Fred Langford, a former member of the Kansas City, Kansas Giants, for his support and recollections of baseball greats from 1907 through 1930; William (Big C) Johnson, a former 24th Infantry member, for his memories of the early years of the Negro National League and the Eastern Colored League; Maurice (Doolittle) Young, a former Kansas City Monarch player for his friendship and encouragement; and John (Buck) O'Neil for his unwavering support of my research.

Special thanks must also go to former Kansas City Monarch Chet Brewer and to baseball researcher David Kemp for their unselfish support and loyalty toward Negro baseball research. I would like also to recognize Newton Allen and Walter Lee (Newt) Joseph whose spirit and abilities were so much admired that my son was named in their honor. My son proudly wears the name Joseph Allen Dixon, and we call him Newt.

Appreciation is also owed the following: Newt Allen and George Giles for information provided on the Kansas City Monarchs; Frank Sykes, college athletes and the Eastern Colored League; Richard Byas and Jack Marshall, Chicago baseball; Roy Partlow, the integration of minor league baseball; David Kemp, baseball in the Upper Midwest and the Northern League; Jay Sanford, the *Denver Post* tournaments; Luis R. Alvelo, professional baseball in Puerto Rico; Lloyd Johnson of the Society for American Baseball Research; Tom Heitz and Pat Kelly of the National Baseball Hall of Fame; Dorsey Moulder and Allen Benson, the House of David; Ted Radcliffe, William Lowe and Lahoma Paige,

Mobile, AL, baseball; Marlin Carter, Rufus Ligon and Alberta Gilmore Penn, the Texas-Oklahoma-Louisiana League; Bob Davids, Mark Rucker and Joe Overfield, nineteenth century baseball; Quincy Trouppe, Normal Webb and James (Cool Papa) Bell, St. Louis and Pittsburgh baseball; Ernest Withers, Verdel Mathis, Bob Boyd and Sam R. Brown, Memphis Red Sox; Kazuo Sayama, Japanese professional leagues; R.L. Posey, college athletics from 1917 through 1928; Jimmie Crutchfield, Pittsburgh Crawfords; Albert Haywood, Cincinnati and Indianapolis Clowns; Chester Blanchard, Dayton Marcos; Julian Bell, Nashville, TN, baseball and college athletics; Maceo Broadnax, Denver baseball; Bob Thurman, Puerto Rican Winter League; Clinton McCord, minor league baseball; Lorenzo Davis, Jim Zapp, Jimmy Britton, Artie Wilson and Rev. William Greason, Birmingham Black Barons; Josh Johnson, Cincinnati Tigers; Robert Bissant and Lloyd Davenport, New Orleans baseball; William Owens, Indianpolis ABC's; Richard E. Jackson, information on George Wilson.

Robert Brasher, Simpson Younger's grandson, provided information from his unfinished manuscript which became the motivation for the nineteenth century research. Mabe Kountze, a former writer for the Associated Negro Press, was helpful, as was his *Fifty Sports Years Along Memory Lane.* Ted Chambers, a former Howard University athletic coach who wrote *The History of Athletics and Physical Education at Howard University,* also deserves thanks.

Several institutions made important contributions and donated many photographs: The Afro-American Museum, Philadelphia; Meharry Medical

College, Nashville; Stearns County Historical Society, St. Cloud, MN; Historical Society of Pennsylvania, Philadelphia; Oberlin College, Oberlin, OH; University of Kansas at Lawrence; Smithsonian Institution, Washington, DC; Mid-America Black Archives, Kansas City, MO; Beinecke Manuscript Library, Yale University, New Haven, CT; Washburn University, Topeka, KS; Michigan Historical Collections, Bentley Historical Library, Lenawee County (MI) Historical Museum.

Several mortuaries were helpful in locating the death records of many former Negro leaguers, including: Thatcher's Funeral Home, Inc., Kansas City, KS; Watkins Brothers Memorial Chapels, Kansas City, MO; T.H. Hayes and Sons, Memphis; and R.S. Lewis and Sons, Memphis.

Wives of a number of players provided information that greatly enhanced this work. I will be forever grateful to Tina Brewer, Clara Bell, Beatrice Joseph Garner, Dorothy Harris, Helen Bankhead, Lydia Williams Edmonds, Georgia Dwight, Dorothy Brown, Gladys Souell, Ora O'Neil, Bertha Wilson, Bernice Duncan, Velma Pinkston, Dorothy Partlow, Elsie Mitchell, Lilla E. Lewis, Nettie Stearnes, Inez Herman, Luvenia Russell, Stella Cooper Bolden, and Lahoma Paige.

Other family members were equally supportive. Several who helped in the research and deserve mention are: Roosevelt Butler, son-in-law of Tobe Smith; Doris Foster, daughter-in-law of Andrew (Rube) Foster; Mamie Pierce, daughter-in-law of Steve Pierce; Harriet Everett and Carolyn Cassio, daughters of Arthur Hardy; the six daughters of Roy Partlow; Minnie Johnston Martin, sister of Wade Johnston; Arthur Taylor, brother of Olan (Jelly) Taylor; Willia Simms, sister of Floyd Kranston; the daughters of Cumberland Posey; Josh Gibson, Jr., son of Josh Gibson and nephew of Jerry Gibson; Francis Hagler, sister of Dan, Fred, Garnett, Joe and Sam Bankhead; Roger Whitworth, son of Richard Whitworth; and Robert L. Williams, son of John Williams.

I would like to thank Joanna Paulsen and Jed Clauss of Amereon Ltd. for believing in this project and for having the patience and faith to see it through; and I would like to thank the Kansas City Royals for giving me the opportunity to work in a major league front office.

I owe my mother, Margaret Dixon, a special thank you for her unwavering support throughout this project. My late father, Arthur Dixon, a longtime Kansas City Monarchs fan (he called "Bullet" Rogan and Frank Duncan "baseball's best battery"), was very proud of this endeavor and provided much inspiration. Also, I will forever be indebted to the late Carroll (Dink) Mothell. This work was conceived with his gift to me of thirteen pictures.

Finally heartfelt thanks to my wife, Kerry. It was her suggestion that I compile a pictorial history. Throughout my years of dedication to this project, she has encouraged me in both a helpful and enthusiastic manner.

I apologize to anyone whose contribution to this work has been overlooked. To everyone who has helped to make this book possible, I thank you from the bottom of my heart. It is my wish that the Lord will continue to bless and keep you.

Phil Dixon
Kansas City, MO
January, 1992

THE
1867

NEGRO

BASEBALL

1955 **LEAGUES**

A Photographic History

Chapter 1

Their game was played under quarantine, far from the madding crowds that embraced professional baseball in mainstream America. Banned by the major leagues because of the color of their skin, these wayward and embittered souls tried to forge their own leagues, playing an exhausting schedule that sometimes included as many as four games in a single day. They were forever on the road, barnstorming from one rock-ridden field to another, all the while earning practically nothing for their efforts. There were Satchel Paige and Josh Gibson and maybe a few others who might have been able to play in the majors, but for the most part the leagues were comprised of players more intent on drawing a laugh than drilling a home run. If it wasn't for Paige, the great pitcher and wildly popular showman, these loosely formed leagues, which were really just a collection of disorganized teams crisscrossing the country, might not have existed at all. As it was, they barely survived, so small were the turnouts for their games.

Such is the folklore that surrounds Negro baseball.

In truth, baseball behind the color barrier provided almost everything that was offered by the major leagues — employment for the athletically gifted and entertainment for their fans. Negro league players were serious-minded baseball men who made the most of a deplorable situation. They didn't wallow in self-pity or anger over the baseball cards they'd been dealt. Their time and energy were devoted to the game they loved, not to the hate that forced their wanton exclusion from the major leagues.

Many of the myths associated with the Negro leagues have been perpetuated by the unavailability of hard historical data. Unlike the major leagues, there are no "Baseball Encyclopedias", no "Book of Baseball Records," no "Baseball Registers" that detail the performances in black baseball. With few exceptions, daily newspapers paid no attention to the activities of black ballplayers. Their exploits were chronicled in weekly black newspapers and magazines, however, and in the last twenty years historians have begun combing the morgues of these publications, searching for an accurate picture of life in the Negro leagues.

The common starting point for any discussion of Negro baseball is usually Satchel Paige. It is unfortunate, but the discussion often ends there, too. There are few baseball players, black or white, as well known as LeRoy Paige. A genuine folk hero, he was blessed with incredible ability and a personality that captivated crowds for more than 40 years. He was 6'3½" tall and weighed only 180 pounds, but he had a whip for a right arm. He walked slow and threw fast, as fast as anyone. Opposing hitters knew they were in for a long day when facing Paige. The fans, meanwhile, knew they could expect an entertaining day at the ballpark with Satchel on the mound.

"They would advertise him all over town when he was coming," said Monte Irvin, a perennial all-star outfielder with the Newark Eagles in the '40s. "People came from miles around to see him. He was the biggest name in the game. He was like Babe Ruth. He had charisma; he had that hesitation pitch, that windmill wind-up, anything to attract the crowd."

Oberlin College's first varsity baseball team, 1881. Top row (L to R): Julian C. Moore, Charles D. Harrison, Welday W. Walker, Merton E. Thompson. Middle row: Moses (Fleet) Walker, Josiah H. Bellows, Willis F. Day, Edward B. Burwell. Bottom row: Charles D. Green, Harlan F. Burket, Arthur T. Packard. "Ubiquitous" was the term used by the college paper to characterize the play of Fleet Walker, who belted a home run, two doubles and a single in the season's opener.

"Once in an exhibition game he called the outfielders all in and told them to sit down in the infield," recounted Ray Dandridge, a teammate of Irvin's who was the finest third baseman of his era. "He had everybody sit down behind him. Then he walked three men, on purpose, mind you. Then he struck out the next three."

And there was the time in the 1934 *Denver Post* tournament, a prestigious semipro event, when Paige, pitching against the Italian Bakery team of Denver, positioned his outfielders just beyond the dirt of the infield — and never let up a hit.

It is the stuff of legends.

Paige, who began his career in 1926 with the Chattanooga Black Lookouts, built his reputation with a crackling fastball, uncanny control and the ability to put on a show. However, as entertaining as it was to see a pitcher wave his outfielders off the

field, or go through a series of wild gyrations before delivering a pitch, it wasn't entirely novel to followers of Negro baseball. Joe Ryan, a sportswriter for the *Sioux City* [Iowa] *Journal*, wrote in 1929 about seeing John Donaldson, fifteen years earlier, walking a couple of men, ordering his outfielders to the sideline, and then striking out the next three batters. As for Satchel's famed hesitation pitch, that wasn't an original, either, having first been thrown by Dick (Cannonball) Redding, a right-hander who began playing fifteen years before Paige debuted professionally.

There is no disputing Satchel's phenomenal talent. Bob Feller, the Cleveland Indians' legendary Hall of Fame pitcher, hooked up with Paige in many barnstorming duels in the '40s. "The prewar Paige was the best pitcher I ever saw," Feller said. Joe DiMaggio was similarly impressed, calling

The Argyle Hotel, Babylon, New York. The site is generally regarded as the birthplace of Negro baseball's first professional team, the Cuban Giants, which was formed from among the waiters who worked at the hotel. Austin Corbin, president of the Long Island Railroad from 1880 to 1896, built the hotel in 1882 as a means to increase train travel. It was named after England's Duke of Argyll, and featured 350 rooms, many with a view of the Great South Bay.

James C. Mathews. Born November 6, 1846, in New Haven, Connecticut, he became captain of the Bachelors Club, an all-black amateur team in Albany, New York. During the summer of 1867, the Bachelors traveled to Philadelphia to play against two other amateur clubs, the Excelsiors and the Pythians, and won both games.

The Penfield Club, Oberlin College's first baseball team, 1867. Standing (L to R): R. Grannis, M.I. Todd, L.B. Platt, Frank Good. Seated: H. Reed, Simpson Younger, Anson Burwell, A.P. Burwell, Frank Stevens. Younger was the left-fielder in 1868. In 1932, in a letter to a teammate, he reminisced about his playing days. "Those days are so indelibly impressed on my mind," Younger wrote, "that it seems but yesterday since we returned from Cleveland, the proud victors, champions of the Western Reserve." Younger died in 1943 at the age of 93.

Satchel "the toughest pitcher I ever faced." Nor can his tremendous impact on the turnstiles be overlooked. For many years, he was the game's top drawing card. However, there was a downside to Paige's pervasive popularity. His stranglehold on the headlines meant that his colleagues, some just as talented, were forced to play in his long shadow.

There were those in the Negro leagues who believed that Satchel might not have even been the best pitcher on his own team when he was with the Kansas City Monarchs. Hilton Smith, a native of Giddings, Texas, was a teammate of Paige's in the 1940s. Apart from entertainment value, Satchel had nothing on Smith, who often worked in relief. "When Hilton Smith came in for Satchel Paige, you couldn't tell the difference," said Roy Campanella, who faced them both as a catcher for the Baltimore Elite Giants in the late '30s and '40s.

Through the years, there were many pitchers who on ability alone were at least the equal of Paige. The *Pittsburgh Courier* conducted a poll of former Negro league players and officials in 1952, asking them to vote for the all-time best player at each position. Paige finished a close second to

Smoky Joe Williams, who pitched from 1897 to 1932 for several teams. Chet Brewer, an outstanding curveball pitcher from the mid-'20s to the late '40s, was once asked to name the two best pitchers he ever saw. "If I had to pick a right-hander, it'd be Rube Currie," Brewer answered. "The left-hander would be John Donaldson."

There were others, too. Wilber (Bullet) Rogan, only 5'7¼", pitched for the Kansas City Monarchs for more than seventeen years, starting in 1920. George Carr, Rogan's catcher early in his career, called him "the greatest pitcher that ever threw a ball. Rogan was a smart pitcher with a wonderful memory. Once he pitched to a batter he never forgot that batter's weaknesses or strong points. And don't think Rogan was nicknamed 'Bullet' for nothing. That guy had a ball that was almost too fast to catch."

Frank Duncan, who also caught Rogan, took extraordinary measures to protect his hands from Wilber's bullets. "I used to buy two three-inch steaks before every game Rogan pitched," Duncan explained. "I would put them in my catcher's mitt and Rogan would pound them into ground beef

Simpson Younger. Above, seated at center, he is flanked by his children. At right, he is with his favorite grandson, Simpson Dotson. On July 2, 1892, the Supreme Court of Missouri ruled against Younger in a case titled Younger vs. Judah, which stemmed from Younger's refusal to be seated in the balcony with other Negro customers at Kansas City's Ninth Street Theater. The court ruled: "Such separation does not necessarily assert or imply inferiority on the part of one or the other. It does no more than work out natural laws and race peculiarities."

Schoharie (Pennsylvania) team, 1886. Mixed clubs such as this one, which featured two nonwhite players, were common during this era.

before the eighth inning."

Willie Foster, a southpaw for the Chicago American Giants, enjoyed a phenomenal career in the '20s and '30s. During one stretch in 1926, Foster won twenty-six straight games and eventually led the American Giants to the World Series championship.

Jose Mendez, Ted Trent, Slim Jones, Frank Wickware, Harry Salmon — there were many who could match Paige on the mound. But it wasn't only the pitchers who were relegated to the background; it was every player in the league, from Josh Gibson to Jud Wilson to Norman (Turkey) Stearnes.

Jocko Conlon, the former major league umpire, saw many of these unsung stars when he was playing semipro baseball in Chicago during the 1920s.

"They had marvelous players, these colored teams," Conlon recounted in his autobiography, *Jocko.* "Oscar Charleston was **THE** great Negro ballplayer then. He would pitch and he'd play first base and center-field. He was a beautiful center-fielder. Josh Gibson played. And a Cuban named [Christobel] Torrienti. What a hitter he was.

"They had Bullet Rogan. And [Oscar] Heavy Johnson, with Kansas City. He was fat, must have weighed 260, and he could hit a ball out of any

park. Oh, they had great ballplayers. [Bingo] DeMoss, the second baseman. They used to drive us crazy. They'd bunt with three men on. DeMoss could drop a bunt on a dime. And [John] Beckwith, a terrific hitter.

"All these colored ballplayers I mention would have been stars in the big leagues today. They would have been stars then if they had been given the chance."

There were occasions, in post-season barnstorming games and in the California and Cuban winter leagues, when these great players were given the chance to test their skills against major leaguers. It has only been in recent years, with the advent of six- and seven-figure salaries, that professional baseball players have not been forced to seek employment during the off-season. Whether they took a job in a factory or with a barnstorming baseball team, players had to find work through the winter months. Those major leaguers who chose to ply their trade year-round frequently found themselves playing against black teams. The results often were revealing.

In 1920, the first year of the Negro National League, the St. Louis Giants and the major league St. Louis Cardinals, managed by Branch Rickey, tangled in a five-game series at the end of their

Unidentified nineteenth century player. Many of the early minority players had learned the game as soldiers during the Civil War. Only two years after the war ended, the first color barrier was raised against nonwhite players.

Bud Fowler (top row, center) in 1885 with Keokuk (Iowa) of the Western League. He was the first black player to cross the minor league color line, pitching three games for Lynn (Massachusetts) of the International Association in 1878. He won one and lost two that season. Fowler played in the minors longer than any other black player during the 1800s. In 1885 the *Rocky Mountain News* reported, "Fowler has two strong points: He is an excellent runner and proof against sunburn. He don't tan worth a cent."

respective seasons. The Giants, led by center-fielder Oscar Charleston, won two of the five games. (Four years later, they filed a $4,208 suit against the Cardinal organization to collect their share of the series' gate.)

The Kansas City Monarchs played two post-season series against minor league teams in 1922, beating Denver of the Western League three out of five games and defeating the Kansas City Blues of the American Association five out of six.

In 1931, Ted (Highpockets) Trent, a right-hander for the St. Louis Stars, faced a team of major league all-stars that included Bill Terry, Paul and Lloyd Waner, Hack Wilson and Babe Herman. In hurling St. Louis to an 8-6 victory, Trent struck out Terry, who'd batted .401 in 1930, and Babe Herman, a .324 career hitter, four times each. In all he struck out sixteen, a major accomplishment in any era.

In a moment of reflection, Satchel Paige once wondered: "How many home runs would Babe Ruth have hit off me or how many more strikeouts would he have had?" The question was rhetorical

but made the point — how would the volumes of major league records have been altered if blacks had been playing alongside whites throughout the history of the game? Would Bill Terry have hit .401 in 1930 if he'd had to face Ted Trent twenty-five or thirty times a year? Would Babe Ruth have slugged sixty home runs in 1927 if he was regularly stepping into the batter's box against Bullet Rogan, Jose Mendez, Willie Foster or even a young Satchel Paige? Maybe Josh Gibson or Mule Suttles, not Roger Maris, would hold the single-season home record. Maybe Pete Rose would have been pursuing the all-time hit records of John Henry Lloyd or Pete Hill, and maybe he wouldn't have caught them.

In 1971 the Baseball Writers Association of America capped a two-year campaign to allow the best of the black players to be inducted into the Hall of Fame. Naturally, Paige was the first. Since then, ten more players have joined him in the hallowed halls of Cooperstown, New York — Josh Gibson (1972), Buck Leonard (1972), Monte Irvin (1973), James (Cool Papa) Bell (1974), William (Judy) Johnson (1975), Oscar Charleston (1976),

John Henry Lloyd (1976), Martin Dihigo (1977), Andrew (Rube) Foster (1980), and Ray Dandridge (1987). There are twenty to thirty more who deserve serious consideration but may never receive it. They were well known within the close confines of Negro baseball, but unlike Satchel Paige, whose acclaim reached both sides of the color barrier, their fame went no further.

In the 1880s, as the major and minor leagues were working diligently to seal all the cracks in the

J.T. Settle. Born September 30, 1850, in the Cumberland Mountains, while his mother and father were en route from North Carolina to Mississippi, he played baseball at Oberlin College in the late 1860s. In *Men of Mark,* a book profiling important contributors to black history, it is written of Settle: "There is not a nobler specimen of manhood in the history of the South than this Southerner." He was nominated by the Republican convention in 1875 for the position of District Attorney of the Twelfth Judicial District of the State of Mississippi.

color barrier, it became apparent that blacks would have to form their own teams if they wanted to pursue a career in baseball. Several of these early clubs, among them the Cuban Giants, combined a degree of showmanship with baseball in an effort to boost their attendance. The Page Fence Giants, a successful team that played in the upper Midwest in the mid-1890s, also relied on "clowning," though usually only against weaker competition. Teams of this ilk, however, faded out quickly.

"The funny man in colored base ball is becoming extinct," wrote Sol White, a former player who in 1907 authored a book titled *Sol White's Official Base Ball Guide.* The book traces the history of blacks in baseball, starting in 1885 with the formation of the Cuban Giants. "Where every man on a team would do a funny stunt during a game back in the eighties and early nineties," White wrote, "now will be found only one or two on a team who essays to amuse the spectators of the present day.

"The majority of colored ball players are now carefully watching the scientific points of the game with a mind to perfect teamwork. Base running, bunting, place hitting and every other department of the game is studied and discussed by the leading colored players which, if continued, will enable them, in the course of a few years, to cope successfully in every particular with the leading teams of the country."

Dave Wyatt, a player-turned-sportswriter, took notice of the trend toward serious baseball in an article he wrote in 1910 for the *Indianapolis Freeman,* a black weekly newspaper that was one of the first to provide extensive baseball coverage. "The class of baseball that the Negro is putting up at this time is very good evidence that he is giving his moral and physical welfare the proper amount of attention," Wyatt wrote. "He has advanced far beyond that brand in which comedy plays the leading part."

In the same issue, Wyatt's words were corroborated by Rube Foster, a great pitcher who later became known as the Father of Negro Baseball for his efforts in pioneering the first successful Negro league. "The people who support the game have advanced far beyond the circus idea in baseball," Foster wrote. "When a team takes the field the fans are there to see baseball, an exhibition of the national pastime, not a farce comedy."

Despite the fact that the curtain closed quickly on the comedy routines, there still exists the perception that Negro baseball was more of a vaudeville act than a serious sporting venture. A share of the blame for that belongs to Satchel Paige, who was renowned for his comical antics on the mound. As the most famous of the black players, his legacy as an entertainer belies the dedication and professionalism that permeated Negro baseball. In fairness to Paige, though, it should be noted that his routines were reserved for non-league exhibition games.

There also were two teams in the late 1930s that

perpetuated the link to comedy. In 1937, when the Italo-Ethiopian War was frequently in the headlines, Charlie Henry, a Kentucky promoter, formed a team called the Zulu Cannibal Giants. In an attempt to authenticate his promotion, Henry had his players put war paint on their faces and wear grass skirts. The "Zulus," who played against semipro teams mostly in the Midwest and South, made a hit at the box office the first few years, but the novelty soon subsided and they folded in the early '40s.

In 1938, Johnny Pierce, the owner of the Miami Giants, attempted to imitate the Zulus' success.

In 1942, both the Negro National League and the Negro American League adopted resolutions that banned their teams from playing against the Ethiopian Clowns. "The painting of faces by the Clowns' players, their antics on the diamond and their style of play [are] a detriment to Negro League baseball," said Tom Wilson, the president of the Negro National League. Others in the league's hierarchy referred to them as "a disgrace to Negro baseball." Only the Kansas City Monarchs of the Negro American League refused to honor the resolution.

When the leagues started to do big business

The Buffalo Bisons, 1887. Frank Grant (bottom row, second from right) led the team in hitting with eight home runs and a .366 average. Paul Stanley of the *Indianapolis Freeman* wrote, "In their day, Clarence Williams and Frank Grant were about the best batters I have ever seen."

Changing the team's name to the Ethiopian Clowns, Pierce passed on the grass skirts but did have his players paint their faces. They wore brightly colored uniforms with a large clown emblazoned on the front of their flannel shirts. It was this team (whose players went by names like Nalahari, Selassie, Wahoo and Tarzan) that may have been most responsible for the close, but unwarranted, association of comedy and black baseball.

during World War II, Syd Pollock, who had purchased the Clowns following Pierce's death, sought entry into the Negro American League. The petition was granted on the stipulation that the Clowns abandon the war paint and silly antics on the field, along with the Ethiopian connection. Pollock complied and moved his team to Cincinnati, renaming them the Cincinnati Clowns. They rented Crosley Field, home of the Reds, and though they retained a couple of nonroster comedians to entertain the crowds, they began playing serious baseball. During the '50s, as the popularity of the Negro leagues waned in the wake of integration, Pollock, who by then had moved the team to Indianapolis, again 'returned to clowning. In the early 1970s, long after the final league had folded, the Indianapolis Clowns continued to tour, providing the last, albeit misleading, vestige of the great black baseball teams.

One of the popular misconceptions about Negro league players is that they performed in virtual seclusion. "It's too bad nobody saw them play," goes the refrain. It simply isn't true. From league games to the countless exhibitions they played, both here and abroad, there were fans flocking to see the "unknown" stars of the game.

In 1943, 51,723 fans packed Chicago's Comiskey Park for the East-West All-Star Game, an annual event that brought together the best players in the Negro leagues. Starting with the inaugural game in 1933, fans increasingly had been swarming to Comiskey Park, usually in August, to see some of the all-time greats. This wasn't just a game; this was a star-studded, glamorous event. Between 1938 and 1948, the East-West Game outdrew the major league All-Star Game on seven occasions.

Nobody saw them play?

As far back as 1925, the Chicago American Giants drew more than 200,000 to their home games at Schorling Park. The Kansas City Monarchs played before 315,000 in 1943. In 1946, the first year of minor league integration, 120,000 saw the Newark Eagles at Ruppert Stadium. Hundreds of thousands more saw these teams when they were playing

away from home, both in league games and barnstorming affairs. Four-team doubleheaders generated tremendous fan support. Crowds of 30,000 or more could be expected for a pair of games at Yankee Stadium or Wrigley Field involving, say, the Homestead Grays, the Pittsburgh Crawfords, the Kansas City Monarchs and the Newark Eagles.

They played in an era when almost every town had a semipro team it felt was worth boasting about. When there wasn't a league game on the schedule, black teams often could be found answering a challenge in some small city or town, playing before a citizenry that likely had never seen a genuine professional club. Often the entire business community closed down for the day to come out and see their local heroes take on the pros. (It should be noted that there was a clear-cut distinction between semipros and professionals. Professional teams were comprised of players who were full-time employees and paid as such, while semipro clubs were made up of players who may have received some compensation but were not reliant on baseball as their primary source of income.)

Robert Higgins (lower left). As the ace of the Syracuse Stars of the International League in the late 1880s, Higgins became embroiled in controversy when two teammates refused to pose with him for the team photograph.

"People only got to see the major leaguers in the big cities," Satchel Paige once commented. "I believe people got a chance to see me everywhere. I played all over, farm fields, penitentiaries, any place in this whole country where there was a baseball diamond they know me and see me."

Paige, of course, wasn't playing alone. Any veteran player could have uttered the same remarks. And it wasn't only in this country where they were seen and known. Beginning in the early 1900s, black players began migrating to Cuba to

The Cuban Giants, 1887-88. Standing (L to R): George Parago, Ben Holmes, Shep Trusty, Arthur Thomas, Clarence Williams, Frank Miller. Seated: Billy Whyte, George Williams, Abe Harrison, manager S.K. Govern, Ben Boyd, Jack Fry, Allen (first name unknown). Wrote Sol White: "Their games attracted the attention of baseball writers all over the country, and the Cuban Giants were heralded everywhere as marvels of the baseball world."

play winter league baseball. Later, they followed the sun to Puerto Rico, Mexico and Venezuela, acquiring new fans at every stop. They may not have been popular with those who limited their baseball scope to the major and minor leagues, but to say that "nobody saw them play" is to belittle the millions who did.

From the time the color barrier was established in the late 1880s and 1890s until 1920, Negro baseball consisted mostly of independent teams playing somewhat haphazard schedules. There were some local leagues, but all attempts to organize on a national basis met with failure. That changed in 1920, when Andrew (Rube) Foster, the founder of the Chicago American Giants, realized a long-held ambition and helped form what became the first successful black baseball league. It was called the Negro National League and chartered franchises from the larger cities of the Midwest. Three years later it was joined by the Eastern Colored League, which fielded teams in New York, Atlantic City, Philadelphia and Baltimore.

The Eastern League disbanded in 1928, while the Negro National League persisted until 1931,

when it fell victim to the Great Depression. It was revived a year later but was composed mainly of Eastern teams. In 1937, it was joined by the Negro American League, whose teams were located in the Midwest and South. These two leagues continued in tandem through 1948, enjoying their most prosperous period during and just after World War II.

As the names imply, the Negro leagues were patterned after the major leagues. They weren't nearly as regimented as the majors and were plagued at times by uneven scheduling and contract jumping, especially in the early years. However, they also weren't as chaotic as they sometimes have been portrayed. Beginning in 1925 they played a splitseason, with the first-half winner meeting the second-half winner for the pennant. Like the majors they played an annual all-star game midway through the season, and, in the good years, they capped the year with the pennant winners meeting in the World Series.

There were many differences between the two ventures, one of them being that Negro league teams always relied heavily on nonleague games for income. If the Kansas City Monarchs were making the long jump to Birmingham for a series

The Bristol Base Ball Club (circa 1880). Standing (L to R): Eugene Wall, Joseph Brown, Charles Davis, Isaac Washington, Manager; Halsey Bradford, John Hunt. Middle row, seated: John Crump, Theodore Smith, James Sims, William Barker. Front row: James Davis, Stephen Tuno, Shadrach Elliot. During this era games between town teams were played only after a formal challenge was issued.

Ann Arbor (Michigan) North Side team was one of many integrated town teams that appeared throughout the nation in the 1890s.

Adrian, Michigan Light Guard team, 1894. Standing in business suit is team manager Gus Parsons. Seated, front row left, is George Wilson. A phenomenal left-handed pitcher, Wilson was 18 when this photograph was taken. The August 8, 1903 issue of the *St. Cloud Times* said of Wilson: "Rube Waddell has struck out 240 men in thirty games. Bill Donovan is second with 122 in twenty games pitched. Wilson of St. Cloud would have Rube skinned in every department, if given a chance." The *St. Paul Pioneer Press* echoed these thoughts in 1905, declaring, "Wilson is undoubtedly one of the best slab artists in the business and but for his race would now be shining in one of the big leagues."

against the Black Barons, they would stop and play six or seven exhibition games along the course of the seven hundred mile journey. These games were played on a percentage basis (P.C. ball, it was called), with the winner usually collecting 60 percent of the gate to the loser's 40, though the stakes could go as high as 100-0.

These barnstorming games have given the players a reputation for being baseball's waifs, men who roamed the countryside in search of a game. In truth, these games were booked during the winter, when both league and exhibition schedules were carefully arranged. Any team that didn't operate in this manner could be reasonably assured of a long and unrewarding summer.

As for the leagues themselves, there were different levels of competition, the highest being the Negro National and Negro American Leagues. The

players, in fact, referred to them as the Negro major leagues. For a young player, they were the ultimate goal, and not many started at the top. Within the framework of Negro baseball, there existed a loosely structured minor league network that fed players to the majors. The Negro Southern League, which supplied hundreds of players through the years. was the most important of the lesser leagues.

The Syracuse Stars, 1888. Standing (L to R): Moses (Fleet) Walker, Silent Dundon, Zip McQuery, Fred Ely, Will Higgins. Middle row: Ollie Beard, Con Murphy, Ratsy Wright, manager George Hacket, Jack Batin, Lefty Marr. Front row: Robert Higgins, Tip Shellbase. Walker's presence on the team helped Higgins, because many white catchers refused to go behind the plate for a black pitcher.

The Page Fence Giants of Adrian, Michigan. They were formed in 1895 and operated through the 1898 season. In 1897 the Giants were reported to have won 82 consecutive games. (L to R) Walker (first name unknown), Charlie Grant, George Wilson, John W. Patterson, Pete Burns, Augustus (Gus) Parsons, Unknown, Grant (Home Run) Johnson, Unknown, Billy Holland, Unknown.

There were also the Texas League and the Texas-Oklahoma-Louisiana League, as well as independent teams like the Gilkerson Union Giants and the Muskogee Hustlers which traveled throughout the Midwest.

John (Buck) O'Neil, a first baseman who also managed the Kansas City Monarchs, spent time in the minors before landing his first big league job. "Our ball would be just like your major league ball," O'Neil explained. "When they go to the major leagues they know how to play 'cause they played minor league ball. So my minor league ball was playing with the Miami Giants, the Zulu Giants, the New York Tigers. This is where you learn — it's like minor league ball."

Like the white major leagues, competition for a roster spot was intense, maybe even more so in the top Negro leagues. Whereas big league teams carried twenty-five players each, the more cost-conscious Negro league clubs were limited to anywhere from fourteen to seventeen players. The small rosters served to create versatile players who could perform at virtually any position. Utility men like Wade Johnston, Hurley McNair, Sam Bankhead, Carroll (Dink) Mothell and others weren't viewed as second-stringers, but, rather, as highly valued contributors. Also, the pitching staffs, commensurate with the sizes of the teams, were comprised of as few as three or four players. As a result, pitchers were expected to finish what they started, no matter how badly they may have been getting battered. And when they weren't on the mound, they were expected to be able to play in the field — and hit, too. Several, such as Bullet Rogan, Bill Lindsay and John Donaldson, were nearly as renowned for their bats as their arms.

"We would stop when Rogan got ready to hit in

batting practice," Buck O'Neil remembered. "It was beautiful the way he'd hit the ball. He'd say: 'I'm gonna hit this one to right, I'm gonna hit this one to center, I'm gonna hit this one to left.' And you could throw the ball any way you want to throw it, cause he's gonna hit the ball the way he says he's gonna hit it. Yeah, he could really hit."

They were lean operations, the Negro league clubs. One serious problem that threatened to destroy them early on was contract jumping. Though there was an agreement among the teams and leagues that forbade tampering with contracted players, it was routinely ignored in the '20s and early '30s. Chet Brewer's story of leaving the Philadelphia Stars illustrates one way a player might engineer a move to another team. Brewer had been fined $100 for an altercation he'd had with an umpire. Unwilling to ante up, he went to team owner Ed Bolden's house and banged on his door, demanding his release so that he could join the Kansas City Monarchs. When Bolden balked,

Brewer tried another approach.

"Bolden told his housekeeper, 'Don't let him in,'" Brewer recounted. "I just pushed on in the door and said, 'Mr. Bolden, if you don't come down here and write me out a release, I'm gonna beat you up till nobody will ever recognize you. Before you can call the police, I'll have you so beat up that you won't even know your own name.'"

Bolden had a change of heart, and Brewer moved on to the Monarchs.

Eventually, the leagues enacted penalties for jumpers that brought the problem under control. In later years, the threat of player raids came not from other teams in the leagues, but from the Mexican League, which relied heavily on black Americans when it started in the '30s.

During the decades of segregated baseball, one of several arguments put forth to justify the ban was that the black players probably weren't good enough anyway. After all, how good could they be,

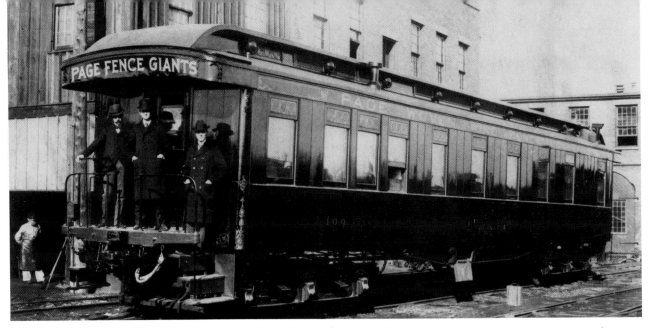

given the fact that their leagues were at best the equivalent of the white low minor leagues? Those in the major leagues who played against them surely knew that wasn't the case, and any serious doubt about the quality of play in the leagues should have been dispelled the first few years after integration. Six of the first seven National League rookies of the year were players who'd been plucked from the Negro leagues. How bad could the Negro leagues have been if they were producing players like Jackie Robinson, Don Newcombe, Sam Jethroe, Willie Mays, Joe Black and Junior Gilliam? Not bad at all.

The Page Fence Giants were right at home as they toured the Midwest in this specially designed private Pullman car during the mid-1890s. According to Sol White, who played during that era and later wrote a book on Negro baseball, "The Giants were formidable opponents to any team. They were hard to beat in '95, as their pitchers were among the best and their fielding excellent."

Much has been made over the years of the miserable conditions with which Negro league players had to contend — the long bus rides, the inhuman accommodations, the exhausting schedule that forced them to play three and four games in a day, the horrible fields, the negligible pay, etc. Add to that the bitterness they surely must have felt over being barred from the major leagues, and a dismal picture of life in black baseball emerges. It is a picture out of focus.

Until the mid-1920s, when bus travel was first introduced, black teams traveled almost exclusively by train, the same mode of transportation used by major league clubs. Some were forced to ride in the black-only Jim Crow cars, though others, such as the Page Fence Giants, the Chicago American Giants and the Kansas City Monarchs, avoided those restrictions by renting or buying their own railroad cars. If they were playing only a short distance from home, large automobiles called "touring cars" were rented.

Once it was determined that buses would provide a more economical and flexible mode of transportation, the players' comfort took a backseat to the owners' opportunity to cut costs and increase revenues. Bus travel enabled teams to expand their schedules beyond the railroad lines to areas previously considered unreachable. Still more games were added to the schedule after the Kansas City Monarchs introduced night baseball in the early '30s. With sunset no longer a factor, teams could play in the afternoon, bus to the next stop and squeeze in another game under the lights.

What should be understood about the rigorous travel and demanding schedule is that both were routinely accepted as being a part of the job. There's no question that many an uncomfortable hour was endured on those buses, but there was also a sense of pride that accompanied the players on their journeys. To board a bus that had "Kansas City Monarchs" or "Newark Eagles" printed in bold lettering on both sides meant they had made it; they'd gone as far as their ability could take them.

There was a degree of drudgery, but the long rides also gave players the chance to discuss upcoming or previous games, catch up on sleep or merely enjoy some of life's simple pleasures.

"We had our good times," recalled Larry Doby, who played for the Newark Eagles in the '40s before breaking the American League color line. "The Negro league players were dedicated athletes playing a game they loved. There was laughter and songs in the bus, new people, fans in every town."

Ray Dandridge, who also played for Newark,

agreed. "We had fun," Dandridge said, "riding the buses, hanging our sweatshirts out the window to dry for the next day's games, singing — we used to have quartets."

Once they got off the bus, some encounters with Jim Crow — the legal, if unethical, system of discrimination against blacks — were inevitable. There wasn't a team that didn't at some point get turned away from a hotel or restaurant. However, that sort of cruel confrontation was easier to avoid than one might presume. Well-organized teams like the Kansas City Monarchs and the Homestead Grays booked their games well in advance, and, as the years wore on, they learned where all the welcome mats were.

Former Monarch Buck O'Neil explains.

"When we played in St. Joseph [Missouri], we'd

The Page Fence Giants, 1896. Top row (L to R): George Taylor, George Wilson, Grant (Home Run) Johnson, Walker (first name unknown). Center row: Billy Holland, manager Augustus S. (Gus) Parsons, Pete Burns. Front row: Fred Van Dyke, Jess Binga, Charlie Grant, Vasco Graham. Home Run Johnson said there were two important qualities a hitter should have, "confidence and fearlessness." Dave Wyatt wrote in the *Chicago Defender*, "With the possible exception of Walter Johnson and Grover Cleveland Alexander, old leaguers will tell you that they never gazed upon a more perfect pitching machine than [George] Wilson."

Fleet Walker. Walker was deeply upset by the treatment he received during his playing days. In 1908 he wrote a book entitled *Our Home Colony*. In it he stated that the Negro, as conditions stood, could never become "a full man or a fit citizen of this Republic."

eat here, in Kansas City. We never stayed in St. Joe. If we played in Topeka, we wouldn't stay in Topeka, we'd go on to Wichita. What happened is we knew all of the places around the country where we could eat.

"Everything was arranged. Our schedule was made so that we would know all of these things — where we were gonna eat, where we were gonna stay — before we got to our destination. It wasn't a case where we were just out there.

"Tom Baird [the team's booking agent] would book all these games in the winter months. [Owner J.L.] Wilkinson then would give the information to [Quincy] Gilmore, the team secretary, who would take care of the arrangements. We always had a private secretary. So actually it was well-organized, much more so than a lot of people would think."

Even in the small towns of the Deep South, according to O'Neil, a good meal and decent lodging weren't that hard to come by.

"Very seldom we had to go to the back door and get the food," said O'Neil, a veteran of more than twenty years in Negro baseball. "We played in places where restaurants didn't want us, but we would play a night game, and it would be ten or

The Moose Jaw team, 1895. Based in Saskatchewan, Canada, this team won the territorial championship. Standing (L to R): Ed Baxter (team secretary), Mr. Tedlock (right-fielder), George Tuxford (left-fielder), Joe Hyland (center-fielder), Bob Franks (right-fielder), W.J. Nelson (manager). Middle row: Bill Simington (shortstop), Bill Lawrence (third baseman), Walter Scott (second baseman), Billy Woods (first baseman). Front row: Bob McCartney (pitcher), Walter Simington (catcher).

Bain (Canada) team, 1898. Top row (L to R): W. Blacklock, William Galloway, H. Barlow. Middle: D. Tipton, C. Culross, Jas. Davis, W. Davis (mascot), Fred Eltom, W. Saunders. Bottom: C. Kickbush, J. Pickard, W. Cristall. In 1899, Galloway, a native of Canada whose nickname was "Hippo," became the last of the nonwhite players to appear in the minor leagues when he played in twenty games for the Woodstock team of the Canadian League.

eleven o'clock before the ball game's over and the restaurant would be closed. So the man would fix a special dinner for us; instead of going in the back door, we would go in the restaurant, but we wouldn't go there when the business was there. And this would happen in Louisiana even. In the cities — Baton Rouge, New Orleans — there were always good places to eat and sleep. When we played the smaller towns a lot of times we would stay at people's houses. But this was arranged beforehand; we didn't go there trying to find a place to stay."

On the occasions when arrangements went awry and players were denied entrance to a restaurant or hotel, they weren't without recourse. Chet Brewer recalled such a situation when he was with the Monarchs in the '20s.

"We were up in Montana and they wouldn't let us eat in the restaurant," Brewer remembered. "They had placards all over that the Monarchs were "World Champions," and they had sold a whole bunch of tickets. We told Wilkinson [who was

white] they wouldn't feed us in the restaurant, and Wilkie told them, 'I'll tell you one thing — you people may as well start getting your money back 'cause we're not playing.' "

The Monarchs enjoyed their meal, and the restaurant owner, according to Brewer, enjoyed "the biggest crowd he ever had in his restaurant, coming to get autographs from us."

As for the fields on which they toiled, there were plenty of the dust bowl variety, but those were usually encountered during barnstorming affairs in small cities and towns. Otherwise, field conditions were far from unplayable. Many teams rented major or minor league parks for their home games and made their schedules according to when their white counterparts were out of town. The Pittsburgh Crawfords and Nashville Elite Giants, built their own stadiums.

Another erroneous notion about life in the Negro leagues is that it was financially unrewarding. While it's true that, with the exception of a few superstars such as Satchel Paige, Josh Gibson and

John W. Patterson (back row, third from right). He played for Plattsmouth (Nebraska) in 1892 as one of eight nonwhite players in the Nebraska State League. Well known in professional baseball circles, Patterson played with the Philadelphia Giants (1903), the Cuban X Giants (1904) and the Quaker Giants of New York (1905), before retiring in 1907. In April of 1909 he became the first minority police officer in Battle Creek, Michigan. He died in 1940 after being injured while capturing an escapee from a local Veterans Administration facility.

Buck Leonard, the players never made as much money as the white major leagues, it's also true that they were better paid than their contemporaries in the black community. That explains in part why careers of twenty years or more were not unusual. There weren't many jobs in the Negro major leagues, perhaps two hundred at most, and a player talented enough to land one wasn't in a rush to relinquish it. However, it wasn't only the money; there was also the prestige. As professional athletes possessing rare abilities, they were admired and respected members of the community.

Judy Johnson, a third baseman in the 1920s and 1930s, once complained that he "hit .392 one year and the man gave me a $10 raise." But he also once wrote, "We played for something greater, that could not be measured in dollars and cents. The secrets of our game were to enjoy and endure."

They made a living playing a game they loved. For most, that was enough to ward off any bitterness over their fate. They were well aware that the color line placed severe limits on their fame and fortune, but they also recognized that segregation extended far beyond major league baseball.

"The big leagues were so far away then that you never even thought about it," said Buck Leonard, the all-star first baseman for the Homestead Grays.

"I didn't think about major league baseball," said James (Cool Papa) Bell, who was so fast it was said he could turn out the lights and be in bed asleep before the room got dark. "It wasn't just baseball then; it was everywhere. I don't feel regrets. That's how it was when I was born. I had to live in that time."

Monte Irvin had a similar outlook. "When I first signed with the Newark Eagles in 1937," Irvin remembered, "there was no talk of playing in the big leagues. Everything was segregated. You just played because you loved baseball. I was signed out of Orange [New Jersey] High School for $150 a month. I thought it was a pretty good deal to be paid anything at all for something I would do for free."

Irvin was fortunate in that by the luck of the calendar he was still young enough when integration came to enjoy a career in the majors. There were many whose careers were winding down when Jackie Robinson broke the major league color barrier in 1947. Yet when they discuss their fate, their words are mostly without acrimony.

"When I was young, all I wanted to do was play," said Cool Papa Bell, who began his career in 1922 and was still playing when Robinson broke into the minor leagues in 1946. "And, thank the Lord, I got the chance to play for half my life, even if it wasn't in the majors. When the doors were opened I was too far over the hill."

"There's nothing greater for a human being than to get his body to react to all the things one does on a ballfield," Buck O'Neil said. "Waste no tears for me. I didn't come along too early; I was right on time."

"When you're doing something you love to do, there's nothing lousy about it," said Jimmie Crutchfield, who retired in 1945 after more than 15 years in the leagues. "I thought [playing professional baseball] was the first step in going to the top of the world."

The story of Negro baseball is one of determination and devotion. It is about strong-willed and dedicated men who refused to accept the preposterous notion that they were unfit to share in the joys of our national pastime. They were ballplayers, first and foremost, who forged a glorious history in an inglorious era. Every man who labored behind the color barrier, from the 1800s to the 1940s, ultimately had a hand in bringing it down.

Joe Greene, a catcher with the Monarchs, put it like this: "They say Jackie Robinson paved the way. He didn't pave the way. We did."

Chapter 2

Sol White earnestly endeavored to chronicle the plight of the early black players in his *Official Base Ball Guide*, which was published in 1907. It is a small book, measuring only 5¾ by 3½ inches, and throughout its 128 pages, photographs and advertisements are liberally displayed along with the text. The book begins with the birth of the first salaried nonwhite team in 1885 in Babylon, Long Island. It was founded by a man named Frank P. Thompson, the headwaiter at the Argyle Hotel in Babylon, who chose his players from among the waiters at the summer resort. Whether carrying the plate or swinging at the plate was more important to Thompson isn't clear, but the Athletics, as they were known that first year, did compile a record of six wins, two losses and one tie against local competition.

The *South Side Signal*, a weekly newspaper in Babylon, reported on the team's exploits throughout the summer. In its August 22 issue, the following story appeared: "A spirited game of baseball was played on the Argyle grounds on Tuesday. The contestants being the National Club of Farmingdale and the Athletics of Babylon, composed of employees at the Argyle. The latter club proved the victors — the score standing 29 to 1 in favor of the Athletics."

Thompson, encouraged by his team's success, scheduled several games when the Argyle, a playground for New York City's rich and famous, closed in September. After a string of impressive victories, the team found a financial backer in Walter Cook, whom White describes only as "a capitalist" from Trenton, New Jersey. Cook renamed the team the Cuban Giants, and paid his players according to the position they played — $18 per week for pitchers and catchers, $15 for infielders and $12 for outfielders. The Cuban Giants, the first in a long line of barnstorming Negro teams, took to the road, playing games against major and minor leaguers, as well as the finest amateur teams, colleges included.

White's book follows the tortuous road of the Giants and other nonwhite teams and players for the next two decades. It is an important and valuable account, but it ignores the play and contributions of some earlier pioneers. To follow the complete orbit of blacks in baseball is to journey back to the period just before the Civil War.

Depending on which theory you ascribe, the game of baseball was either invented by Abner Doubleday in 1839 in Cooperstown, New York, or by Alexander J. Cartwright, a surveyor and amateur athlete who staged the first game in Hoboken, New Jersey, on June 19, 1846. According to *The Baseball Encyclopedia*, Cartwright's game marks "the only acceptable date of baseball's beginning."

Exactly when blacks became involved in the game isn't known, but it has been documented that about six months before the Confederates fired on Fort Sumter in Charleston, South Carolina, on April 12, 1861, two black teams squared off against one another on a diamond in Brooklyn. According to baseball historian Harry Simmons, a game was played on September 28, 1860 "between former slaves living in Brooklyn. One team was the Unknown Club of Weeksville, the other the Union

Club of Williamsburg. The Unknowns won, 11-0."
As proof that the game was played between blacks,
Simmons offered a letter written by a member of
the Unions to a newspaper, advising the editor that
the team's real name was the "colored Union Club.
We do not want to be confused with a white Union
club of the same name."

From 1861 to 1865 the country's focus was
riveted to the battlefield. Some baseball was played
among the troops, but it wasn't until the summer of
1865, with the war ended, that the game began to
intensify its grip on the country. It was then that the
seeds were planted for what would become a lush
history for Negro baseball.

Two amateur baseball clubs, the Moniter Club of
Jamaica (Queens) and the Bachelor's Club of
Albany, New York, were organized that summer.
Within the next few years other teams began to
assemble. There was the Blue Sky Club of Camden,
New Jersey; the Excelsiors and the Pythians of
Philadelphia; the Monrovia Club of Harrisburg,
Pennsylvania; the Hannibals of Baltimore; the

Tecumsehs of Alexandria, Virginia; and the Mutuals
and Alerts of Washington, D.C. (The Mutuals
featured Charles and Fred Douglass, sons of
Frederick Douglass, a former slave who became
the first nationally known black leader.) In the
Midwest, the Uniques formed in Chicago and the
Rialtos in Detroit. The Rialtos often traveled to
London, Ontario, to play Canada's first nonwhite
club, the Goodwills. Most of these teams were
comprised of former soldiers who had learned the
game at army camps during the war.

Shortly after the Excelsiors of Philadelphia were
organized in 1866, local competition arose from a
team called the Pythian Baseball Club, which was
sponsored by Jacob C. White and Major Octavius V.
Catto, teachers at the Institute for Colored Youth. In
1867 the Excelsiors and the Pythians invited the
Bachelors of Albany to Philadelphia to match skills
on the field. James C. Matthews, captain of the
Bachelors, accepted and brought his team 260
miles to the City of Brotherly Love. The Bachelors,
who paid their own expenses, "swamped both the
Excelsiors and the Pythians in a merciless way,"

The original Kansas City Monarchs, 1908. (L to R): William Houston, Bert Wakefield, Tully McAdoo, West Wilkins, Bill Lindsay, Thomas McCampbell, Arthur Pullam, Frank Evans, Tom Stearman, Ernest McCampbell, Fred Lee, R. (Frog) Lindsay. The Lindsay brothers were coal miners from Lexington, Missouri, before turning to baseball. In 1909 Bill Lindsay struck out sixteen in a game against the powerful Leland Giants. McAdoo, who was just beginning a long career in baseball, developed into one of the game's premier first baseman, starring for Charlie Mills' St. Louis Giants.

according to a newspaper account.

For the local community in Philadelphia, the games not only were athletic competitions, but social events, as well. As historian William Carl Bolivar recalled, "The women were interested and lent value by numbers and general attractiveness both at the games and in social features. There were picnics, dances and lunches showered upon the players, and the visitors' stay covered more than a week." When the Mutuals and the Alerts, both of Washington, D.C., visited the Philadelphia teams in 1867, the Pythians spent $26 on amenities for the Alerts and $58 for the Mutuals. The money went toward ham, chicken, ice cream, cake, cigars and beer for the post-game picnic.

During this era prospective games usually were initiated by a formal challenge. In 1867 the Mutual Baseball Club sought to engage the Pythians in a contest. A letter, written by the team's secretary, was sent to the Philadelphia club, stating, "The Mutual Base Ball Club of Washington, D.C., has instructed me to address you a friendly note, congratulatory of the high position you, as an organization, have attained in our National game, and to request that I will enter our Club as a friendly competitor for its honors." The Pythians, friendly competitors that they were, accepted the challenge and traveled to the nation's capital, where they beat both the Mutuals and Alerts.

The Pythians finished the 1867 season with a record of nine victories and one loss. In an effort to improve on that mark, the demanding Catto, who was also the manager, held pre-season practices and brought in two new players, John Cannon and George Brown. The result was a 7-0 record in 1868. Cannon, according to a *Philadelphia Tribune* story, was "considered by the whites a baseball wonder." Brown was referred to as "a pitcher, the best amateur of his day, a strong scientific batter and a fielder of much cleverness."

After their undefeated season, the Pythian Club received notice that several white baseball clubs were meeting in Harrisburg, Pennsylvania, in December, to organize a new league. Team member Raymond J. Burr was dispatched to make his pitch for the Pythians. Burr submitted his team's

The Jenkins Sons team of Kansas City (Missouri), 1907. Standing (L to R): West Wilkins, Thomas McCampbell, William Houston, Bill Lindsay, Frank Evans. Kneeling: Ernest McCampbell, (unknown), Roy Dorsey, Thomas Stearman. Seated: Arthur Pullam, Tully McAdoo. The Jenkins Sons, who were backed by a local music store, met the Kansas City Blues of the American Association in 1907 and lost, 16-2. Though they were overmatched, the *Kansas City Times* gave Tom Stearman a glowing, but stereotypical, report: "The left-fielder of the Jenkins team certainly made himself solid with the bleachers. He ate up everything that landed anywhere in the vicinity of his chicken yard. He gobbled up long, high fly balls and gathered in hard beeline raps with one hand while running at full speed. Each time the player came in the bleacherites [cheered]. He tipped his cap each time and wore a watermelon grin."

35

The Darkies Too Swift

The Topeka giants, the colored aggregation of ball players, were here Monday to show our boys a few new tricks in the art of base ball playing. At the start of the game it looked as though it would be close and interesting, no scores being made in either of these innings but in the third the fireworks started and it was a chase around the diamond one after the other, until the finish. At the close of the sixth inning the score was seven and seven but in the next the dark complected boys did some hard batting and piled up five more scores. Our boys got only one more man over the rubber during the balance of the game, the colored fellows making another score in the ninth, the game finished 13 to 8. It seemed as though the colored fellows had their rabbit foot with them and Neal, Relihan nor Mathes could keep them from pasting the ball on the nozzle whenever it came over the plate. The largest crowd turned out to see this game that has been at a ball game here for some time, the receipts amounting to $139 of which the giants got 60 per cent. Score by innings.

```
                1 2 3 4 5 6 7 8 9
Topeka giants...0 0 3 3 1 0 5 0 1—13
Smith Centre....0 0 2 0 3 2 0 1 0— 8
```

(Left) Clipping from the *Smith Centre* [Kansas] *County Newspaper,* July 25, 1907. The white press used various racist names to describe black baseball teams.

(Right) Rube Foster. As the Father of the Negro leagues, he became the most powerful and influential man in the game. In 1909, Foster wrote, "Three years ago, when I brought the now Leland Giants to Chicago, Mr. Frank C. Leland then owned the club. He made me a proposition to come to Chicago and manage the Lelands. Finally, I consented to come. I released his entire club and brought my team all from the East. How well we have succeeded is history."

(Below) The Philadelphia Giants, 1904. Standing (L to R): Grant Johnson, Rube Foster, Emmett Bowman, Walter Schlichter, Sol White, Pete Booker, Charlie Grant. Seated: Dan McClellan, Pete Hill, Tom Washington, Mike Moore, William Monroe. Behind the pitching of Foster and McClellan and the hitting of Pete Hill, they finished the season with a record of 81 wins 43 losses and 2 ties. The following year their record improved to 134-21-3.

Tobe Smith. He was the owner of the Kansas City (Kansas) Giants, the first professional Negro team in Kansas City. After the great season of 1909, when his team won 54 consecutive games, his manager, Topeka Jack Johnson, moved to Kansas City, Missouri, and organized the Royal Giants. Several other members of the team joined the newly formed Oklahoma Monarchs.

application, despite warnings that the delegates would not approve a nonwhite team. The credentials committee ignored Burr's request but was reminded by E. Hick Hayhurst of the Philadelphia Athletics that the Pythians' application had not been submitted to a vote. The issue was tabled until the evening when more delegates would be in attendance.

At the night session it was decided that the Pythians would not be allowed to join the league, that organized baseball should be composed of white teams only. According to Burr, "All expressed sympathy for our club." While no representatives stated personal opposition to the Pythians' application, only the Philadelphia Athletics supported it. The remaining delegates claimed that they were not expressing their own feelings, but those of their team members.

Members of the Pythian Club telegraphed a message to Burr, telling him to "fight if there was a chance." However, the Pythian representative was

The Philadelphia Giants, 1905. Top row (L to R): H. Smith, Mike Moore, Emmett Bowman, Sol White, Tom Washington, Dan McClellan. Middle row: Grant (Home Run) Johnson, Charlie Grant, Walter Schlichter, Andrew (Rube) Foster, Pete Hill. Front row: William Monroe, Pete Booker. Walter Johnson of the Washington Senators once received $600 to pitch for a black team against the all-black Lincoln Giants. He took along his catcher, Gabby Street. According to Johnson, "Gabby was from Huntsville, Alabama, and didn't like the idea of playing colored baseball, but the $300 he got was too much to overlook. I'll never forget the first hitter I faced. They called him 'Home Run' Johnson, an outfielder. Up at the plate he says, 'Come on, and throw that fast one in here and I'll knock it over the fence.' And that's just what he did, too."

The Jenkins Sons team, 1906. Standing (L to R): Unknown, Unknown, West Wilkins, Gertha Page, William Houston, Unknown. Middle row: Roy Dorsey, Thomas Stearman, Unknown, Unknown. Front row: Ernest McCampbell, Arthur (Chick) Pullam, Thomas McCampbell. On March 13, 1933, a man named William Wright walked into the office of Dr. Thomas McCampbell, then a druggist on Vine Street in Kansas City, and robbed the cash register. Armed with a pistol, he fired several shots as he was leaving, killing McCampbell. The amount in the register was $1.78. Wright was caught and became the first man in Missouri to be hanged for murdering a black man.

advised by his lone supporter, Hayhurst, that it would be better "for us to withdraw than to have it on record that we were blackballed." Burr withdrew the application, and baseball's initial color barrier was erected.

The Pythians continued their excellent work in 1869, compiling another undefeated record. Teams from as far away as Chicago ventured to Philadelphia to test the Pythians. Though none were successful, the Pythians' reign as champions of black baseball would prove to be short-lived. Philadelphia, like the rest of the country, was in the throes of a volatile era, as if confronted the new

freedoms that had been granted blacks. The Fifteenth Amendment, which prohibited voting discrimination, was ratified in 1870, a development that angered many whites. While there had been no violence that year on election day, chiefly because a company of marines had been summoned to keep order, the following year the City of Brotherly Love turned into a war zone on October 10. Blacks and whites battled in the streets and by election day's end three blacks were killed and many more of both races were injured. Octavius Catto, 31, the Pythians' leader who was also a force in the civil rights movement, was among the dead,

Action at a Cuban Giants-Boston Red Sox game, 1905. As reported in the text, there was little that was Cuban about the Cuban Giants. According to a *Philadelphia Tribune* story in 1912, "The people of Cuba sent up an awful howl and protested to the Spanish Minister at Washington, D.C., to use his best efforts to stop the club from using Cuba's good name to fool the American public."

having been shot by a white man he'd argued with as he was leaving the Institute for Colored Youth. The Pythians, devoid of leadership, soon disbanded.

While the Pythians were building a strong reputation in the East, a young man named Simpson C. Younger was etching his name in baseball history in the Midwest. Younger was born into slavery on May 17, 1850, in Jackson County, Missouri. His mother was a twenty-year-old mulatto slave named Elizabeth, who had two light-skinned children by a wealthy white landowner named Charles Younger. In 1852 Charles Younger, who was the grandfather of "the Younger Brothers," a band of Midwestern outlaws, recorded a will with the state of Missouri that mentioned the two children born to his slave. In the will, which called for all of his other slaves to be sold off, Younger bequeathed a farm to Elizabeth and declared that their children, Simpson and Catherine, should be freed. The will stated:

An unidentified Cuban Giant infielder reaches for a ground ball, 1905.

Sampson, shown here warming up, was an outstanding pitcher for the Cuban Giants. In his *Base Ball Guide* Sol White said that both Sampson and Best, pitchers for the Cuban Giants, were considered to be two of the top hurlers.

Salt Lake City Occidental team, 1909. Occidental was the only nonwhite team in the semipro Utah League and featured shortstop Sam Hawkins, the league's only .400 hitter. Standing at center, in suit, is heavyweight boxing champion Jack Johnson. According to the *Indianapolis Freeman*, Johnson, before his July 4, 1910 fight with Jim Jeffries in Reno, Nevada, told a group of blacks in Oakland, California: "I want to advise every one of you to bet on me, but not to bet on the duration of the fight. Don't bother about the number of rounds; just get your money down that I will bring home the bacon and then sit back and wait until the time comes to cash in." Of the fight, which ended in the fifteenth round, novelist Jack London wrote, "As he lay across the lower rope while the seconds were tolled off, a cry that had in it tears and abject broken pride went up from many of the spectators. 'Don't let the Negro knock him out!' was the repeated cry. There is little more to be said. Jeff did not come back."

"It is my will and desire that the slaves Catherine and Simpson in addition to their freedom absolutely at my death, it is my will and desire, that my executor herein after named shall as soon as convenient after my death take said Catherine and Simpson to a free state and place them in a respectable school."

Thus, shortly after Charles' death in November of 1854 the two children were separated from their mother and taken by a guardian to Oberlin, Ohio. According to a letter written to Oberlin College on November 21, 1907, by Mrs. Elisha Gray, an acquaintance of Simpson and Catherine's, the Younger children "were test cases in the education of Negroes as whites and with whites." The Youngers attended white schools and had "no associations with Negroes."

In 1864, at age fourteen, Simpson Younger joined the 27th Colored Infantry. Overall, there were more than 186,000 black soldiers in the Union Army, according to Thomas Sowell's *Ethnic America*. Twenty-one blacks received the Congressional Medal of Honor during the Civil War. Private Younger was discharged on September 21, 1865, at Smithville, South Carolina, and returned to Oberlin to continue his education, first in the preparatory school and then at the college.

Oberlin College's first baseball team, which was called the Penfield Club, was started in 1867. Simpson Younger was a left-fielder on that team, making him, if not the first, then certainly one of the first of his color to play college baseball.

The Cuban Giants, 1905. Top row (L to R): Brown, Williams (outfielder), J.M. Bright (manager), R. Best (pitcher), William Galloway (second baseman). Middle row: Kelly (outfielder), F. Watkins (first baseman), Gordon (third baseman), Rawlins (outfielder), Satterfield (shortstop). Front row: Lyons (pitcher), Sampson (pitcher), Bradley (catcher). Galloway, a native of Canada, was also a highly regarded hockey player in the Ontario Hockey Association in 1899.

According to Younger, in a letter written to the school in 1932, "that club was made up mostly of upperclassmen, who played the game for exercise, not caring much for the glory of conquest." Simpson sought to change that.

The following year, in the words of Younger, "us ambitious boys, seeking other worlds to conquer, were not satisfied to play for exercise alone and finally organized what we named the Resolute Club, resolved that we would be known outside of the baseball diamond, on the college square at that time. I was selected as pitcher of the club and was in that position in all the games played by the club till I left in 1870."

According to Oberlin College records, the Resolutes played their first game on July 21, 1868, defeating the Occidentals of Cleveland, 43-13. They were awarded a rosewood bat with the players' names engraved on it and a silver ball with an inscription that read: "Championship Western Reserve won by Resolute B.B. Club 1868." During

Simpson Younger's stay at Oberlin, thirteen games were recorded, with the Resolutes winning ten and losing three, all to the Forest City Club, a professional team in Cleveland. In 1871, the Forest City Club became a member of the National Association of Professional Baseball Players, the first league of its kind.

Oberlin also was given a silver bat for a game it won in Sandusky, Ohio, on September 11, 1868. The Resolutes again had their names engraved on the trophy. The players listed were A.S. Burwell, H. Reed, S.B. Platt, F. Stevens, S. Younger, F.A. Good, A.P. Burwell, G.H. Grannis and J.T. Settle.

J.T. Settle's full name was Josiah Thomas Settle. Known as Joe, he was born September 30, 1850, in Tennessee and was also a child of mixed ancestry. His father, Josiah, was a slave owner in Rockingham, North Carolina. His mother, Nancy, "belonged" to his father and together they raised a family. After moving to Mississippi, he freed his children and their mother. The State of Mississippi, however,

The Cuban X Giants. They were the first black team to visit Cuba. While there in 1900 the Giants played eighteen games, winning fifteen and losing three. They made a return visit in 1903, and the improved Cubans won nine of eleven games. Dan McClellan (seated, second from right), while with the Philadelphia Giants, pitched a perfect game July 17, 1903 in York, Pennsylvania, one of the earliest known "perfectos" by a nonwhite.

Charlie Grant. In the early 1900s, Grant, along with John Henry Lloyd and Frank Grant, was one of the most colorful and sure-handed fielders in baseball.

forbade free Negroes from residing there, so in March of 1856 Settle moved his family to Hamilton, Ohio, where he spent summers with them and the remainder of the year on his Mississippi plantation.

In 1866, Joe Settle entered the preparatory school at Oberlin. He enrolled at Oberlin College in 1868 and joined Simpson Younger on the baseball team, though it is uncertain how many games he played with the Resolutes. Settle left Oberlin after his freshman year and moved to Washington, D.C., where he enrolled as a sophomore at Howard University. He was graduated from Howard in 1872 and subsequently enrolled in the Howard Law School. He was admitted to the bar in Mississippi in 1875 and began a long and distinguished career both as a lawyer and a politician.

In 1909, Settle, then an officer for the Solvent Savings Bank in Memphis, Tennessee, sent his old friend Simpson Younger a letter in which he reminisced about their days at Oberlin. "I shall never forget those dear old days at Oberlin," Settle wrote, "when the old Resolute base ball club was in its glory and you and I were the only ones of the 'brethren' on it. Life was young with both of us then; we had not tasted any of its bitterness and disappointments."

Four hundred miles east of Oberlin, in Cooperstown, New York, of all places, a boy named John W. Jackson was learning to play the game that would take him to almost every corner of the United States. Jackson, the son of John and Mary Lansing Jackson, was born on March 16, 1858, in Fort Plain, New York. By 1860 the family had moved to Cooperstown, where they remained at least until 1870. At some point, for reasons unknown, the young Jackson began calling himself John Fowler. He would later be nicknamed Bud, the name he used to address most everyone else.

Bud Fowler's niche in baseball history was carved near Boston in 1878, two years after the National Baseball League was founded. At the time Fowler was a pitcher for a team in Chelsea. The Lynn (Massachusetts) Live Oaks of the International Association, baseball's first minor league, were in need of a replacement for their pitcher, who was ailing, and acquired Fowler from Chelsea to fill the void. According to a *Boston Globe* report on May 18, "Fowler, the young colored pitcher of the Chelseas," shut down the Tecumsehs of London, Ontario, holding them to two hits until the eighth inning when the Canadians objected to an umpire's ruling and left the field in protest. When Bud Fowler walked to the mound that day, it marked the first time a black man had participated in a professional baseball game.

Charlie Grant. In 1933, a story in the *Chicago Defender* told of Grant's versatility. "No one can deny Mathewson the right to fame as the first big-timer to toss the 'fadeaway,' nor will anyone deny old Doc White the honor that goes with originating the knuckleball. Any oldtimer will argue until doomsday that Charlie Grant was the guy who threw the first screwball. Grant served as a pitcher for about two years before he became a recognized 'big league' infielder. Had Grant cared to continue pitching he would have been one of the game's greatest. No batter could successfully solve the twisting motions of the screwball in that day."

John Henry Lloyd in Cuba, early 1900s. According to a report in the *Indianapolis Freeman*, the Cubans learned a lot from visiting black players. "The Cubans are very clever ball players when it comes down to squeeze playing," an article stated. "And who learned them all they know? Take it from me — the American Negro. I will also tell you why it is so hard for the big league teams to defeat these Cuban Clubs. Simply because a majority of their teams consist, in a greater part, of American Negro star ball players such as Lloyd and [catcher Bruce] Petway."

In breaking the minor league color line in 1878, Fowler didn't have it any easier than Jackie Robinson did sixty-eight years later. In 1881, Fowler signed to pitch for the otherwise all-white Maple Leafs of Guelph, Ontario. His teammates, upon hearing that they'd be sharing the field with a man of color, threatened the owner with a "him-or-us" ultimatum; Fowler was promptly released. The *Guelph Herald* was sympathetic: "We regret that some members of the Maple Leafs are ill-natured enough to object to the colored pitcher Fowler. He is one of the best pitchers on the continent of America and it would be greatly to the interest of the Maple Leaf team if he were reinstated. He has forgotten more about baseball than the present team ever knew and he could teach them many points in the game."

Rev. Andrew Foster, father of Rube and Willie Foster. He was presiding elder of the United Methodist Church in southern Texas.

It seems the teams in Canada, like those who rejected the Pythians in Harrisburg, Pennsylvania, twenty-three years earlier, were less interested in promoting the game than they were in promoting their own prejudices.

After leaving Guelph, Fowler continued his odyssey through the minor leagues. In 1884 he signed with Stillwater (Minnesota) of the Northwestern League. His team lost their first sixteen games, but won their next four, all with Fowler on the mound. He stayed with Stillwater until the team disbanded in August.

The year before Fowler signed with Stillwater, the pennant in the Northwestern League (a minor league) was won by the Toledo Blue Stockings. The catcher for the Blue Stockings was a former Oberlin College student named Moses Fleetwood Walker. Fleet Walker was born October 7, 1857, in Mt. Pleasant, Ohio. His father, Moses W. Walker, a physician, moved the family to Steubenville, Ohio, where three years later another son, Welday, was born. At age twenty, Fleet began taking a preparatory course at Oberlin College, and in 1879, nine years after Simpson Younger had finished his education at Oberlin, Walker enrolled as a full-time student. It's not known what had become of the Resolutes, the school's original baseball club, but in 1881 Oberlin formed its first varsity team. Fleet was the catcher and his brother Welday was the right-fielder.

Fleet Walker left Oberlin the following year and enrolled at the University of Michigan, where he earned varsity baseball letters in 1882 and 1883. After leaving Ann Arbor he signed with the Blue Stockings, batting .251 in sixty games. In 1884 Toledo dropped out of the Northwestern League and joined the American Association, which had been formed three years earlier. By 1884 the American Association had bullied its way to major league status, which until then had been the private domain of the National League. The upstart league undercut the senior circuit's prices (from fifty to twenty-five cents) and scheduled Sunday games, which was taboo in the National League. Player raids by both leagues became a constant threat. After the '83 season, A.G. Mills, the National League president, worked out a national agreement with the American Association that afforded both leagues protection for player contracts.

Fleet Walker remained with the Blue Stockings in 1884, and thus became the first black player in the major leagues. The second black to grace the big leagues was Welday Walker, who was rushed into service when several of the Blue Stockings were injured. After the 1884 season, the Toledo team, beset by financial problems, folded. Fleet Walker played forty-two games in the major leagues, batting .263 in 152 appearances at the plate, while brother Welday, in six games, was

The Kansas City (Kansas) Giants, 1909. Standing (L to R) Wilbur (Ashes) Jackson, Arthur Hardy, Felix Payne, Topeka Jack Johnson, Tobe Smith, Unknown, Unknown. Seated: Dee Williams, Unknown, William Tenny, Unknown, Worthy Smith, Unknown, Unknown, Unknown, Robert (Ginney) Robinson. On August 20, 1921, in Topeka, Kansas, Sam Langford, "the Boston Tar Baby", met Topeka Jack Johnson, who also fought professionally, in a boxing exhibition. As Langford entered the ring, someone asked if he wanted some lemonade. The fighter smiled and said, "Thanks, but I've got some corn whiskey." The duo battled to a six-round draw.

credited with four hits in eighteen at-bats. Until 1947, that would remain the sum total of the Negro experience in the majors — forty-eight games, 170 at-bats.

The mid-1880s was a period in which several minority players dotted the rosters of otherwise all-white minor league teams. Jack Frye, an out-fielder, played for Reading (Pennsylvania) of the Interstate Association in 1883 and for Lewiston (Pennsylvania) of the Pennsylvania State Association in 1886. Another player to cross the color line was George Washington Stovey, a left-handed pitcher who signed with the Eastern League's Jersey City team in 1886. Stovey's earned run average with Jersey City was a slim 1.13, but he evidently did not receive much support from his teammates; his won-loss record was only 16-15. On August 28 his blazing fastball accounted for fifteen strikeouts in a two-hit victory over Newark (New Jersey), and in an exhibition game against Bridgeport (Connecticut), he fanned twenty-two. Small wonder that the following year he was signed by Newark of the two-year-old International League, which was one of the top minor circuits. There he was joined by Fleet Walker, who had played with Cleveland of the Western League and Waterbury (Connecticut) of the Eastern League in 1885 and 1886. Stovey won thirty-four games for Newark in 1887, an International League record that still stands today.

Another player who broke into the minor leagues in 1886 was Frank Grant, who debuted with Meriden (Connecticut) of the Eastern League. Born in Pittsfield, Massachusetts, in 1867, he was a sure-fielding second baseman who swung a power-ful bat and was one of the best players of the era. Standing 5' 7½" and weighing 155 pounds, Grant never batted below .313 in a six-year minor league career. His first team, Meriden, folded in midseason, and Grant was immediately signed by the Buffalo Bisons of the International League. In his Buffalo debut on July 14, he was installed as the cleanup hitter and belted a triple that helped the Bisons post an 8-3 victory. He went on to play forty-nine games for Buffalo, batting .344, third best in the league. The next year, Grant led the league in home runs with eleven and stole forty bases.

After Buffalo played an exhibition game in Boston in 1887, the *Boston Post* noted, "Grant, the sensational colored second baseman, attracted a large attendance and was enthusiastically greeted. He fielded and batted finely and showed himself to be a first-class ballplayer."

Jackson, who signed with Oswego (New York); and William Renfro, a pitcher who joined Bud Fowler, by then a nine-year veteran, at Binghamton (New York). Elsewhere, in the Ohio State League, Sol White was starting out as a third baseman with Wheeling; Welday Walker hooked on with Akron and Richard Johnson signed with Zanesville.

Higgins, Jackson and Renfro had first come to prominence in the Southern League of Colored Base Ballists, a loosely assembled circuit which was formed in 1886 and holds the distinction of being the first Negro league. It featured teams representing Memphis, Tennessee; Jacksonville, Florida; Savannah, Georgia; Atlanta, Georgia;

The Leland Giants, 1909. Standing (L to R): Pete Hill, Andrew Payne, Pete Booker, Walter Ball, Pat Dougherty, Bill Gatewood, Andrew (Rube) Foster. Seated: Danger Talbert, Mike Moore, Frank C. Leland, Bobby Winston, Sam Strothers, Nate Harris. During the 1908 Cuban Winter League season, Winston led the league in at-bats (177) and stolen bases (33). Teammate Pete Hill paced the league in runs scored (53), hits (60) and triples (five), and batted .343. Both Winston and Hill appeared in 45 games for the league champion Havana team.

Sol White, who made his professional debut in 1887, was especially impressed with Grant's ability, both in the field and at the plate. White wrote of Grant: "In those days he was a baseball marvel. His playing was a revelation to his teammates, as well as the spectators. In hitting he ranked with the best and his fielding bordered on the impossible. Grant was a born ball player."

Others who managed to land spots on International League rosters in 1887 were Bob Higgins, a pitcher for the Syracuse Stars; Randolph (Andy)

Charleston, South Carolina; and New Orleans, Louisiana. The *Memphis Appeal*, which credited the Eclipse Club of Memphis with winning the championship, reported on June 24 that Renfro, its star pitcher, "has won every game he pitched but one, averaging twelve strikeouts a game for nine games. In his game against Chattanooga he struck out the first nine men who came to bat. He has great speed."

While 1887 could be considered a good year for the minority players, with at least twelve playing

Mr. and Mrs. Mack Richardson
request your presence at the marriage
of their daughter
Sarah Watts
to
Mr. Andrew Foster
Thursday evening, October the twenty-ninth
nineteen hundred and eight
at eight o'clock
214 South 8th Street   Temple, Texas

Andrew (Rube) Foster took a break from baseball in 1908, just long enough to get married to his sweetheart, Sarah, in Temple, Texas. Two months later he was off to Cuba, playing for Havana in the Cuban Winter League. He led the circuit with eight victories and nine complete games.

Rube Foster. "Many of the [independent] white teams in the East and West tried to get [Foster] to play with them and they offered him a good salary," said Dave Malarcher, who played under Foster in the 1920s. "Foster told them he refused because it was his duty to stay with Negro baseball and to keep it developing to a high point so that when the time came to go into the major leagues we would be ready."

Main Street, Calvert, Texas. From the dirt roads of this small Texas town came a baseball legend, Rube Foster.

The Hilldale Athletic Club, circa 1915. Located in Darby, Pennsylvania, the team's motto was "Clean Baseball." Edward Bolden owned and operated the club, which played in its own park at 9th and Cedar Streets.

in the minors, it was also a year in which antiblack sentiment rose to such echelons as to nullify all gains. The story of Bob Higgins provides an ugly illustration.

Higgins, the Syracuse Stars' pitcher, hurled his first International League game on May 25 in Toronto, losing 28-8. The *Toronto World*, in its account, accused the Stars of throwing the game to make Higgins look bad. Twenty-one of Toronto's twenty-eight runs were unearned, and according to the story Syracuse "distinguished itself by a most disgusting exhibition. Marr, Bittman, and Beard seemed to want the Toronto team to knock Higgins out of the box, and time and again they fielded so badly that the home team was enabled to secure many hits after the side should have been retired. In several instances these players carried out their plans in the most glaring manner. Fumbles and muffs of easy fly balls were frequent occurrences, but Higgins retained control of his temper and smiled at every move of the clique." Though the

Syracuse manager, Joe Simmons, fined the Stars' catcher $50 and suspended him for his blatant errors, Higgins' troubles were far from finished.

A week later the Stars were scheduled to have their team picture taken. Photography was still somewhat of a novelty in 1887, and a formal atmosphere existed around any picture-taking session. Two of the Syracuse Stars, Henry Simon and Doug Crothers, refused to pose with Higgins. A furor erupted, and the recalcitrant Crothers was suspended after punching Joe Simmons, his manager. Crothers offered this explanation for being camera shy: "I don't know as people in the North can appreciate my feelings on the subject. I am a Southerner by birth, and I tell you I would have my heart cut out before I would consent to have my picture in the group. My father would have kicked me out of the house had I allowed my picture to be taken in that group."

Somehow, Higgins managed to block out the hatred and finish the season with a 20-7 record,

The Minneapolis Keystones, circa 1910. They were owned by Col. Edward F. (Kidd) Mitchell and were among many independent teams that played in the upper Midwest. Their rivals were the powerful St. Paul Gophers, to whom they lost city championships in 1908 and 1909. The Keystones played their home games at Nicollett Park.

The Brooklyn Royal Giants, 1905. The team was owned by John W. Connors, shown here in suit. Connors also operated the Royal Cafe and Palm Garden which was located at 176 Myrtle Avenue in Brooklyn. He was said to have been swindled out of the Royals' ownership by Nat Strong, a powerful East Coast booking agent. Connors returned to baseball in 1919, starting the Bacharach Giants of Atlantic City, New Jersey. The Giants, with a wardrobe of five different colored uniforms and designs, were undoubtedly baseball's best dressed team.

St. Cloud (Minnesota) team, 1903. This semipro club was led by right-handed pitcher George Wilson (bottom row, second from right). In his only season of minor league play, as a member of Adrian of the Michigan State League in 1895, Wilson, then age nineteen, led the circuit with a 29-4 record, with 280 strikeouts in 298 innings. While with the Page Fence Giants in 1896, he threw a no-hitter against a team from Defiance, Ohio.

second-best winning percentage in the league.

William Renfro, like Higgins, also was victimized more by his teammates than the opposition. On June 2, 1887, Renfro lost, 7-6, to the Syracuse Stars, and the Binghamton *Daily Leader* indicated that the Binghamton players were not putting forth their best effort. "The Bings did not support Renfro yesterday, and many think the shabby work was intentional," said the *Leader*. Evidently, the turmoil continued — a month later Renfro and teammate Bud Fowler were released.

Frank Grant had his share of problems during his two and one-half year stay with Buffalo. In 1886, he, too, had been involved in a flap over a team picture, with the Bisons balking at his presence in the photograph. The next year Grant faced a torrent of abuse in Toronto, where, according to a newspaper report, crowds screamed, "Kill the nigger,"

when he stepped on the field.

The nonwhite players were not only attacked verbally, but physically, too. Grant became such a frequent target at second base that he was said to be responsible for two innovations in the game: the feetfirst slide and shinguards. Until the mid-1880's, the conventional method of sliding was to go into the base headfirst. With Grant covering second, many white players, hell-bent on inflicting injury, began sliding feetfirst in hopes of sinking their spikes into Grant's legs. After suffering numerous cuts and bruises, Grant began wrapping his shins with wood. The ever-industrious base runners, though, started sharpening their spikes and often were able to split the shinguards.

Newark's George Stovey became embroiled in a controversy in 1887, when he was scheduled to pitch an exhibition game against the Chicago

White Stockings of the National League. The White Stockings were led by Adrian (Cap) Anson, arguably the game's best player and certainly the most well known. He started with Chicago in 1876, and by the time he retired as a player in 1897, he'd had a cigar and a candy bar named after him. He also was an avowed proponent of the color line. When he learned that the White Stockings would be facing Stovey, Anson, who was also the manager, threatened to pull his team off the field. Newark's management, fearful of losing a large gate, refused to call Anson's bluff. Stovey suddenly succumbed to a mysterious illness, the game went on and, because of Anson's resolve, the segregationists had an important feather in their cap.

That incident wasn't the first time Anson tried to infuse the game with his racist attitude. In 1883 he had made a similar demand when the White Stockings scheduled an exhibition against Toledo, which had Fleet Walker on the roster. On that occasion, however, the Toledo team refused to accede to Anson's ultimatum, and the game was played — with Walker behind the plate.

Shortly after the incident in Newark, the International League, responding to the growing sentiment against blacks, held a meeting of team representatives in Buffalo. The *Newark Daily Journal* reported the significance of the meeting under the headline: *The Color Line Drawn in Baseball.* The story said, "The International League directors held a secret meeting at the Genesee House yesterday, and the question of colored players was freely discussed. Several representatives declared that many of the best players in the league are anxious to leave on account of the colored element, and the board finally directed Secretary White to approve of no more contracts with colored men."

Those players already in the league would be allowed to remain with their teams, but it was clear that the "whites only" sign, so prominent in all other areas of American society, soon would be hung throughout organized baseball.

Frank Grant remained with Buffalo in 1888, leading the team in batting with a .346 average. His superb work at the plate, however, wasn't enough to get his teammates to join him in front of the camera; they again balked at posing with him for the team picture. Undoubtedly he was the Bisons' best player, and he sought to capitalize on that in

Tobe Smith and family. Smith was responsible for bringing Negro professional baseball to Kansas in 1906. As the owner of the Kansas City Giants, he operated the only pro team to play in Kansas. He booked such teams as the Leland Giants, the Buxton (Iowa) Wonders, the New Orleans Eagles, the Minneapolis Keystones, the San Antonio Black Broncos and the St. Louis Giants.

1889, refusing to play unless he was paid $250 a month. His teammates threatened rebellion if the team capitulated, so Grant bade farewell to Buffalo and played the rest of the season with the Cuban Giants, who were based in Trenton (New Jersey) as members of the Middle States League. In 1890, he played for Harrisburg, a mixed team in the Eastern Interstate League, and the following year returned to the Cuban Giants, who had joined the Connecticut State League and Atlantic Association, playing in Ansonia (Connecticut). That League folded in midsummer, sending the Giants back to the barnstorming trail.

Also traveling with the Cuban Giants that summer was George Stovey who had been released from Newark despite winning thirty-four games in 1887. He played briefly for Worcester of the New England League in 1888, for Trenton of the Middle States League in 1889 and for Troy of the New York State League in 1890, before joining the Cubans.

Of all the early black players, none was as well traveled as Bud Fowler, whose roots were in Cooperstown, but whose career branched out across the entire country. The scrappy second baseman, who'd played with Topeka in 1886, was with Binghamton in 1887. As mentioned, the team gave less than their best effort when William Renfro was on the mound. Naturally, Fowler had his share of problems, too. On one occasion, several teammates refused to play unless he was dropped from the team. Although the rebels were fined $50 apiece, Fowler, who was hitting at a .350 clip after thirty-four games, was released shortly thereafter, possibly at his own request. The July 5 *Rochester Democrat and Chronicle* reported that, "Fowler . . . has been released upon condition that he will not sign with any other international club." The fact that such a condition was a part of the release indicates that racial tensions on the team may have heightened to the point that Fowler asked to be let go.

After a brief stay with a team in Montpelier, Vermont, Fowler went to Indiana for the 1888 season, playing with Crawfordsville and Terre Haute in the Central Interstate League. When that league folded in July, Fowler continued west to the territory of New Mexico, playing for Santa Fe in the New Mexico League. Following his stint with Santa Fe, he traveled with another team through the Southwest. On November 24 it was noted in a California newspaper that Fowler was playing in San Bernardino, California. In 1889, he was off to

Michigan for a tour of duty with Greenville of the Michigan State League.

While he was with Greenville, the *Grand Rapids Democrat* offered these insights into Barnstorming Bud:

"Fowler, the colored second baseman of the Greenvilles, is a tricky player. When at the bat he turns his head occasionally and catches the sign made by the catcher to the pitcher and lays his plans accordingly. [The catcher] discovered the act yesterday and fooled him several times. It is said he has played in nearly every state in the Union, coming here from Texas. He has a peculiarity or, perhaps a superstition, about striking at the first ball over the plate and always strikes at it whether over the plate or over his head."

In 1890, Fowler played first for Galesburg (Illinois) of the Central Interstate League, then, when that team disbanded, he went on to Sterling (Illinois) of the Illinois-Iowa League. He later returned to the revived Galesburg club and finished the season with Burlington (Indiana) After a four-hit game against Dubuque on July 28, the Dubuque *Daily Times* had this to say about Fowler: "And how some of them ran the bases, especially that man Fowler. Just think, five stolen bases . . . in one game. If he had only been painted white, he would be playing with the best of them."

Fowler played with an independent team in Findlay, Ohio, in 1891, but was back in the minors the next year, signing with Lincoln of the Nebraska State League. He achieved a measure of notoriety during a game against Grand Island (Nebraska) on May 29. A Grand Island player named Joe Rourke was on first base when a ground ball was hit to Fowler at second base. Instead of stepping on second, Fowler, perhaps responding to some earlier rough treatment, "pounded both fists and the ball into Rourke and knocked the wind out of him," according to the Grand Island *Independent*. "Rourke's temper took flight and then it looked like a coroner's inquest would follow. It was a disgusting exhibition all around. Both men are equally to blame."

The Nebraska State League folded in July, and Fowler hooked up with a touring team. He was back with the independent team in Findlay in 1893-94 before closing out his minor league career with Lansing of the Michigan State League in 1895. Fowler would continue playing for several more years, but almost exclusively for the all-black teams that were beginning to proliferate.

Royal Poinciana Winter League Club (circa 1904). Standing (L to R): Dan McClellan, Unknown, Rube Foster, Unknown, Mike Moore, Grant Johnson. Bottom row: Pete Hill, Bill Monroe, Sol White, Unknown, Charlie Grant. In 1934 Bill Yancey wrote of McClellan: "In 1923 I joined the Philadelphia Giants as a second baseman under Danny McClellan. I admired McClellan, as all ball players do, for his frankness and squareness with every ball player. No ball player has ever had an unfavorable word to say about Danny."

Bob Higgins, the strong-armed pitcher of the Syracuse Stars, was back with his team for the 1888 season, but the steady diet of racial ridicule was beginning to take its toll. Higgins, complaining of homesickness, threatened to surrender his $200 a month salary and return to his barbershop in Memphis. According to Robert Peterson's *Only the Ball was White,* which cited a report in the *Sporting News,* Higgins was fined $100 for "failing to appear on time for a road trip, but finished the season." Another version of the story, this one recounted in 1910 by David Wyatt, renowned sportswriter for the *Indianapolis Freeman,* a weekly black newspaper, said Higgins actually left the team in midseason. According to Wyatt: "Syracuse was well out in front for the pennant, when Higgins jumped the Syracuse Club. The management offered every kind of inducement for Higgins' return, but he refused, and the only excuse he gave for not staying with the club was that he was homesick."

Wyatt attached special significance to Higgins' "illness." "That case of homesickness," Wyatt wrote,

"cost every colored player his job in the International League at the close of the season in 1888."

Wyatt was definitely wrong on one point: there was one black player remaining in the International League in 1889. Fleet Walker had signed with Syracuse in 1888 and returned in 1889, his final season in baseball. He caught seventy-six games in 1888, but no doubt was embittered by another incident with the hateful Cap Anson. The Stars hosted an exhibition against the Chicago White Stockings on September 27. Since the episode with George Stovey in Newark, Anson's practice of keeping the field free of "darkeys" and "coons," terms he used freely, had become accepted. Walker, Syracuse's number one catcher, was not permitted to play against the (Lily) White Stockings.

In the games he was allowed to play that year he batted .170. Most catchers in that era were not known for their prowess at the plate, and Walker was no exception. Players did not wear gloves at that time, so injuries, especially to catchers, were frequent. It must have been difficult to swing the

Waseca Eaco Flour team, Minnesota Independent Champions, 1901. Standling, far left, is George Wilson. Seated, far right, is Bill Holland with Robert Foote next. Wilson pitched a five hitter, striking out nine as he and Holland collected four of Waseca's eight hits in defeating Litchfield, Minnesota, 9-2 at St. Paul before 10,000 fans in the state title game.

bat effectively after catching fastballs bare-handed all day. In 1889, Walker bowed out of baseball with a .216 average in fifty games. There would not be another black player in the International League until 1946, when Jackie Robinson suited up for the Montreal Royals.

With his playing days over, Walker remained in Syracuse and worked as a railroad clerk. Trouble found him in April of 1891 when he became involved in an altercation outside of a bar. Walker, after getting punched in the face by a man named Patrick Murray, pulled out a knife and plunged it into his assailant's groin. Murray died and Walker was charged with second-degree murder. Two months later a jury found him not guilty, and shortly thereafter he returned home to Steubenville.

Back in Ohio, Walker and his brother, Welday,

managed a hotel and became owners of several movie houses. On a questionnaire from Oberlin College which he filled out in 1920, Fleet Walker noted under "accomplishments" that he had devised several inventions in the "moving pictures industry." No mention was made of his achievements in baseball.

In a similar questionnaire filled out by Welday in 1908, the brothers' involvement with a newspaper called the *Equator* in 1902 was noted. Welday listed himself as the "Local Editor" and Fleet as the "Editor."

Fleet Walker, baseball player, businessman, inventor and journalist, became an author in 1908. Tapping the experiences of his broad background, he offered an enlightening and incisive slice of social commentary in a forty-seven page book titled *Our Home Colony — A Treatise on the Past, Present and Future of the Negro Race in America.* The word "baseball" does not appear in his book, but surely he drew on his sometimes bitter experiences in the game. His book presented a fatalistic view that, among other things, called for his race either to return to Africa or face extermination in America. His confrontations with racism prompted Walker to write:

"If there does not exist in the community absolute social, political and industrial equality among the people it is proof positive of an illegitimate association of the races, and certain evidence of the existence of a damnable and blighting caste spirit.

St. Cloud (Minnesota) team, 1902. Walter Ball (seated on floor, far left) was born in Detroit, Michigan, on September 13, 1877. He began his professional career with the St. Paul (Minnesota) club in 1893. In 1899-1900 he played in the Red River Valley League (semipro) as a member of the Grand Forks team, winning 25 of the 28 games he pitched. After ten years of playing on mixed teams, Ball signed with the all-black Chicago Union Giants in 1903.

John W. Patterson. Known to all as "Pat," he played with the Columbia Giants of Chicago, serving as team captain in 1899 and 1900.

Battle Creek (MIchigan) team, 1901. John W. Patterson (standing, third from left) learned the game on the sandlots of Omaha, Nebraska. He played for the Lincoln (Nebraska) Giants before joining the Page Fence Giants in 1895.

"Without social equality there is social inequality and that means that in all the relations that exist between man and man he is to be measured and taken not according to his natural fitness and qualification but that blind and relentless rule which accords certain pursuits and certain privileges to origin or birth."

There certainly was enough evidence to indict the national pastime for "a damnable and blighting caste spirit." The last of the unwanted minor leaguers was purged in the late 1890s, not for "fitness and qualification," but rather for "origin." The ostracized players turned down the one avenue that allowed them to pursue their passion, the all-black teams.

The caste spirit be damned.

Chapter 3

As hope for the individual Negro player was disappearing in the late 1880s, a new source of optimism was beginning to manifest itself — the all-Negro teams. To those with even the thickest of skin — the Frank Grants, Bud Fowlers and Fleet Walkers — it was becoming as clear as a beanball that the white players did not want to share their rosters with them, no matter how good they were.

As mentioned, the Cuban Giants, founded in 1885 in Babylon, N.Y., were the first all-black professional team. According to Sol White, the team, then known as the Athletics, was comprised of Ben Holmes, third base, Captain; A. Randolph, first base; Ben Boyd, second base; William Eggleston, shortstop; Guy Day, catcher; George Parego, Frank Harris and R. Mortin, pitchers; Milton Dabney, left-field; and Charles Nichols, right-field. Center-field was manned by one of the idle pitchers.

After completing their first "season" at the Argyle Hotel, the Athletics, with nine games of experience, felt they were ready for the big time. They traveled to New York City for a game with the Metropolitans, who'd finished in seventh place in the major league American Association. The "Cubans" were beaten soundly, 11-3, but their business manager, John F. Lang, was undaunted, and took his Athletics to meet Philadelphia's Athletics, who'd come in fourth in the American Association. The result wasn't much better, with the visitors losing, 13-7. While in Philadelphia, Lang scheduled a game against a local black semipro team named the Orions. After posting a 6-4 victory, Lang staged a small coup by signing three of the Orions' best players — second baseman George Williams, shortstop Abe Harrison and pitcher Shep Trusty. According to Sol White's *Official Base Ball Guide*, the raid on the Orions was an important step for the Athletics. "It made the boys from Babylon the strongest independent team in the East," White wrote, "and the novelty of a team of colored players with that distinction made them a valuable asset."

It seems that Walter Cook of Trenton, New Jersey, concurred. Cook, a businessman, took control of the team and put the players on salary in 1886, renaming them the Cuban Giants. There was nothing Cuban about the Cuban Giants, just as there was nothing Spanish about the language they spoke on the field. Cook called them Cuban because he felt fans would be more inclined to come out to see Latin players than black Americans. To further the ruse, he had his players speak their own made-up language — a cross between Spanish and gibberish — with an accent on the latter.

As for their surname, it no doubt came from the National League's New York Giants, who were very popular at the time. In later years it would become **THE** name in black baseball. There were the Cuban Giants, the Page Fence Giants, the Philadelphia Giants, the Brooklyn Royal Giants, the Chicago American Giants, the Lincoln Giants, the Leland Giants and the Kansas City Royal Giants, to name a few. Why Giants? It's likely the word was used as a marketing device, a quick identifier geared toward fans who might be looking for Negro baseball in newspapers or on billboards.

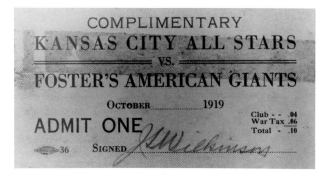

This ticket was from a three-game series in which a major league all-star team won 2-of-3 games from the Chicago American Giants. Playing for the all-stars were Cot Tierney, Zack Wheat, Roy Sanders, Dutch Zwilling, Rolla Mapel and Casey Stengel. The American Giants salvaged the final game with the aid of Jimmie Lyons' grand slam.

Arthur (Chick) Pullam. He was a catcher with the original Kansas City Monarchs and the Kansas City Royal Giants. He recommended to his son that he seek a career outside of baseball. "Frankly, I don't see the day when Negroes will be accepted into the major leagues," he told his son.

(L to R) Elwood Knox, sports editor of the *Indianapolis Freeman*; Rube Foster; J.D. Howard, sports editor of the *Indianapolis Ledger*, and C.I. Taylor, manager of the Indianapolis ABCs. Photograph is from 1916 "World Series," which was won by ABCs. In 1922, when Taylor died, the *Chicago Whip* offered these words in memorializing the much-respected manager: "He fought for baseball. He lived for baseball. He died for baseball."

The Homestead Grays, 1913. Cumberland Willis Posey (second row, third from left) had a unique look about him. Besides being very light-skinned, he also had blue eyes. Cum, as he was commonly called, dedicated his life to the game, first as a player and then as manager of the Grays, who were located in the Homestead section of Pittsburgh.

In 1886 the original Cuban Giants took to the roads of the Northeast playing their version of "triple A" baseball — anyone, anywhere, anytime. Aside from the few black players who were on minor league rosters, the Cuban Giants had the best talent available, including the outstanding battery of catcher Clarence Williams and pitcher Billy Whyte. George Stovey also played with them briefly before moving on to Jersey City of the Eastern League. Their exciting brand of baseball began to receive notice.

"Their games attracted the attention of baseball writers all over the country," Sol White wrote, "and the Cuban Giants were heralded everywhere as

Rube Foster. He was known for his aggressive style of managing. According to his brother Willie, "Rube would start his man from first, and have his man that was hitting lay the ball down the third base line. Since you were already stealing you [were expected to] make it to third and pick up the extra base."

Arthur Hardy and his wife, Effie Grant Hardy. While working his way through Ohio State University, Hardy, who originally played for the Topeka Giants, took a job as a Pullman porter. While on a run to Los Angeles, he met Bill Hart, the famous cowboy actor who was also known as a small tipper. Hardy did all he could to make his customer comfortable, listening to his stories and answering his questions. At the end of the trip Hart gave Hardy his usual tip —twenty-five cents. But at the end of the summer, when Hardy was back in Chicago, several large packing cases arrived at his room. They held a dozen suits, along with shirts and socks, all gifts from Bill Hart.

Ed Bolden (standing, center, in suit) and the Hilldale Athletic Club, circa 1915. In 1910, Bolden, a postal clerk in Darby, Pennsylvania, agreed to keep score for a game between some local youths and a team from Philadelphia. Afterwards, the locals asked Bolden to manage their team. Bolden consented and eventually built the team into an eastern powerhouse. According to a 1920 story in the *Philadelphia Tribune*, "Bolden has sure put Darby on the baseball map and his team will go down in history as did the famous Cuban Giants." Bolden later served as President of the Eastern Colored League from 1923 to 1927.

marvels of the baseball world. They were not looked upon by the public as freaks, but they were classed as men of talent."

It was the success of the Cuban Giants that provided the impetus in 1887 for the National Colored Baseball League. Recognized as an official minor league, it was protected under the terms of baseball's National Agreement. The plans were drawn up in 1886, and by May of 1887 league president Walter S. Brown had eight teams ready to play ball: the Lord Baltimores of Baltimore, the Resolutes of Boston, the Browns of Cincinnati, the Falls City of Louisville, the Gorhams of New York, the Pythians of Philadelphia, the Keystones of Pittsburgh and the Capital City of Washington, D.C. The Cuban Giants, not wanting to tamper with their success, chose to continue as an independent.

The organizers dreamed that one day the major leagues would begin tapping the circuit's talent as they did other minor leagues. More realistically, they hoped to give the Negro an opportunity to play professionally the game he loved. Alas, neither

The Hilldale Club, 1917. Otto (Mirror) Briggs, (standing, second from right) began a long tenure as captain of the team beginning in 1917. A native of North Carolina, Briggs joined the Indianapolis ABCs while playing winter ball in Palm Beach during 1914. However, upon arriving in Indiana, Briggs signed with the West Baden Sprudels. As the leadoff hitter for Hilldale in the 1925 World Series, he batted .414, getting twelve hits and posting an on-base percentage of .452, all Series high. Also pictured are Neal Rhodes (front left), a former catcher for the Cuban X Giants, and Frank Sykes (standing, far left), a native of Decatur, Georgia.

The Chicago American Giants, 1919. Standing (L to R): Elwood (Bingo) DeMoss, Leroy Grant, Dave Brown, Rube Foster, Oscar Charleston, Richard Whitworth. Middle row: Dave Malarcher, Bobby Williams, Unknown, John Reese. Front row: Unknown, Jimmie Lyons, Bill Francis, Unknown, Unknown. Whitworth was originally a third baseman for the Palace Colts, an amateur team in Kansas City, Kansas. One day in practice he was shagging fly balls in deep center-field and unleashed a throw that sailed all the way to the backstop. Fred Palace, the team's manager, looked at Whitworth and said, "If your're going to be throwing like that, you might as well start pitching."

Letterhead of the Chicago American Giants, which featured the names of Rube Foster's hand-picked diamond stars of 1915.

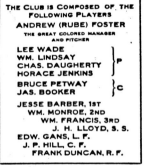

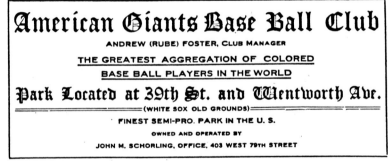

Chicago 6/26/15   191

Mr.J.V.Brasfield,Mgr,

Henry Greys-B.B.Club,

Dear Sir:-

      Your letter confirming the date there-wednesday-July 14-also

accepting the terms-of a gaurantee of Sixty Dollars-(Same to be paid in

case of rain,or no game) received,replying to it-beg to say,I will try

and not play in the Immediate vicinity of Henry-before playing there--

but am trying to fill out a week,around there,so as to make it pay-hence

the terms to you--send me a list of some of the good places around,also

the days that they play---I will pitch the game there for you,providing

I am not sick-or disabled--The terms are with option of Fifty percent

of the gross receipts--   Respectfully Yours-

                                   Andrew Foster

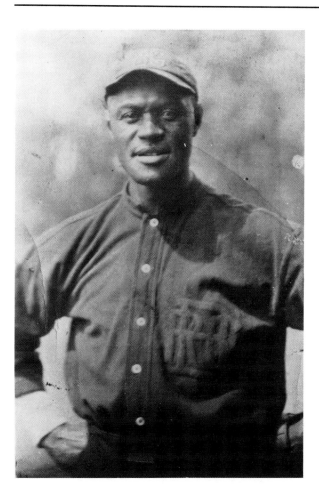

John Henry Lloyd. In 1910, the *Indianapolis Freeman* wrote: "Lloyd, former second baseman of the Philadelphia Giants, is considered by every manager in the country to be a wonder of the 20th century. He contains a ball team within himself."

scenario unfolded. The league opened May 6 in Pittsburgh, with the New York Gorhams defeating the Keystones, 11-8. Thirteen days later, after a total of thirteen games had been played, it collapsed in financial ruin, brought about by insufficient financial backing, poor attendance and a rainy spring. Two teams, the Cincinnati Browns and the Capital City Club of Washington, D.C., never played a game. Another, the Boston Resolutes, played their first game in Louisville, but did not have enough money to make the trip to Baltimore for their second game.

Their high hopes dashed, several of the clubs, such as the Keystones of Pittsburgh and the Gorhams of New York, chose to keep swimming rather than sink with the league. They remained intact and went on to establish reputations as strong independent teams.

The Cuban Giants, meanwhile, continued on their independent way in 1887. One of the high-

The Browns Tennessee Rats, 1914. This team was run by a man the players called "Uncle Walt" Brown. The Rats, who were based in Warrensburg, Missouri, also performed a medicine show that featured Brown on cornet and a female singer. According to Manvall (Buzz) Boldridge, a member of the team in 1924, Brown's wife, "Aunt Mert," used to cook for the team, and she was known for her tough steaks. The Rats of 1914 featured William (Plunk) Drake (standing, fourth from right) and Hugh Blackburn (sitting, third from right).

The Parson (Kansas) Smart Set, 1918. Standing (L to R): John Johnson, Ben Preston, Unknown, Unknown, Unknown, Clarence Glass (manager). Middle row: Unknown, Ross (first name unknown), Raymond Preston, Unknown. Front row: Norman Johnson (bat boy), Unknown, Dewey Bonner, Brownie Carr. John Johnson, who also played for the St. Louis Bloomer Girls, was renowned for his underhand rise ball. He said he was once paid $50 to teach this pitch to a white player who later became a major leaguer.

The Lincoln Giants, 1911. Standing (L to R): William Pettus, Jude Gans, Pete Booker, Johnny (Steel Arm) Taylor, Spottswood Poles. Seated: Dick Redding, George Wright, John Henry Lloyd, Leroy Grant, Louis Santop. Front: Bill Francis, Mascot, Mike Moore. In the May 7, 1910 issue of the *Indianapolis Freeman,* J.E. Allen wrote: "I think Pettus is the greatest colored catcher that ever put on a mask, for he is not only a heady catcher, but throws like a shot and is one of the fastest base runners that ever put on a uniform, and when it comes to hitting that horsehide he is one of the very best." Pettus also fought professionally, once battling heavyweight Jim Flynn.

The Chicago White Sox, 1913. William Buckner (far rght), the team's trainer since 1908, held the job until 1916, when Eddie Collins is said to have asked for his removal. Buckner then opened the Famous Colonial Barber Shop at 3437 State Street in Chicago, which in its heyday employed three shifts of one dozen barbers. He returned to the White Sox in 1920 and remained until 1933. He became the first black person ever to draw a pension from a major league club.

Indianapolis Freeman cartoon, 1916. During the "World Series" between the Indianapolis ABCs and Chicago American Giants in 1916, a dispute erupted when an umpire told American Giants manager Rube Foster to remove his mitt from his hand while coaching first base. Foster refused and took his team off the field, and the game was declared a forfeit. At the next game, Foster was allowed to wear the glove. In Foster's words, the ruling "vindicated me in withdrawing my team during the previous game. Thus the series should remain tied with no advantage to Indianapolis." The umps disagreed and the forfeit stood. The ABCs went on to win the series, 5-4.

AN ATTEMPTED HOLD-UP.

The 25th Infantry baseball team. Front row (L to R): Unknown, Wilber (Bullet) Rogan, Lemuel Hawkins, Unknown, Oscar Johnson. When the 25th Infantry met the 1st Infantry (white) for the post championship in 1915, 7,000 soldiers were on hand to see the game, which was played at Schofield Barracks in Hawaii. Johnson's home run helped the 25th march to a 7-3 triumph.

lights for the Giants was a Western trip in which they played games in Cincinnati and Indianapolis, beating all-white big league teams in both cities. They also played in Wheeling, West Virginia, and Pittsburgh, where they lost to the Keystones. Another significant test for the Giants came against Detroit, the National League champion. With Billy Whyte on the mound, the Giants carried a 4-2 lead into the eighth inning before breakdowns in the field allowed Detroit to rally for a 6-4 victory. Nevertheless, it was becoming clear that the black players, whether on mixed or all-black teams, could compete on equal terms — at any level.

In 1888, the Giants were under new management. Walter Cook had died in 1887 and the team was taken over by J.M. Bright. The change had little

effect on the team, which was joined by the New York Gorhams in the battle for Eastern supremacy. The big event that year was a four-team tournament in New York City, with the winner to receive a silver ball donated by Bright. The combatants were the Cuban Giants, the Keystones of Pittsburgh, the Gorhams of New York and the Red Stockings of Norfolk, Virginia. In sweeping their three games, the Giants avenged their loss to the Keystones and took the trophy.

The following year the Cuban Giants signed Frank Grant, the standout second baseman who had left the Buffalo Bisons after a salary dispute. The Giants, along with the Gorhams of New York, decided to test their skills in "organized baseball." Surrendering their "independence," both teams

Richard Whitworth. In 1919, he was known as the world's greatest Negro pitcher. When asked about his manager, Rube Foster, he remarked, "In 1916, I snapped a tendon in my elbow. I had decided I was done. Foster said, 'No, you are not done, for you have not yet started. What you need is a good rest.' I followed his advice, laid off for a while, rested and returned to the game. I was delighted to find Foster right again."

The Hilldale Athletic Club, 1919. Standing (L to R): Dick Lundy, "Pud" Flournoy, George Johnson, Ed Bolden, Tom Williams, James (Yank) Deas. Kneeling: Jim York, Toussaint Allen, A.C. (Chick) Meade, Otis Starks. Sitting: Elihu Roberts, Unknown, McKinley (Bunny) Downs, Phil Cockrell. To Bolster his lineup in 1919, Bolden recruited Starks, a southpaw from Chattanooga, Tennessee; Meade, an infielder from Buffalo, New York; and Roberts, an outfielder from Atlanta, Georgia. The switch-hitting Lundy started his professional career with the Jacksonville (Florida) Giants in 1915. From 1925 to 1928 he managed the powerful Bacharach Giants, leading them to two Eastern Colored League pennants. Cockrell, whose real name was Philip Williams, was a graduate of Paine College in Augusta, Georgia. A spitball pitcher, he threw four no-hitters in his career.

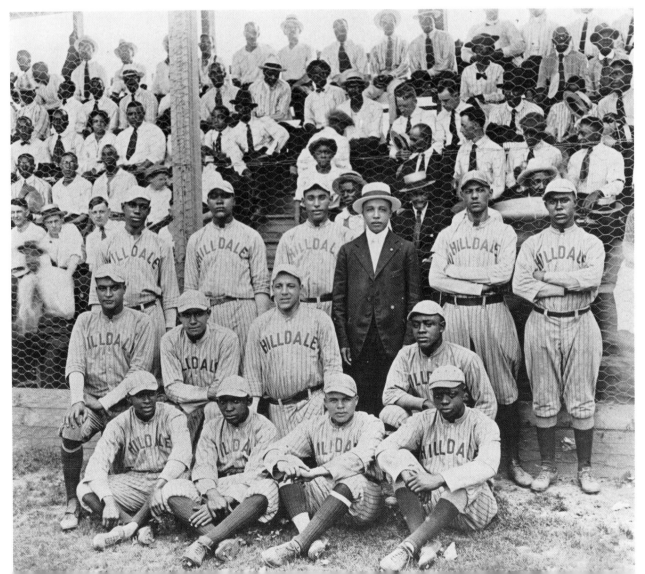

The original Mohawk Giants, 1913. Standing (L to R): Wesley Pryor, Frank Wickware, Bill Smith, Frank Dunbar, Harry Buckner, Johnny Pugh. Seated: White (first name unknown), Unknown, Phil Bradley, "Uncle Rich" Richardson, William M. Wernecke II, Henry Wernecke, "Nix" Jones, George (Chappie) Johnson, Mollett (first name unknown). The Mohawk Giants were based in Schenectady, New York. Chappie Johnson was the originator of the feather mitt. He lined the inside of his catcher's glove with goose feathers. According to former player Fred Langford, "Johnson went around the country teaching all the black players how to line their catchers' mitts with the feathers."

joined the Middle States League, a minor league comprised of otherwise all-white Pennsylvania teams from Harrisburg, Lancaster, Philadelphia, Reading and York. Harrisburg and the Cuban Giants, representing Trenton, New Jersey, waged a bitter battle for the pennant, and the season ended with both teams claiming the championship. A dispute of this nature was not uncommon during the 1800s. With no radio or television, and newspapers not as focused on sports as they became in later years, forfeits and even results of games may have gone unreported, all of which provided little solace for the Cuban Giants. By ruling of the league president, Harrisburg was awarded the flag, despite Giant protests that their rival had been given credit for two games they had not won.

In 1890 the Middle States League was transformed into the Interstate League. While the Gorhams resumed playing an independent schedule, the Cuban Giants reenlisted and represented York, Pennsylvania. Known as the Monarchs of York, they lost the services of second baseman Frank Grant and catcher Clarence Williams, who despite cries of protest, were lured to league rival Harrisburg. The Monarchs replaced Grant by signing Sol White, who was described in the June 3

issue of the *York Gazette* as "in every respect a second baseman equal to Grant." Other member cities of the league included Lancaster, Altoona, Lebanon, and Easton.

The Monarchs, backed by J. Monroe Kreiter, rolled into the season with strong local support, drawing 2400 to their opening series against Altoona at York's East King Street field. Shortly after the season started, they further fortified their roster by adding shortstop William Terrill, pitcher Billy Whyte, and Oscar Jackson, an outstanding centerfielder.

The team was red-hot in June, winning nine straight during one stretch, and by July 21, the Monarchs led the league with a 40-16 record. Harrisburg, which was second at 38-24, decided at this point that it had had enough of the Interstate League and jumped to the Atlantic Association. Harrisburg's move, coupled with the earlier collapses of the Lancaster and Easton franchises, effectively doomed the league.

Sol White, a witness to the league's brief existence, felt that Harrisburg's decision was strictly a face-saving measure. Wrote White:

"It was quite a race for the lead the first month between York, Harrisburg and Altoona; after which the colored boys gradually pulled away until July, when they were so far in the lead that Harrisburg jumped to the Atlantic League to save them the shame of being left so far behind in a race for the pennant."

The Giants finished out the summer barnstorming through Pennsylvania.

It was also in 1890 that the first black professional team in the Midwest was formed. The team was called the Lincoln (Nebraska) Giants and it played against white teams throughout the region. According to White:

"The Lincoln Giants were strong in batteries, hard hitters and fast runners. They were hard to beat unless a strong pitcher was against them. The Lincoln Giants made a great record during the season of 1890 playing Western League and State League teams."

Despite their success, financial troubles forced the team to fold at season's end.

The Cuban Giants, meanwhile, opted to continue in the minors in 1891, as they represented Ansonia (Connecticut) in the Connecticut State League. Now called the Big Gorhams, they re-signed Frank Grant, catcher Clarence Williams and pitcher George Stovey. It wasn't long, however, before the Big Gorhams were back on the open roads. Like so many other leagues that were springing up in the late 1800s, the Connecticut State League folded midway through the season.

From 1892 to 1894 the Cuban Giants remained the number one team in black baseball. Late in the summer of 1894, however, Bud Fowler, who'd broken the minor league color line in 1878, initiated efforts to start a new team, one that would threaten the Cuban Giants' reputation. Fowler, then thirty-six years old and playing for an independent team in Findlay, Ohio, joined forces with a twenty year old teammate named Grant (Home Run) Johnson. They had hoped to start the team in Findlay and play as the Findlay Colored Western Giants, but with the nation still reeling from the stock market crash of 1893 they were unable to find backing.

While in Adrian, Michigan, for a game in August of 1894, Fowler alerted the press that he might be

Joseph (Smoky Joe) Williams. Satchel Paige used to tell people that Williams was "the greatest pitcher that I've ever seen." Williams came from Amarillo, Texas, where he played his first professional game with the Texas All-Stars. As a youngster, he shut out the powerful Leland Giants, 3-0. The opposing pitcher was Rube Foster.

willing to locate his prospective team in Adrian "if enough support was given him by businessmen." According to the Adrian *Daily Times and Expositer*, Fowler received a favorable response to his feeler. "Local baseball enthusiasts are much interested in the enterprise and it is not improbable that Fowler's scheme may succeed," the paper wrote. On September 21, 1894, it was announced that Fowler and two white businessmen, L.W. Hoch and Rolla L. Taylor, had contracted with the Page Wire Fence Company, located in Adrian, and an unidentified bicycle company in Massachusetts to form a black professional baseball team. In return for the free publicity, the two companies agreed to supply the necessary funds to start the team.

The team was called the Page Fence Giants. Bud Fowler was appointed player/manager and Grant Johnson was named captain. Fowler, with funds in hand, spent the off-season looking not only for top-shelf talent, but also for players of strong character. According to the manager, none of his players drank alcohol and only two used tobacco. The players, five of whom were college graduates, were paid approximately $100 per month, an

impressive sum considering that the country was in the throes of a depression.

The team, which was without a home field, played all of its games on the road, mostly in Michigan, Ohio and Indiana. Business manager Gus Parsons scheduled 130 games for the 1895 season, which ran from April to October. That meant a lot of time was spent riding the rails between games. But with the team on solid financial ground, at least in the beginning, travel was made easy in a custom-made, dark brown railroad car with "Page Fence Giants" emblazoned in white letters on its front. The luxury coach had sleeping quarters, a cook and a porter — all the comforts of home, on the road. This group didn't live on the wrong side of the tracks; they lived on the tracks.

When the Page Fence Giants arrived at their destination, their first order of business usually was to work on bolstering the gate for that day's game. This they achieved by hopping on their bicycles, which were all the rage then, and parading down "Main Street." Once they'd made their presence known, all that remained was to put on an

The Indianapolis ABCs, 1915. Standing (L to R): Russell Powell, Ben Taylor, Dick Redding, Elwood (Bingo) DeMoss, Morten Clark, Dan Kennard. Seated: Oscar Charleston, Dicta Johnson, C.I. Taylor, Jimmie Lyons, Tom Allen. Front: George Shively, James Jeffries. In 1916, Charleston collected six straight hits off Chicago American Giant pitchers before Frank Wickware struck him out to end the streak.

When Rube Foster returned to his hometown of Calvert, Texas, in 1910, his name alone attracted the largest crowd ever to witness a baseball game in that community.

The Breakers team (Palm Beach Florida), 1914. Top row (L to R): Walls, Jude Gans, Bruce Petway, Bill Francis, John Lloyd, Pete Hill, Louis Santop. Front: Unknown, Unknown, Bill Gatewood, Pete Booker, Joe Williams, Leroy Grant, Unknown. Gatewood used to go behind the dugout, in full view of the crowd, turn up a corn whiskey bottle, then pitch nine innings and never show any effects. After observing this ritual on several occasions, one rookie asked him: "Why do you always drink before every game?" Gatewood replied, "This is only water. The people think it's liquor, and they are amazed how I can still pitch. It's all for show."

Sarah Foster. If Rube Foster was the Father of Negro Baseball, then it could be said that his wife, Sarah, was its Mother. The door to their home was always open to the American Giants players. When Bobby Williams, the team's shortstop, married in 1918, the Fosters gave the newlyweds a room in their house, which was located at 3242 Vernon Avenue in Chicago.

Rube Foster. He taught his teams that the game is won in one rally. "Now is the time," he would say, "and you shouldn't throw away the opportunity by doing the wrong things. You don't have to get three hits a day for me, or even two. I only want one at the right time."

entertaining performance on the field.

The Giants played many of their games against overmatched amateur and semipro teams, which not only enabled them to compile a gaudy record but to add some showmanship as well. Pitcher Billy Holland was described by an Adrian newspaper as being "funnier than an end man on a minstrel show." At times, when victory was safely secured, they would even let their cook and porter play.

A slow start in April of 1895 did not diminish their owners' support. Early losses were blamed on "trouble in teamwork, arising from lack of practice together," and bigoted umpires, who, in the words of co-owner Rolla L. Taylor, were "invariably home players, and hate to see a colored team beat a white one." Two of those defeats, on April 11 and 12, were administered by the National League's Cincinnati Reds. The Giants stayed fairly close in the first game before losing, 11-7, and then were thoroughly thrashed the following day, 16-2. Nevertheless, they made a favorable impression on the Cincinnati *Enquirer* writer who covered the first game and interviewed Bud Fowler. According to the *Enquirer* of April 12:

"It was a great game. Bud Fowler, the veteran, has got together a great team of players. They will win more than they will lose . . . . Fowler has been playing baseball for the last twenty-six years, and he is yet as spry and as fast in his actions as any man on the team. He has no charley horses or stiff joints, but can bend over and get up a grounder like a young blood . . . . Altogether, he is a wonder.

The Washburn (Kansas) University team, 1910. Arthur Hardy (front row, far left), who played for the Kansas City (Kansas) Giants and Topeka Giants, and Thomas McCampbell (front row, third from left) were members of this team.

The Brooklyn Royal Giants, 1917. (L to R): Frank (Doc) Sykes, Louis Santop, Andrew (String Bean) Williams, Charles Earle, Pearl F. (Speck) Webster, Ernest Gatewood, William Kindle, Joe (Buck) Hewitt, William Handy, Harvey, Johnny Pugh. Sykes was a graduate of the Howard Medical School. A great baseball and basketball player, he turned professional when schoomate Bill Wiley, who was manager of the Lincoln Giants, offered him a starting pitching position. Sykes called teammate Johnny Pugh "the toughest and meanest man I have ever seen in all my years of baseball."

Hurley McNair. His career in baseball spanned twenty-eight years. In 1911 McNair pitched a one-hit shutout against the Kansas City Blues of the American Association. He played in more contests against the Blues than any other black player. In fourteen games against the minor league club, McNair hit for an average of .382, with four doubles and two home runs. He also was a master of the scuttle fish slide in which the player slid into the base and stood up in one motion. The technique was popularized by black players.

Fowler attributes his remarkable condition to the fact that he has always taken care of himself. Wine, women and song have played a very little part in the life of this veteran of the diamond."

After the Cincinnati series, Fowler made some roster adjustments, including the signing of Sol White, that helped the Giants improve their play as the season progressed. All was well: the team was winning and drawing an average of 1,500 fans per game, which helped sell a few more fences and bicycles and kept everybody associated with the team happy.

In his book White recalled that the Page Fence Giants "were hard to beat in '95 as their pitchers were among the best and their fielding excellent." However, he muted his applause somewhat by adding, "Owing to the weakness of the teams in Michigan and Northern Ohio and the great strength of the Page Fence Giants they had easy sailing during the season and won as they pleased."

Their success evidently wasn't enough to satisfy Fowler, the baseball waif. On July 15 the founder of the Page Fence Giants inexplicably abandoned his creation for what would be his final stint in the minors, this time with Adrian of the Michigan State League. Despite losing their manager, the Page Fence Giants continued on a prosperous path through the Upper Midwest, concluding the season on October 10 in Detroit against a team of major leaguers. Though they lost badly, 18-3, their owners

The Hilldale Atheletic Club, 1917. The team recruited some of the greatest players in the game, but it wasn't long before several were called to military service, including McKinley (Bunny) Downs, Louis Santop, Frank Sykes, Otto Briggs, Dick Lundy and Pearl F. Webster. At the time of his induction to the military, the freckled Webster, who was nicknamed "Speck," was one of the game's fastest players. The *Phildelphia Tribune* reported in 1919 that corporal Webster "died recently in France from pneumonia."

Clarence (Kid) Ross. A member of the Oakland (California) Pierce Giants in the early '20s, Ross refused to move east when Steve Pierce, the team's owner, purchased the Detroit Stars. Only three of the Pierce Giants joined their owner in Detroit, the most famous being Harold (Yellowhorse) Morris.

and promoters were happy with the return on their investment and pledged to continue their support in 1896.

The following year the Page Fence Giants maintained their busy schedule, but also were able to improve their lineup with the addition of two key players, Charles Grant and George Wilson. Grant was a first-rate infielder making his debut as a professional. Wilson, the son of former slaves, was a talented pitcher who in 1895 played with Adrian of the Michigan State League where he was a teammate of future Hall of Famer Honus Wagner. Described as an "earnest student of the science of curves and drops" by an Adrian newspaper, Wilson won twenty-nine games and lost only four during his only year in the minor leagues.

While Wilson joined the Page Fence Giants, teammate Bud Fowler returned to Ohio and resumed playing for a mostly white independent team in Findlay. He remained there until 1899, when his white teammates fell into place on the color line. According to a July report in the *Sporting News*: "The white members of the Findlay ball club have drawn the color line and have demanded of Dr. Drake, their backer, that Bud Fowler, colored, be ousted from the team. They will quit if their demand is not heeded."

OH! YOU . CHICKEN

Two other important players played starring roles in 1896. They were Homer A. Plessy and John H. Ferguson. It's doubtful that either man slugged many home runs, but the result of their "game" proved to have far-reaching effects on racial discrimination in America for more than a half century.

Plessy, who contended that he was seven-eighths Caucasian and one-eighth African, was arrested on June 7, 1892, in New Orleans for refusing to comply with a railroad conductor's order to ride in a coach designated solely for blacks. He was brought before Judge Ferguson of the Criminal District Court for the Parish of Orleans. On the basis of Louisiana's Acts of 1890, which required railway companies to provide equal, but separate, accomodations for whites and nonwhites, Ferguson found Plessy guilty as charged. Plessy's appeals, which cited the Thirteenth and Fourteenth

Kansas City Star cartoon, 1910. While the Philadelphia Athletics and Chicago Cubs were battling in the World Series, some members of the media were trying to convince their readers that Negroes were playing for nothing more than a meal. Actually, the Kansas City Royal Giants and Kansas City (Kansas) Giants were playing for the celebrated championship of Kansas City, won by the K.C. (Kansas) Giants.

John Donaldson. A native of Glasgow, Missouri, John Donaldson emerged in 1915 as the greatest pitching prospect of his generation. His season's accomplishments included a thirty strike-out game in Sioux Falls, South Dakota, twenty-five strike-outs in a game at Kansas City, a twenty-one strike-out victory in Cando, North Dakota, and two no-hitters in one month, one of which went twelve innings — thirty-six batters without allowing a hit.

Amendments, took him first to the Louisiana Supreme Court and then to the Supreme Court of the United States.

The Supreme Court upheld the lower court's ruling. Separate transportation facilities for white and black, as long as they were equal, was ruled a legal concept. From the trunk of that decision would grow the limbs of segregation that denied blacks access to lodging, schools, restaurants, even a simple drink of water. It was the stamp of approval that allowed Jim Crow, the systematic discrimination by whites against blacks, to rule the South for the next fifty-eight years. The facilities for blacks and whites were separate, but they were not often equal. For the Negro baseball player, already on the verge of extinction in organized baseball, the Supreme Court's ruling would serve to further encumber his migratory existence.

Even if they'd been based in Mississippi instead of Michigan, the Page Fence Giants would not have been adversely affected by the Supreme Court's decision. With their own railroad car and a personal chef who provided three squares a day, the Giants were traveling first class. Newcomers Charles Grant and George Wilson, along with Grant Johnson and Sol White, helped the team pile up victories at an even greater rate than during the previous year. By August 1 they'd posted eighty-two wins against nineteen losses and were ready to test their skills on a higher level. It was time, they felt, to bring on the Cuban Giants, the team generally recognized as the best in black baseball. The "Cubans" accepted the challenge, and it was decided that a fifteen-

The Detroit Stars, 1919. (L to R): Unknown, Unknown, Frank Warfield, Unknown, Pete Hill, Jose Mendez, Tenny Blount, Frank Wickware, Rodriques (first name unknown), Unknown, Bruce Petway, John Donaldson, Sam Crawford. As a manager, Crawford was a strict disciplinarian who didn't allow his players to drink and forced them to observe a curfew. Few players had the nerve to challenge this tough man, but in 1917 Christobel Torrienti fought Crawford during a Detroit-Chicago American Giants game. The fight lasted twenty-five minutes on the field and continued afterward when the players left the park. It didn't end until hours later when both players were arrested for throwing bricks at one another.

game series would be a fair test for bragging rights. The games were played from September 15 to October 2 at various sites, mostly in Michigan.

The Cuban Giants stormed into Hudson, Michigan, for the opener and lived up to their reputation as they roughed up starting pitcher Billy Holland in a 20-14 slugfest. It turned out to be one of the few high points for the Easterners. The Page Fence club bounced back the next day in Quincy and evened the score with a 26-6 drubbing of their own. On September 16, the series shifted to Lansing, where the teams split two games, with the Page Fence Giants winning the opener, 5-2, behind the sharp pitching of Wilson. The upstarts from Michigan then took over, winning the next three games to go up 5-2. After losing the eighth

John Donaldson. In 1915, John McGraw, manager of the New York Giants, stated: "If Donaldson were a white man, or if the unwritten law of baseball didn't bar Negroes from the major leagues, I would give $50,000 for him — and think I was getting a bargain." Donaldson was one of the top southpaws in baseball.

game, they won three more in a row to effectively stake their claim to the championship. They finished out the series with the Page Fence Giants winning ten of the games. Each player received an engraved silver medal that read: 1896 Page Fence Giants Champions. Now regarded as the best team in black baseball, the future should have been bright for these kings of the rails. Appearances proved deceiving.

The team had lost a great deal of revenue throughout 1896 because of rainouts. Champions or not, that money could not be recovered. They were on shaky financial ground going into the 1897 season and never stabilized, despite winning eighty-two straight during one stretch. With America crippled by the depression, the public was putting tickets for baseball games low on its

The Royal Poinciana Baseball Club, 1915. Back row (L to R): Jess Barber, Pearl F. (Speck) Webster, Spottswood Poles, Jules Thomas, Unknown, William Pettus, Bill Pierce. Front row: Bill Handy, Dell Clarke, Charles Earle, Frank Wickware, Harvey, Wesley Pryor, Andrew (Tacky) Payne. The famous Royal Poinciana winter resort in Palm Beach, Florida, attracted many of the wealthiest people in America, including the Astors, Vanderbilts and Morgans. The Breakers Hotel, which was also located at the resort, fielded a team as well. The two hotels provided seasonal employment for 800 blacks.

The Bacharach Giants, 1921. Standing (L to R): Unknown, manager Dick Redding, Maurice Busby, McDonald (first name unknown), William Pettus, Jess Barber, Brown (frist name unknown), Unknown. Seated: Oliver Marcelle, Jimmy Fuller, James (Yank) Deas, John Connors, George Harvey, Andrew (String Bean) Williams, Johnny Pugh. Front: Julian Rojo, George Shively, Graham (first name unknown). A rare faded print of one of baseball's outstanding teams. On May 16, 1920, the Giants became the first Negro team to play at Ebbetts Field in Brooklyn. Redding shut out the Lincoln Giants, 5-0, there on July 11 of the same year.

priority list. Another financially difficult season followed in 1898, and the team disbanded.

It was also in 1898 that black teams took their final bow in otherwise all-white leagues. The Acme Colored Giants, who were located in Celoron, New York, a small town just north of Pennsylvania in the western part of the state, were the last of this genre. The team was organized by a white man named Harry Curtis, who entered the Giants in the Iron and Oil League. The Acme Colored Giants were faced with a problem that was even more difficult to overcome than their skin color: they were a bad baseball team. By July 5 they were buried in the league's basement with a record of 8-41. Harry Curtis had seen enough and disbanded the team the following day.

Arthur Hardy. He played on the 1910 Washburn University baseball team in Topeka. Because of AAU regulations, Hardy had to play much of his professional baseball under the name of William (Chin) Norman, using that name when he played for the Leland Giants. Hardy was graduated from Washburn University with a bachelor of arts degree in 1914 and later received a masters degree from Ohio State University.

The St. Louis Giants, 1916. Standing (L to R): Bill Gatewood, William Drake, Harry Kimbro, Tully McAdoo, Sam Bennett, Lee Wade. Seated: Bunny Downs, Frank Warfield, Dan Kennard, manager Charles Mills, Richard Wallace, Jimmie Lyons, Charles Blackwell. In 1922 the Giants played a best-of-three series against the Detroit Tigers of the American League. According to Cool Papa Bell, then playing for the Giants, a lady in attendance was so confident the Tigers would win that she bet her rent money on them. When Sam Bennett belted a pinch-hit triple to win it for the Giants, the woman fainted. After regaining consciousness, she said, "I'm fine, just don't let Bennett bat again." The Giants won the series, 2-1.

The Leavenworth (Kansas) military team, 1917. The national pastime had been popular with U.S. soldiers since the Civil War. In 1894 the 25th Infantry became the first non-white military team. By 1902 the 25th was being managed by Major Arlington Erasmus Pond, a former pitcher with Baltimore of the National League. The team defeated all other American troops and reigned as the dominant baseball power on the Phillipine Islands from 1899 to 1918.

The last of the nineteenth-century black individuals to appear in the American minor leagues were Bert Jones and Bert Wakefield. Both players played in the Kansas State League in 1898; Jones, a pitcher/outfielder, with Atchison (Kansas), and Wakefield, a second baseman, with Salina (Kansas). One player, outfielder Bill Galloway, participated in twenty games for Woodstock of the Canadian League in 1899. From the time of Galloway's last game until April 18, 1946, baseball's color line,

both on the major and minor league level, went uncrossed.

With the dawn of the twentieth-century, Negro baseball was composed of many amateur teams but just five professional teams. The Cuban Giants were still playing, though they were known as the Genuine Cuban Giants. There were also the Cuban X Giants, who were based in New York; the Red Stockings of Norfolk, Virginia; the Chicago Unions and the Columbia Giants, who played out of

Horton (Kansas) All Nations team, 1918. Clubs like this one tried to cash in on the popularity of the original All Nations team, which was formed in 1912 by J.L. Wilkinson.

Chicago and were made up mostly of players from the defunct Page Fence Giants.

The shortage of professional teams should not be interpreted as a lack of enthusiasm on the part of blacks. At the time, 90 percent of the black population lived in the South. As the primary focus on baseball was located in the North, it was difficult for black teams to develop the fan support needed to operate a professional organization. All that was beginning to change.

As race relations in the Jim Crow South were continuing to deteriorate, employment opportunities were increasing in the industrial North. A mass black exodus from the South was in its early stages, and with that march north would come the two basic ingredients essential to the success of any professional sport — players and fans.

Black baseball was about to take off.

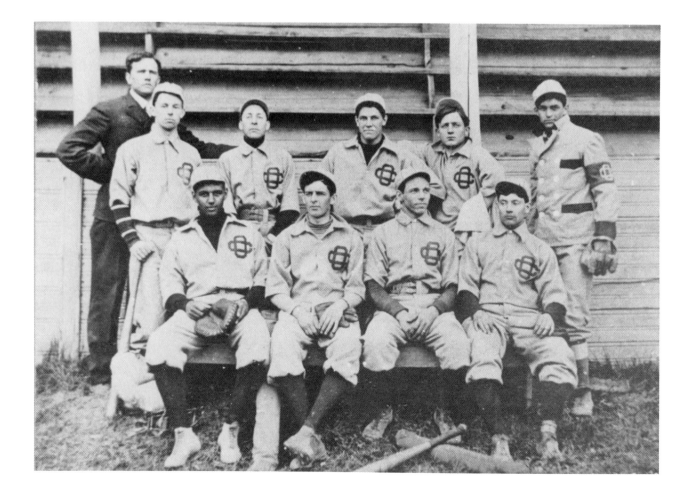

Simpson Younger's delegate certificate to the Farmers National Congress, 1907. Younger, who played for Oberlin College's first baseball team in 1867, was chosen by Oklahoma's first governor, Frank Frantz, to attend the national convention. Younger was a published poet, whose poems appeared in the *Afro-American Newspapers* as late as 1930.

(Upper left) The St. Paul Gophers, 1909. Standing: Robert Marshall (third from left), Johnny (Steel Arm) Taylor (fifth from left). Seated: Jim (Candy) Taylor (second from left), Felix Wallace (far right). In 1909 the Gophers defeated the Leland Giants in a three-game series and declared themselves the "Colored World's Champions." Rube Foster, manager of the Leland Giants, disagreed. "No one in their right mind would consider the Gophers as colored champs," Foster said, "or they would think the class of colored baseball to be very poor." The Gophers posted records of 92-14 in 1907 and 116-28 in 1908.

(Lower left) The Olivet (Michigan) Baseball Club, 1906. Many semipro teams were not influenced by the major and minor leagues' "unwritten rule."

Oscar Charleston. He first played in Cuba in 1915 when the Indianapolis ABCs, led by C.I. Taylor, made their first trek to the island. In addition to swinging a powerful bat, the Hoosier Comet, as he was known, was a phenomenal outfielder.

From the *St. Louis Argus*, 1920.

Chapter 4

Black baseball exploded across America in the first decade of the twentieth-century. The country's industrial revolution was in full swing, with the population continuing to shift more and more away from the agricultural areas to the urban manufacturing centers. By 1900 only a third of the nation's seventy-six million people were working the soil. In the 1890s Southern blacks, seeking to capitalize on these new opportunities, had begun moving in great numbers to the larger cities of the North and South. As this migration gathered momentum, blacks, despite their rude treatment from "organized baseball," began to embrace the game as never before. By 1910 there were more than sixty black professional teams crisscrossing the country, playing as many games as they could cram into a season.

For the career-minded athlete, boxing was the only alternative to professional baseball. A few, such as Jack Johnson, Joe Gans and Sam Langford, chose to study "the sweet science," while the rest turned to baseball, usually starting with a local semipro team and playing their way up the ladder. On the top rung were the big-city teams — Chicago, Philadelphia and New York. It was often a long struggle for a player to reach this level, as the career of Elwood (Bingo) DeMoss illustrates.

DeMoss, who was recognized as one of the finest second baseman and the game's best bunter, started with the Topeka Giants as a sixteen year old in 1905. He played on teams in Kansas City (Kansas), Oklahoma, West Baden (Indiana) and Indianapolis before finally getting his big chance

with the Chicago American Giants in 1917.

There were few leagues during this era, but there was an abundance of games. Opponents could range from a major league barnstorming team to a rival black team to a local amateur or semipro team, white or black. Some of these clubs played as many as 150 games over the course of a year. With the automobile industry in its infancy and the Wright brothers taking their first flights over Kitty Hawk, teams traveled exclusively by railroad, sometimes embarking on journeys for as long as a month at a time. If the Kansas City (Kansas) Giants scheduled a series in Chicago against the Leland Giants, they would also schedule games against semipro teams at every whistle-stop along the way. It was a major event in these small towns when a black team stopped off to play the locals.

In the large cities, taking in a baseball game was becoming a popular form of entertainment, especially on Sundays, the only idle day of the week for most people. When teams from other cities visited, Sunday crowds of anywhere from 4,000 to 10,000 could be expected.

It was also during this era that some teams began migrating to Florida, California, and even Cuba when the cold weather arrived in the fall. As early as 1903, the Cuban X Giants, the best of the teams in the Northeast, played a nine-game series in Havana, where the game was undergoing a similar surge in popularity. Spring training trips, designed to prepare a team for the upcoming season, also became commonplace.

The Hilldale Giants, (L to R): Jesse Hubbard, Biz Mackey, John Beckwith, Herbert (Rap) Dixon and Clint Thomas. Photograph was taken in the mid-1920s during the California Winter League season. In 1921 Beckwith, at age nineteen, became one of a select few to hit a home-run over the left-field wall at Cincinnati's Redland Field. He was given a great ovation by the 5,000 fans in attendance, some of whom showered him with money. It turned to be a $25 home run.

With independent teams scattered all over the country, there were many billing themselves as "Colored World Champions." In 1902 a team from Atlanta called the Deppins forged a record of fifty-five wins and thirteen losses. According to a short story in the *Indianapolis Freeman* of September 20, their manager, P.A. Thomas, was convinced that his team was the best in black baseball. That was an upgrade of an earlier boast he'd made in the May 10 *Freeman* when he claimed after a three-game sweep of the Nashville Villains that the Deppins were the champs of the South.

In 1903, while Boston was defeating Pittsburgh

in the major leagues' inaugural World Series, the Algona (Iowa) Brownies, who were led by the brilliant pitching of Billy Holland, were laying claim to being the best black team in the West. This claim was fortified by series wins over the all-black Chicago Union Giants and Winnipeg, champions of the Northern League, an all-white minor league. The Brownies, who had started out as a mixed team in 1901, were comprised solely of black players by 1903.

The Cuban X Giants, who were based in the Northeast, and Sol White's two-year-old Philadelphia Giants engaged in an eight-game series in

Walter (Dobie) Moore and Hurley McNair. Moore (standing, third from left) and McNair (standing, second from right) were mainstays of the Kansas City Monarchs in the '20s. Moore was an outstanding shortstop who led the Monarchs in home runs from 1920-1926. McNair was a superb left-handed outfielder from Marshall, Texas.

1904 to determine the "colored championship of the world." According to White's *Official Base Ball Guide*, the Cuban X Giants clinched the series in seven games to capture the coveted crown. Of course, no other regions besides the Northeast had any input into the final determination. The same year, a team in Kentucky called the Paducah Giants was billing itself as the "champions of the South." And in the Midwest, Frank Leland, an important pioneer, was of the opinion that his Chicago Union Giants were without peer.

Within a particular region these assertions of supremacy proved to be effective drawing devices. In 1909 the Leland Giants, formerly the Chicago Union Giants, were recognized as the preeminent team in the Midwest. In August of that year they carried that mantle with them to Kansas City for a three-game series with the Kansas City (Kansas) Giants. The strong Kansas City club had won fifty-four straight games during one stretch of the season, and anticipation was running high in the days before the first game. The *Kansas City Journal* proclaimed on the day of the opener that the series was "for the colored championship of the United States and a purse of $1,000."

Five thousand fans poured into Riverside Park,

Hurley Allen McNair. He was known by his colleagues as "the best two-strike hitter in baseball." According to George Giles, a 1927 Monarch teammate, "Mac could have taken two strikes on Jesus Christ and base-hit the next pitch." McNair, whose greatest years were in the early days of the Negro National League, played from 1911 to 1939.

Wilber (Bullet) Rogan. In 1921, the *Chicago Whip* wrote, "There are few pitchers in the game today, regardless of color, who look as good on the mound as Rogan. His stand is beautiful. His wind-up, perfect. He is a great twirler, we venture to say another Matty [Christy Mathewson] or Foster [Rube]."

located at Second Avenue and Franklin Street, for game one. They couldn't have been too thrilled to see their Giants go down meekly as Walter Ball shut them out, 5-0. The locals squared matters the next day in front of 6,000. Bill Lindsay, ace of the K.C. staff, struck out sixteen and allowed only four hits and one unearned run in a 3-1 victory. The Kansas City *Journal* offered an exuberant report the following day:

"Riverside Park was the scene of one of the best games of baseball that has been witnessed on a local diamond when the Kansas City, Kansas, Giants turned the tables on the Leland Giants yesterday afternoon, winning by a score of 3 to 1."

In game three, Kansas City scored three runs in the eighth inning to eke out a 5-4 triumph before 5,000. The colored championship of the United States was theirs. Or was it?

Similar claims that year were submitted by the Philadelphia Giants and the St. Paul (Minnesota)

The Topeka Giants, 1918. Carroll (Dink) Mothell (standing, far left) was one of several Negro leaguers to get his start in Topeka. Bingo DeMoss, Tully McAdoo, Roosevelt (Duro) Davis and Topeka Jack Johnson also debuted there. In 1924, Mothell homered off Major League's Jess Barnes of the Boston Braves, in an exhibition game in Topeka.

Bazz Owen Smaulding (left) and George Franklin Giles, 1927. In 1929, Giles, having married recently, asked Kansas City Monarchs owner J.L. Wilkinson for an increase in pay. Wilkinson replied: "I could get three ball players in the South for what you're asking." Giles approached Robert Gilkerson of the Gilkerson Union Giants, an independent team, and was able to get his price. Smaulding, a native of Seattle, Washington, attended the University of Idaho from 1924-1926, and later managed the Piney Woods Country Life College baseball team.

Gophers, who'd also beaten the Leland Giants. According to the *Indianapolis Freeman,* a weekly which was attentive to black sports, the Gophers had "the strongest claim." In its September 11, 1909, issue, the *Freeman* reasoned that St. Paul "beat the Lelands in a five-game series the last week of July. The other two teams defeated the famous Chicago aggregation after they had surrendered the title." But that was just one newspaper's opinion. The *Kansas City Journal* continually referred to "their" Giants as the "colored world champions" throughout 1910.

Of all the teams that year, the Kansas Citians probably had the most legitimate claim to the brass ring. Formed in 1907 by a local businessman named Tobe Smith, the Kansas City Giants emerged as a first-rate team two years later, when Smith hired Topeka Jack Johnson of the Topeka Giants to manage the team. Johnson brought many of his Topeka players with him. They played 147 games and lost just nineteen against the best of the black teams, and anyone else they could get a game with throughout Kansas, Missouri, Oklahoma, Nebraska, Iowa, Illinois and Texas.

Once a club joined the ranks of the elite, it became increasingly difficult for it to retain its personnel. If a team was consistently beating the opposition, there was little doubt that eventually it was going to get raided. There were no long-term contracts, and there were no reserve clauses binding a player to the team that held his contract.

Oliver Riggins (left) and Dave Brown. This photograph was taken while the pair were in Cuba for the 1924 winter league. In 1921, the *Chicago Whip* offered this glowing report on Riggins: "Of all the new recruits developed by the major colored league, none have shown better form than shortstop Riggins. He is a flashy handler of difficult rolling grounders, a slashing hitter and possesses one of the greatest throwing arms in baseball. Riggins, like many of the great ball players, is a coal miner by trade and hails from southern Illinois."

Players, if they had a contract at all, were signed for a year at a time, but those deals were easily broken. If Frank Leland or Tobe Smith or Sol White wanted another team's player, they'd flash him some sign language — dollar sign, that is — and would usually be able to strike a deal.

"Wherever the money was, that's where I was," said John Henry Lloyd, a feared hitter who played for more than ten teams in a career that spanned twenty-six seasons.

In 1909 the Leland Giants lost important series to the St. Paul Gophers, the Kansas City (Kansas) Giants and the Philadelphia Giants. By the time the 1910 season opened, Leland, who had lost several players when his manager formed a new team, had four former Gophers and one former Kansas City Giant on his team. Two of the former St. Paul

The Kansas City Royals, 1922. (L to R) Piney Brown, Wilmer Fields, Unknown, Unknown, Unknown, Unknown, Unknown, Roosevelt (Chappy) Gray, Unknown, Unknown, Herlan Earl Ragland, Unknown. On and off the field, Gray was one of baseball's most unforgettable characters. A well-traveled semipro catcher from Kansas City, he was known for his colorful comments. During one game, as the opposition's power-hitter stepped to the plate, a locomotive chugged by beyond the centerfield fence. Gray offered these words of caution to his pitcher: "Don't let this man derail that train."

James (Cool Papa) Bell. He was born James Thomas Nichols on May 17, 1903, outside of Starkville, Mississippi. In 1920, he began using his father's last name, which was Bell. He soon became recognized as the fastest man in baseball, taking that distinction from aging Jimmie Lyons.

players were members of the famed Taylor family, James (Candy Jim) Taylor and his brother John (Steel-Armed Johnny) Taylor. Candy Jim started his professional career as a third baseman with the Birmingham Giants and went on to enjoy a forty-four year career in the game as a player, manager and administrator. Two other Taylor brothers, Charles I., the oldest, and Ben, the youngest, also had long and distinguished careers in the game.

Jumping from team to team was a common practice until several years after the first established league was formed in 1920. No one used the practice more, or did more to curtail it in later years than a man named Andrew (Rube) Foster.

Rube Foster was born in Calvert, Texas, on September 17, 1879. He died on December 9, 1930 in Kankakee, Illinois. During his fifty-one years he was relentless in his pursuit to legitimize and elevate interest in baseball, first as a player, then as a manager, and finally as the founder of the first nationally recognized league — the Negro National League. Foster was a large, broad-shoul-

dered man, standing six feet tall and weighing well over two hundred pounds. He was an eloquent spokesman for the game and wrote frequently in the black journals of the day, extolling the virtues of Negro baseball. As a pitcher, he was a hard-throwing right-hander who was a fierce competitor. As a manager, he was an innovator and a stern taskmaster who demanded total compliance from his players. As an adminstrator, he was an iron-willed dictator who brought order to a segment of sport that had been operating largely without regimentation.

Foster began his professional career in 1897 with a team called the Waco (Texas) Yellow Jackets, who toured the South playing other black teams. While Foster was in Hot Springs, Arkansas, in the spring of 1902, Frank Leland took notice of Foster's ability and invited him to Chicago to play for Leland's newly formed Chicago Union Giants. Foster accepted but found that he wasn't quite ready for the higher level of play. After getting hit hard in his first few outings, he and teammate Dave Wyatt left the Union Giants to join a mixed semipro team in Michigan. During the latter part of that

Walter (Newt) Joseph, 1924. A third baseman, he was called "Blood and Guts" by his Kansas City Monarchs' teammates because he played the bunt so close to the hitter. Once, while Joseph was being interviewed on the radio in his hometown of Muskogee, Oklahoma, the announcer asked him, "If you could go to the major leagues today who would you take with you?" He replied, "The entire Monarchs team."

season, he signed to play for E.B. Lamar's Cuban X Giants. It was with the Cuban X Giants that Foster emerged as a dominant pitcher.

As mentioned, the "Cubans" beat Sol White's Philadelphia Giants for the "colored championship of the world" in 1903. Rube Foster dominated that series, winning four of the five games. White took notice, and the following year Foster was pitching for the Philly Giants. The two titans of Eastern baseball again met for the championship, this time in a three-game series played in Atlantic City, and Rube again made the difference, winning two games to give Philly the title.

In 1905 Foster, still with the Philadelphia Giants, enjoyed the best year of his career. In a 1907 story written by Frederick North Shorey in the *Indianapolis Freeman*, Foster talked of the phenomenal record he had compiled two years previously, not only against black teams, but against major league teams as well.

"I won fifty-one out of fifty-five games I pitched for that season, and that was doing pretty well," Foster said. "We played the New York Giants, the Philadelphia Athletics, the Brooklyns [all major league teams], the teams of the Tri-State Leagues

[minor league clubs] and cleaned 'em all up. It was when we beat the Athletics, with Rube Waddell pitching, that they gave me the name of the colored Rube Waddell."

Waddell, one the best pitchers in the major leagues in the early 1900s, led American League pitchers in wins (twenty-six) and strikeouts (287) in 1905.

Foster, in the same story, tried to explain his success: "I don't rely on any kind of [pitch], and I don't use any kind of system. I just kind of size up the batter and give him what I think he can't hit. Sometimes it's a curve, sometimes it's a straight ball, but I can almost always tell, sort of by instinct [what to throw]."

Arguably the best pitcher of his time, Foster had harbored aspirations early in his career of playing in the major leagues. That, of course, never happened. By 1907 Foster was resigned to his fate,

Wade Johnston, Baltimore Black Sox, 1924. During the 1920s he was one of the best left-handed leadoff hitters. According to pitcher Chet Brewer, his success was due to his philosophy. "Johnston always tried to hit the first ball that the pitcher threw to begin the game," Brewer said. "Since most pitchers threw their best pitch, in an attempt to start the game off with a strike, Johnston felt confident that if you hit this first pitch well you would have a mental advantage on the pitcher all day."

Emma McNair. The wife of Monarch outfielder Hurley McNair, she is pictured here in Association Park in Kansas City. Both the Monarchs and the Kansas City Blues of the American Association shared this field. For the Blues' home games, signs were posted around the park that stated where Negro fans were allowed to sit. When the Monarchs played, the signs were covered.

telling an interviewer in the *Freeman*: "Five or six years ago, I think I'd have been a first-class pitcher, but I found then I'd gone as far as I could go and that there was no hope of getting into the big league, so I kind of let myself go."

Of all the black players of this period, none came closer to crossing the color line than Charlie Grant, one of Rube's teammates on the Philly Giants. Grant, an outstanding infielder who had debuted professionally with the Page Fence Giants in 1896, was between seasons with the Columbia (Chicago) Giants in 1902, working as a bell boy and playing ball during the winter months in Hot Springs, Arkansas. It so happened that manager John McGraw brought his Baltimore Orioles of the American League to Hot Springs for spring training that year. The American League, an outgrowth of the minor league Western Association, was in its second year of operation and its first as a recognized major league in direct competition with the National League. McGraw saw the light-skinned Grant playing on the hotel grounds one day and was so impressed with his glovework that he

immediately began scheming to circumvent the color barrier.

McGraw figured that a change of name and heritage might accomplish his objective. Charlie Grant, he decided, would no longer be Charlie Grant, American Negro; he would be Charlie Tokohama, full-blooded Cherokee Indian. The plan almost worked. Grant, though, was well known in Chicago baseball circles, having played several years there with the Columbia Giants. His reputation proved his undoing. "Tokohama" practiced with the Orioles for the rest of the spring, but as the season approached, Charles Comiskey, president of the Chicago White Sox, heard of the ruse and exposed it. Grant was promptly dropped from the Orioles and returned to the Columbia Giants for the 1902 season. Evidently, Comiskey's racial attitude had hardened since his playing days. As a first baseman for the St. Louis Browns of the American Association in 1884, he had played against Fleet Walker of Toledo.

Charlie Grant was by no means the only black player who caught the eye of major league officials. Many of his comtemporaries heard the unfair, but familiar, refrain: "If only you were white." There were genuine superstars in Negro baseball, stars that would have made an impact on any major league team.

One of those superstars was George Wilson, who'd pitched for the Page Fence Giants in the

(L to R) Crush Holloway, Jud Wilson, Oscar Johnson, John Beckwith. In 1933, Al Moses of the Associated Negro Press asked Babe Ruth for his opinion on Negro baseball players. "I played against the Homestead Grays while with Eddie Mack's All-Stars, and would say that Vic Harris and Oscar Charleston would make any big league team," Ruth said. When asked which of the black players were the hardest hitters, Ruth responded, "Beckwith — not only can Beckwith hit harder than any Negro ball player, but any man in the world."

The Hilldale Club, 1920, Louis (Big Bertha) Santop (standing, third from right), a good-hitting, good-fielding catcher, started his career in 1909 with the Fort Worth Wonders. He played briefly in Oklahoma before moving east in 1911 to play for the Philadelphia Giants. In 1916, he signed with Hilldale, playing there for a year before joining the navy. He reenlisted with Hilldale in 1920 and stayed until 1926. During those years, "Top" was a big drawing card at white semipro parks.

The Hilldale Club, 1924. Standing (L to R): George Carr, Toussaint Allen, Judy Johnson, George Johnson, Ed Bolden, Biz Mackey, Jesse Winters, Rube Currie, Louis Santop. Kneeling: Joseph Lewis, Clint Thomas, Holsey Lee, Frank Warfield, Rocky (the mascot), Jake Stephens, Otto Briggs, William Campbell, Merven Ryan. Ed Bolden had worked for years to put together a strong team. In 1924 Hilldale faced the Kansas City Monarchs in the first Negro World Series. The *Kansas City Journal* refused to use his picture with a story headlined, "Principals in the Negro World Series." Instead, it printed a picture of Charles P. Spedden, the white owner of the Baltimore Black Soxs, and used Bolden's name under it. In 1922 Rube Currie had this to say about Rube Foster: "Fortunately, in our league, we have a president [Rube Foster] who knows baseball from every angle. True, we can't all play for him, but we do have the opportunity and pleasure of playing against him."

mid-1890s. Wilson, a native of Palmyra, Michigan, was a fastball pitcher who threw both overhand and submarine-style. He was a teammate of Charlie Grant's with the Columbia Giants for a few years and pitched several no-hitters during his career, prompting one newspaper to call him "a marvel of the day." In 1903, while pitching for St. Cloud (Minnesota), an otherwise all-white semipro team, Wilson recorded ten shutouts and struck out more than fifteen batters eight times. Wilson's talents

were such that he was able to earn more pitching for these white semipro teams than he could with the black professional teams.

And there were plenty of others who had the talent but not the tint to play in the majors: John Henry Lloyd, a sure-fielding shortstop who was perhaps the finest hitter of the early 1900s; Bruce Petway, who by all accounts was the finest catcher of the early 1900s; Jose Mendez, a native of Havana who was an overpowering right-handed fastball

Above left: Paul (Jake) Stephens. He started with Hilldale in 1921 after sending team owner Ed Bolden a letter which stated, "I am the best short-fielder that ever matriculated among the White Roses of York, Pennsylvania." Bolden was so impressed by the player's confidence that he signed him. In addition to playing with Hilldale, Stevens also starred with the Philadelphia Stars from 1934-37.
Above center: Louis Santop. According to Ed Bolden, owner of the Hilldale Club, Santop was "a sweet hitter and a brainy catcher."
Above right: Holsey (Scrip) Lee. A submarine-style pitcher, Lee made his professional debut in 1920 with the Norfolk Stars, who were managed by Chappie Johnson. He joined Hilldale in 1923 after a stint with the Philadelphia Stars.
Right: Raleigh (Biz) Mackey. A native of San Antonio, he joined the Indianapolis ABCs in 1920. With the ability to play every position on the field and switch-hit, he proved to be an immediate sensation. He had a terrific arm and was rated one of the league's top catchers.
Next page, left: Clinton (Hawk) Thomas. He received his first introduction into pro ball with the Brooklyn Royal Giants in 1920 and moved to the Negro National League in 1921 and 1922, playing first for the Columbus Buckeyes then the Detroit Stars. Thomas, a superb outfielder and solid hitter, was lured to Hilldale when the Eastern Colored League started in 1923.
Next page, center: Jesse (Nip) Winters. Born in Washington, D.C., he was rated as one of the greatest southpaws. He began as an amateur with the Detroit Tigers in his native city, then was signed by Chappie Johnson, manager of the Norfolk Stars, in 1919. Winters played for the Bacharach Giants, the Philadelphia Stars

and Harrisburg before landing with Hilldale in 1923. He led the Eastern Colored League in 1925 with a record of 18-7.
Next page, right: Merven (Red) Ryan. After beginning with the Pittsburgh Stars of Buffalo, New York, in 1915, he went on to play for the Brooklyn Royal Giants, the Lincoln Stars, Bacharach Giants and the Harrisburg Giants before joining Hilldale in 1922. A native of Brooklyn, he weighed only 158 pounds but delivered the fastball of a heavyweight.

The Montgomery Wards Monitors, 1925. This semipro team operated out of Kansas City and featured three former professional players: Richard Whitworth (standing, center), Otto Ray (standing, far right) and Hugh Blackburn (kneeling, far right). Whitworth won thirty games in 1914 as a member of Peterson's Chicago Union Giants and pitched a no-hitter against the Chicago Giants in 1915.

The Harrisburg Giants, 1924. Oscar Charleston (standing, far right) was the team's player/manager from 1924-26. In 1929, Rollo Wilson, a sportswriter for the Pittsburgh Courier, wrote of Charleston: "Big, aggressive, intelligent, highly efficient — that's the Hoosier Hustler. He is without technical fault and as near perfect as ball players ever come." Also pictured are Herbert (Rap) Dixon (top row, second from left), team owner Colonel C.W. Strothers (top row, third from left), "Ping" Gardner (middle row, far left), Edgar Wesley (middle row, second from left), Dalti Cooper (front row, far left) and Clarence (Fats) Jenkins (front row, second from left).

pitcher; Joe Williams — Cyclone Joe or Smoky Joe to those who stepped into the batter's box against him — you couldn't see the ball, but you could smell the smoke; John Donaldson, a left-hander with a blazing fastball and sharp-breaking curve. All these and many more had the ability to play in the major leagues — "if only they were white."

Rube Foster remained with the Philadelphia Giants through the 1906 season. The Giants again were the self-proclaimed champs by virtue of their dominance over the Cuban X Giants, the Brooklyn Royal Giants and the Wilmington (Delaware) Giants. Their proclamation, no doubt, was on the money. In addition to Foster, they had another outstanding hurler in Dan McClellan. A right-hander, McClellan became the first black to pitch a perfect game on July 7, 1903, when he set down all twenty-seven batters in a game against York (Pennsylvania) of the Tri-State League. Philadelphia's infield displayed the talents of second baseman Charlie

Grant and shortstop Grant (Home Run) Johnson, who along with Bud Fowler had started the Page Fence Giants in 1896. They also had Preston (Pete) Hill, an outstanding, lefty-hitting center-fielder. Philly's reign, however, came to a sudden end at the close of the season.

Foster, unhappy with the players' cut of the action, decided to shop his services and found a taker in Frank Leland. Leland, president and general manager of the Leland Giants, was born in Memphis in 1868. He moved to Chicago in 1887 after attending Fisk University in Nashville. Along with W.S. Peters and two other men, Leland formed the Union Base Ball Club in 1887. Renamed the Chicago Unions the following year, the team didn't turn professional until the mid-1890s. In 1902, Leland bolstered his team by drawing the best players from the Columbia Giants (formerly the Page Fence Giants), who had disbanded. Now called the Chicago Union Giants, the team perennially was regarded as the class of the Midwest. In

1905 the Union Giants played 122 games and won 112, including forty-eight straight during one stretch.

Before leaving the East, Foster effectively decimated his former team by securing the services of six members of the Philadelphia Giants. The defectors included catcher James (Pete) Booker, first baseman Mike Moore, second baseman Nate Harris (considered by many to be the finest at his position in the country), center-fielder Pete Hill, right-fielder Andrew (Tacky) Payne and shortstop George Wright.

In his second stint in Chicago, Foster, who also served as the team's manager, captured the hearts of Chicago's fans. With Rube on the mound, Leland could be guaranteed a crowd of anywhere from 4,000 to 6,000 for Sunday games. During August of 1908, the Leland Giants and Mike Donlin's All-Stars scheduled a six-game series that energized the community. Donlin, a twelve-year major leaguer who sat out the 1907 season, had formed a team comprised of ex-major leaguers and area semipros. There was much anticipation as game one of the series approached. The *Indianapolis Freeman*, in its account of the opener, stated:

"For weeks the colored population of Chicago have been saving their money to go to the great series between their favorites and the All-Stars. A large amount of money was up between the two teams, and there was intense rivalry between the two aggregations."

Big money was at stake not only on the field, but in the bleachers as well. Backers of both teams were willing to support their gloved ones with cold cash. According to the story, one fan of the All-Stars stood up before the game and announced: "I've got $20 that says the chocolates won't win." The challenge brought a flurry of action from Giant supporters.

When the Giants took the field in the first inning, Foster, ever the showman, remained out of sight until his teammates reached their positions. He then began a slow stroll to the mound, the ovation getting louder with each step. "Rube Foster was the whole thing," wrote Frederick North Shorey in the *Freeman*, "and, what is more, he knows it."

And so did the adoring fans who filled the park to watch this master of the mound. He could throw overhand, sidearm or submarine-style. He had

The Bacharach Giants. Herbert (Rap) Dixon (standing, second from left) was a power-hitting outfielder. His career in baseball started one day when his high school science teacher announced that the class was going to dissect a cat. Dixon, feeling squeamish, exited quickly and went straight to a sporting goods store. With the money he had earned working weekends at the Bethlehem (Pennsylvania) Steel Company, he purchased a glove and bat, took a train to Atlantic City and joined the Bacharach Giants.

The Kansas City Monarchs, 1921. Top row (L to R): Rube Currie, John Donaldson, Frank Blattner, Sam Crawford, George Carr, Walter Moore. Middle row: Wilber Rogan, Bartolo Portuando, Zack Foreman, Hurley McNair, Lemuel Hawkins, Otto Ray. Front row: Sylvester Foreman, Robert Fagan. Both Hawkins and Ray were traded to the Chicago Giants for catcher Frank Duncan shortly after this photograph was taken. Hawkins was killed in 1934 while attempting to hold up a beer truck in Chicago. Ray later became a detective in Kansas City.

superb control of a good fastball and a sharp curve, which he delivered from either a full windup or no windup, sometimes even quick-pitching an unsuspecting batter.

Against Donlin's All-Stars that August afternoon, Foster was brilliant, limiting them to three hits in a 3-1 Giant victory. Late in the game he conspired with first baseman Mike Moore and executed the hidden-ball trick, catching an All-Star taking a lead while Moore had the ball stashed in his glove. Rube's philosophy, whether playing or managing, was to use any means necessary to win. Rube's way became **THE** way in Negro baseball. It was an aggressive style that relied heavily on the hit-and-run, the squeeze play, steals, double steals, taking the extra base, and even hidden-ball tricks. All were woven into the fabric of the game by Rube Foster.

The fans developed a great appreciation for Foster's methods. After the Giants' victory over the All-Stars, the *Freeman* reporter, in his enthusiastic account of the game, wrote:

"As for Rube Foster, well, if it were in the power of the colored people to honor him politically or to raise him to the station to which they believe he is entitled, Booker T. Washington would have to settle for second place."

Foster, whose Giants won four of the six games against Donlin's All-Stars, was a good bet to pack the house whenever he was scheduled to pitch. In game two, which he did not pitch, attendance dropped to 4,000 — 1,000 less than the opener. In the finale, with Foster back on the hill, 6,500 poured through the gates.

Foster continued to manage Leland's Giants through 1909, when the two clashed over Rube's role. Foster wanted more input into the administrative end of the business, which Leland considered his private domain. Irreconcilable differences forced a split between the two Chicago baseball giants. Oddly, after a court case, it was Foster who was allowed to retain the name "Leland Giants." Leland started a new team called the Chicago

Above: Rube Foster. Several owners of Negro National League teams were unhappy with Foster's management of the league. Foster, as the league's booking agent, collected five percent of the gate from every league game. In the first year, 1920, Foster earned $11,220 for his efforts.

Right: Rube Foster in Havana, 1916. In 1925 he told a group of fans at Stark's Shoe Shine Parlor in Kansas City, "We are going to defeat your great [Bullet] Rogan 1-0 today." Later that afternoon, the American Giants took a 1-0 lead into the bottom of the ninth. Walter Moore of the Monarchs stepped to the plate. "Pitch him high and tight," Rube yelled to his pitcher. And then, to the bat boy, he said, "Stack 'em up, darling." On the next pitch, Moore hit a shot that Bobby Williams grabbed in the hole at short and threw to first, barely getting the out.

Left: Foster and wife Sarah in front of their home on Michigan Avenue in Chicago. Sarah said, "Whenever my husband was in town he never stayed out past 11:00 p.m. He was not a drinker; however, he did have a weakness for gingersnaps and milk." Foster's guidance of the Negro National League proved to be an immediate success. At the second annual league meeting, the treasurer reported that the club had 616,000 paid admissions in 1920.

William Drake. A star pitcher for the St. Louis Giants and the Kansas City Monarchs, he used to shine his baseball shoes before every game for good luck. He was a member of the undefeated 1919 805th Regiment baseball team and rejoined the St. Louis Giants in 1920 having originally signed with them in 1916. In 1922 Drake defeated the Kansas City Blues of the American Association and pitched a no-hitter against Sioux Falls, a minor league team that was a member of the Dakota League. In 1929, he managed the Tulsa Black Indians of the Texas-Oklahoma-Louisiana League.

with a Southern trip. Rube, of course, was at the vanguard of any new trend. On this journey, his Leland Giants played thirty-one games in five weeks, barnstorming through Texas, Arkansas, Louisiana, Mississippi, Alabama, Florida, Tennessee and Kentucky. Thirty-one games in thirty-five days; the team was ready, and Rube knew it.

In the May 21 issue of the *Freeman*, he issued the following challenge:

"Rube Foster's Leland Giants challenges any ball club in the world for a series of games to decide the championship, for a side bet of $500 to $3,000, or for 75 per cent to winner and 25 per cent to loser, or for all the gate receipts. The Lelands will play on the above terms any place in the United States. I offer this inducement to all the so-called champions; I want the public to be convinced as to who is really the champion.... I want the readers of the *Freeman* to be convinced once and for all that all the clubs that are advertising how great they are are only looking for advertising and are afraid to play

Giants, though he kept most of the players from the 1909 Leland Giants.

In his first effort as an administrator, Rube, who continued to pitch and manage, assembled a team of superstars. Foster was the ace of a staff that included standouts Frank Wickware and Pat Dougherty. Rifle-armed Bruce Petway was the catcher. In the infield were Home Run Johnson and John Henry Lloyd. Pete Hill, who had batted .350 in the 1909 Cuban Winter League, was the center-fielder.

After tapping the rosters of the Philadelphia Giants and the Brooklyn Royal Giants, Foster led his newly formed troops on a tour of the South to get ready for the upcoming season. More and more, teams were tuning up in March and April

Carroll Ray (Dink) Mothell. After the 1923 season, Kansas City Monarchs owner J.L. Wilkinson, who also operated the All Nations team, decided to break up his second club. The St. Louis Stars picked up Willie Bobo in the liquidation for almost nothing. When the Stars made a bid for Mothell, Wilkinson balked. The Stars even offered Cool Papa Bell for several Monarchs and Mothell. "Mothell was the greatest utility man in the game of baseball," Bell said. "He could step in at any position, except pitcher, and you'd never notice that the regular player was missing."

Ed Mackel and the New York Giants, 1921. With the exception of 1903, when he served one season as trainer of the Cincinnati Reds, Mackel (seated, far left) spent twenty-three years working for John McGraw. He began his career as an athletic trainer in 1899 at Johns Hopkins University in Baltimore. In 1922, McGraw gave the eulogy at Mackel's funeral, stating: "I have not merely lost a great club trainer, but also a good and irreplaceable friend."

us. We are open to play any place or any club. Now watch them all crawl in their hole. If our challenge is not accepted this year, we will claim the undisputed right to championship of the world."

They were strong words, but the 1910 Leland Giants could back up any of their effusive manager's boasts. In 129 games they compiled an incredible record of 123-6, a .954 winning percentage. Clearly, Foster's team was the "undisputed champion of the world."

Nevertheless, Foster, a perfectionist, couldn't resist signing Bill Lindsay, ace of the Kansas City (Kansas) Giants, late in the season. The K.C. club, so dominant in 1909 when they'd won fifty-four straight, already had been weakened by the departure of manager Topeka Jack Johnson, who'd

jumped to the rival Kansas City (Missouri) Royal Giants. The Royals evidently weren't faring too well, either. In the July 9 *Freeman*, this advertisement, under the headline *Base Ball Players Wanted*, appeared: "Pitcher, Catcher and Short Stop. Must be able to play in fast company. Send reference and salary wanted. Address Jack Johnson, Mgr., 1005 McGee St., Kansas City, Mo."

In the East, the Philly Giants and the Brooklyn Royal Giants had been decimated by player defections, mainly to Foster's Leland Giants. Philadelphia had even lost the services of manager Sol White, who became manager of the Brooklyn Royal Giants after a dispute with Philly owner Walter Schlichter.

After dusting off the local competition in 1910, Foster packed his champions off to Cuba for ten

The New York Giants, 1923. After the death of veteran trainer Ed Mackel, the Giants added two more black trainers — Walter Irvin (front row, far left) and Emmett Parker (second row, far right).

games against Havana's finest, Almendares and Havana. Baseball had been popular on the island since the early 1880s. By the 1890s major league teams were paying winter visits to play local teams, and in the early 1900s the Cuban X Giants began taking a regular winter tour. During the same period, Cuba began sending a team of all-stars to compete in America. The Cuban Stars, as they were called, played the Negro circuit.

Playing in Cuba, and later Puerto Rico, Mexico and other Latin American countries, was a study in contrasts for the Americans. When the Leland Giants visited Cuba in the fall of 1910, they encountered no color barrier, no discrimination, no Jim Crow. They were not viewed as "black Americans"; they were simply Americans, who were to be afforded treatment equal to that of any other visitor. Back home in May of that same year, the National Association for the Advancement of Colored People (NAACP) was beginning its long fight for equality. "The problem of the twentieth century is the problem of the color line," said W.E.B. Du Bois, the Harvard-educated civil rights leader. Back home in July of 1910, race riots broke out all over the country when black heavyweight boxer Jack Johnson successfully defended his title against Jim Jeffries, the Great White Hope.

Their stay in Cuba also provided the players with a welcome change of pace. There were no grueling trips on the small island and double-headers were a rarity. When the Leland Giants played there in 1910, their ten-game series, which took place in Havana, was played over twenty-five days, a far cry from the frenetic pace of their summer schedule. In Cuba they also were routinely given the opportunity to compare skills not only with the fine Cuban players but with major leaguers as well. They measured up on both counts.

Against the Cuban teams that fall, the Giants won five games, lost four and tied one. John Henry Lloyd batted .400 in forty at-bats. Third baseman Wes Pryor was the only other player to bat higher than .300. Bill Lindsay won two games, while Foster, Frank Wickware and Pat Dougherty split two games each.

The Hilldale Club, 1923. (L to R) John Henry Lloyd (manager), Red Ryan, Pud Flournoy, Clint Thomas, Raleigh (Biz) Mackey, Jake Stephens, Jesse (Nip) Winters, owner Ed Bolden, Judy Johnson, George Carr, Frank Warfield, Toussaint Allen, Holsey (Scrip) Lee, Louis Santop. In 1923, the first year of the Eastern Colored League, Hilldale won the pennant with a record of 32-17 and finished with an overall mark of 137-43-6 that included a split of a two-game series with the major league Philadelphia A's. During the inaugural World Series in 1924 against the Kansas City Monarchs, Winters, a left-hander, won three games and lost one, while striking out 21 in 38 innings.

Fannie Robinson. She was the wife of Bill (Bojangles) Robinson, the famous tap dancer and owner of the New York Black Yankees. Whenever the Robinsons were in Kansas City, they stayed at the home of Quincy Gilmore, secretary of the Kansas City Monarchs. This photograph was given to the Gilmores in 1923.

After concluding the series, several of the Giants were invited to play for the Havana team in a six-game set against the Detroit Tigers. The Tigers, who had finished third in the American League that year, were led by Ty Cobb, recent winner of his fourth straight batting crown, and "Wahoo" Sam Crawford, the league's RBI leader. Their pitchers included twenty-one-game winner George Mullin, Ed Willet, who'd won sixteen, and Ed Summer, twelve. Havana used John Henry Lloyd at shortstop, Home Run Johnson at second, Bruce Petway behind the plate and Pete Hill in the outfield.

The teams split the six games, with all of the black players making important contributions to the Cuban cause. Lloyd stroked eleven hits in twenty-two at-bats for a .500 average, Johnson was 7-for-17 (.412), Petway 7-for-18 (.389) and Hill 6-for-22 (.273). Cobb batted .368 but twice was cut down on steal attempts by Petway.

When Cuba opened its winter league to foreigners in 1907, it had a profound effect on the Negro player, who like the major leaguers was paid only from April to October. The option of going to Cuba in the winter, where the season ran from late December or early January to early April, offered him the opportunity to work at his profession

almost year-round. Participation was by invitation only, though; no mediocrity wanted. Since each team was allowed only a few Americans, they didn't want to waste their allotment of foreign attractions on anything less than an outstanding player. Once there the black players played side by side not only with the fine Cuban players but major leaguers also, an occurrence unheard of at home.

The baseball-crazy fans of Havana were color-blind in their adulation of the imported stars. John Henry Lloyd, a longtime favorite, was just as bright a star as Ty Cobb. Nicknamed "El Cuchara" (The Shovel) for his habit of scooping up dirt along with ground balls, Lloyd made his first trip to Cuba in 1908. He played a total of twelve seasons, the last in 1930. From the early 1900s until Fidel Castro closed the doors after the 1959-60 season, hundreds of players cashed in on the Cuban Winter League.

For the early players, those of the 1900-1920 era, the journey to the Caribbean offered them their only exposure to something other than independent baseball. There were set schedules, culminating with a pennant winner. The local papers covered the action diligently, printing the box scores and standings, and offering statistics on the batting and pitching leaders. Back home there were plenty of games for black players, but they basically were playing exhibition baseball. Without a league, with little press coverage, with no official crown passing from team to team at season's end, there was a sense that Negro baseball was

William Ross, pitcher. He had a tendency to lose his control at times. While playing a game with the ABCs Ross hit a player in the head early in the game. Several innings later, as he walked past the other team's bench, he stopped suddenly and proclaimed, "Look, that man has one of our balls under his hat." Ross approached the player and pulled his hat off, revealing a large lump from the errant fastball he had thrown earlier.

The Chicago American Giants, early 1920s. (L to R) John Reese, Otis Starks, Robert Poindexter, Floyd (Jelly) Gardner, George Dixon, Jimmie Lyons, Dave Malarcher, Christobel Torrienti, Jack Marshall, Jim Brown, Elwood (Bingo) DeMoss, Tom Williams, Dave Brown, Leroy Grant, Tom Johnson. Torrienti was one of the top sluggers of the era, though he was hot-tempered. The American Giants eventually became fed up with his outbursts and traded him to the Monarchs in 1926. While in Kansas City, Torrienti sued trainer James Floyd and the team for allegedly losing his diamond ring, which was valued at $250. The Monarchs released him at the end of the season, though he continued to play for ten more years.

unimportant.

Some local leagues did exist, among them the Chicago City League. The Leland Giants were perennial powers in that circuit, which was made up of area semipro teams, both black and white. The Cuban Stars also played in it during the years when they made Chicago their home base. In New Orleans, in 1903 and 1904, there was a four-team league that played for Bayou bragging rights. There was also a league in Boston in 1903 and 1904 called the Greater Boston Colored League. But these were local efforts that failed to generate national interest. Virtually all teams remained unattached. Increasingly, though, voices were calling for these clubs to come together under one banner.

David Wyatt of the *Indianapolis Freeman* recognized the need to bring structure to this loose confederation. In the March 5, 1910 *Freeman* he penned a poetic plea under the headline: *Let's Organize*:

> We have players who can bat and players who can field. We have players who can pitch and who can run, we have magnates with the glad hand, also the baseball fan; we have coaches who can make a lot of fun. We have umpires, we have scribes, the

John Henry Lloyd. In 1921, Rube Foster persuaded Lloyd to move west and manage the Columbus Buckeyes. Lloyd managed the team to a sixth-place finish and then decided to return to the East the next season, which infuriated Foster. "Lloyd received more money than I have ever paid a player on the American Giants to manage this club," Foster stated. "Lloyd has never been a successful manager and never will be." Responded Lloyd: "I do not want Foster to make money off my ability."

The Chicago Giants, 1920. Standing (L to R): Unknown, Horace Jenkins, Unknown, Unknown, John Beckwith, Butler White, James Davis, Unknown. Kneeling: Bob Winston, Bob Anderson, Unknown, Joe Green, Unknown, Willie Green, Jack Jennings. Joe Green was the owner of this team, which at one time belonged to Frank C. Leland. As a player during the Leland Giants 1909 series against the Chicago Cubs, Green broke his leg while sliding into third base. Noticing that the ball had eluded Harry Steinfeldt, the Cubs' third baseman, Green made a great effort to score by hopping within a yard of home before leftfielder Jimmy Sheckard's throw to Pat Moran nipped him at the plate. Green dropped to the ground and was carried from the field. The Giants went on to lose the game, 4-1.

Frank Duncan. The Monarch catcher was married to jazz recording artist Julia Lee. According to Milton Morris, a Kansas City jazz promoter, when Julia was appearing at a white club, "Frank had to carry a horn case and sit in the bandstand to see his wife perform, because Negroes were not allowed in the audience."

latter to criticize; we have cranks and also enthusiasts; but of all this, the one we need most is the man who will say, 'Let's organize.'

Big leagues all have grounds and players of wide renown; they have their Wagners and their Crawfords and their Stahls; they have magnates with money to burn and others eager to earn. They are organized and that's the best of all. They've got us on the run in this game, more work than fun. This fact, no doubt you have surmised, so while running in this race, why not keep up with the pace? Get together and proceed to organize.

The importance of this plea sooner or later you'll surely see, that it's timely and directed at the right place; so while you have the chance, accept opportunities to advance and uphold the rapid progress of our race. The game is honest, the game is square, a point we all declare, so we need not dwell on that at any length; from out of our slumber let us arise and treat our friends to a grand surprise — be up and doing! Let's organize.

Rube Foster, who ultimately answered the call, was another outspoken and ardent supporter of the cause. In the April 16, 1910, edition of the *Freeman*,

The St. Louis Stars, 1922. Standing (L to R): Joe (Buck) Hewitt, Bob Fagan, Unknown, Unknown, Unknown, Unknown, James (Cool Papa) Bell, Unknown, Logan (Eggie) Hensley. Kneeling: Unknown, Branch Russell, Unknown, Unknown, John Reese, Unknown, Otto Ray. Front: Unknown, George Scales. Russell spent seven years as an army track man and baseball player before Casey Stengel recommended him to the Kansas City Monarchs in 1922. The St. Louis Stars traded their ace pitcher, Bill Drake, to Kansas City to obtain Russell, who was a solid outfielder and contributor to the Stars' pennant-winning seasons in 1928, 1930 and 1931.

which was dedicated to the upcoming season, Foster wrote an article in which he made note of the strides blacks had made in the game. He concluded with a petition to the business community:

"In my opinion the time is now at hand when the formation of colored leagues should receive much consideration. In fact, I believe it is absolutely necessary. What we need is the proper financial backing and encouragement.... The business end of the game has lagged along to such an extent that we now find ourselves in a dangerous predicament. We have a country full of colored ball players, well-developed as to playing; but the places for giving employment to them are being promoted with such an eel-like pace, and the majority are founded upon such an uncertain business principle, that it is having a tendency to throw a dense cloud over the Negro .... The players have, through all sorts of adverse conditions, been able to bring our race to the notice of thousands who are interested in the game. Now will our businessmen and friends of the profession make an effort to help us to reach the coveted goal of complete success, or will they stand by and see us fail? Which

shall it be?"

For the next ten years, there was not failure, but there was by no means complete success, either. From 1911 through 1919, it was basically business as usual, including the familiar claims made by "world champions." As noted, Rube Foster's Leland Giants compiled an awesome record of 123-6 in 1910. The following year Foster formed a partnership with a man named John Schorling, who handled business matters, while Rube maintained control of the baseball department. They renamed the team the Chicago American Giants and played their games at the Chicago White Sox's former park, which Schorling rebuilt into a 9,000-seat stadium and renamed Schorling Park.

Frank Leland, meanwhile, reclaimed the name "Leland Giants" for his team, and by June of 1911 confusion reigned.

The Leland Giants, knowingly or otherwise, were being billed as the "colored world's champions." The counterfeit champs traveled to Kansas City in early July and lost a series to the Kansas City (Kansas) Giants. The *Kansas City Journal* reported that the K.C. club was "entitled to the claim of being the champion Negro team of America." Their reign lasted until Foster brought his American Giants to town later in the month and took three of four to reclaim the crown they'd never really lost in the first place.

Rampant jumping continued. One reason for this was that new teams were continually forming. And what better way to stock a club than by going after proven stars? Given the flimsiness of most contracts (if they existed at all) players essentially were free agents, ready, willing and able to sell their services to the highest bidder. The Lincoln Giants, formed in Harlem in 1911, became an overnight power-house in just this manner.

Their founder was Jess McMahon, a white boxing promoter who had a keen eye for talent and was committed to building a championship baseball team in Harlem. No club was spared as he conducted one raid after another.

Rube Foster, never timid about pilfering players, had his own pocket picked by McMahon, who grabbed John Henry Lloyd, Grant (Home Run) Johnson and Pete Booker from the American Giants. Frank Leland lost the services of Smoky Joe Williams and Bill Pettus, while the Philadelphia Giants lost Cannonball Dick Redding, Louis Santop and Spottswood Poles.

Clarence Everett. He had tryouts with the St. Louis Stars and the Kansas City Monarchs before being signed by the Detroit Stars in 1925. Everett spent most of his career with the Gilkerson Union Giants, an independent team.

The Estavan Team, 1921. This was a mixed team that played in Canada. Standing second from right is Joe Davis.

Right: Wilber (Bullet) Rogan (left) and George Carr. Rogan played only one season in the Cuban Winter League. In the 1924-25 campaign, he pitched eighteen games for Almendares, finishing with a 9-4 record. George Carr was a great all-around player, who also had a reputation for being a great all-around drinker. Teammate Clint Thomas once said of him: "On payday, every time you saw Carr he had a fish sandwich in one hand and a pint of liquor in the other."

Below, left: George Alexander Sweatt. His two triples in the sixth and seventh games of the 1924 World Series helped the Monarchs win their first championship. After the 1925 season, Sweatt was traded to the Chicago American Giants for Christobel Torrienti. The Chicago American Giants went to the World Series in 1926 and 1927, making Sweatt one of two players to perform in all four of the Negro World Series games played during the 1920s. The other was Rube Currie, who played for Hilldale in 1924 and 1925, then for the American Giants in 1926 and 1927.

Below, right: Mr. and Mrs. Richard Rogan. They were the parents of Bullet Rogan. Originally from Oklahoma, they moved to Kansas City in search of a more prosperous environment.

Next page, below left: Newton Allen (left) and Robert Fagan. Fagan, a second baseman, was a member of the 24th Infantry baseball team before joining the Kansas City Monarchs in 1921. The following season he was traded to St. Louis. Allen eventually replaced him at second. When Allen first visited Cuba in 1923, he had an excellent season, batting .313. The Cubans nicknamed him "The Black Diamond." He liked the name so much that when he returned home, he had a dentist cap one of his front teeth in gold and place a diamond in it.

Next page, below right: (L to R) Neil Pullen, Herbert (Rap) Dixon, Crush Holloway. Pullen was a catcher and the home run king of the California Winter League. Although he received many offers to move east and play in one of the leagues, Pullen refused to leave California. The most renowned player to join the Negro National League from the Coast League was George Carr.

Pitchers Joe Williams and Dick Redding were enough to make the Lincoln Giants a threat against any team. Smoky Joe, from San Antonio, Texas, was twenty-five years old when he went to Harlem, having spent most of his early pro career playing with obscure Texas teams. He was playing in Los Angeles in the winter of 1909 when Leland signed him for the 1910 season. He was a 6'5" right-hander with a sizzling fastball and sinker. Cannon-ball Dick, born in Atlanta in 1891, was playing for a team in his native city when the Philadelphia Giants discovered him on a southern trip in the spring of 1911. He came north with them and jumped to the Lincoln Giants later in the season. Another speedballer, Redding ran off seventeen straight victories after joining the Harlem club.

Louis Santop, also plucked from the Philly Giants, was a lefty-swinging, power-hitting catcher. He was rated just behind Bruce Petway as a receiver, but had a more potent bat. Spottswood Poles, another former Philadelphia Giant, was a quick outfielder who was spectacular at the plate. In his first year with the Lincolns, "Spot" led the club in hitting — batting over .400 — and also stole forty-one bases.

The Lincoln Giants, with their star-studded lineup, quickly established themselves as the premier team in the East. In 1913 six of their players, John Henry Lloyd, Spot Poles, Jude Gans, Billy Francis, Smoky Joe Williams and Dick Redding, were invited to play for Fe of the Cuban Winter League. All except Francis contributed mightily to a pennant-winning season. Poles batted .364, Gans .346 and Lloyd .341. Williams won nine games in fourteen decisions, while Redding chipped in with seven victories.

At home their only true competition for national supremacy came from Foster's Chicago American Giants. In 1913, the two powers settled the issue in a head-to-head confrontation won by the easterners. Rube Foster, in a year-end summary in the *Indianapolis Freeman*, called it the greatest spectacle since 1904, when the Philadelphia Giants recaptured the title from the Cuban X Giants. Rube, who didn't take losing well, was surprisingly gracious in defeat, writing, "I am one who takes his hat off to the victorious Lincoln Giants. Their great playing and wonderful defense was never surpassed, if equalled, on any diamond."

The year 1913 also marked the passing of one of baseball's important pioneers. In the March 1 edition of the Frankfort [New York] *Evening Telegram* the following obituary was published:

"The death of John W. Jackson, which occurred yesterday at the home of his sister, Mrs. John Odom, removed from this life a man who at one time was one of the most famous ball players of the country and who always took great pride in his baseball record . . . . In baseball circles he was known as 'Bud Fowler.' "

The man who was the first to cross the color line, the founder of the Page Fence Giants who practiced his craft in all corners of the country, was fifty-four years old when he died of pernicious anemia. His life was a monument to the game he loved. Even in his final years, while battling serious illness, he had been trying to organize another team but was unable to obtain the financial backing.

Joe Williams. In the West, he was known as Cyclone Joe; in the East, he was Smoky Joe. One thing the two regions agreed on was that Joe Williams, a tall right-hander who was active from 1905 until the late 1930s, was one of the best pitchers who ever lived. He was also the pitcher whom Satchel Paige admired above all others.

Ty Cobb. In 1923 the Chicago American Giants played the American League Detroit Tigers in a three-game set without the services of Cobb. The *Chicago Defender* hinted as to why he would be missing when it declared, "Of course old Ty Cobb of Georgia won't show up."

The Negro league players did not receive the publicity or pay of their major league counterparts. However, they were able to take pride in their skills, knowledge and commitment to the national pastime. From the *Pittsburgh Courier,* 1924.

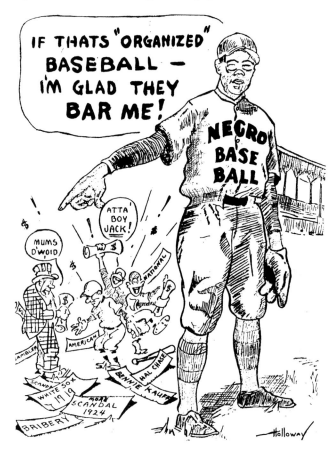

The Rogan Family. Wilber Rogan, pictured here with wife Kathryn and son Wilber Rogan, Jr., led the Kansas City Monarchs in batting (.317 average) and pitching (two wins) during the 1924 World Series. In 1925, he missed the entire Series when he accidentally stuck a needle into his knee while playing with his son the day before the first game. The Rogan-less Monarchs lost the Series to Hilldale in six games.

while two of C.I.'s brothers manned the corners, Ben at first and Candy Jim at third. Anchoring the pitching staff were Cannonball Dick Redding of Lincoln Giant fame and William (Dizzy) Dismukes, a right-hander who threw submarine-style. It was a formidable — and fiery — outfit.

In late October of 1915 the ABCs played against a team of touring minor leaguers. The game proceeded smoothly enough until the fifth inning, when an umpire called one of the minor leaguers safe at second on a steal. DeMoss disagreed — violently. He charged the ump, gave him a push and then took a swing at him. The second baseman and umpire had their fists up when center-fielder Oscar Charleston, on a dead run, streaked into the infield and delivered an overhand left to the face of the arbitrator, knocking him to the ground and opening a cut on the side of his face. Bedlam erupted.

Another team that began developing a rich history during this era was the Indianapolis ABCs. The club, which was named for its original sponsor, the American Brewing Company, was managed by Charles I. Taylor. C.I., as he was commonly called, was a native of Anderson, North Carolina who had been the skipper of the Birmingham Giants from 1904 to 1912 before moving north to manage the West Baden (Indiana) Sprudels. After a successful two-year stint there, he was lured to the ABCs.

Widely regarded as one of the game's top managers, Taylor also was a pretty fair talent scout, as he proved in 1915 when he assembled one of the best teams in the country. Perhaps his most important move was the signing of a nineteen year old local product named Oscar Charleston. From the start of his illustrious career Charleston was an impact player who could sway a game with his strong arm, raw speed or powerful bat. Bingo DeMoss, a peppery second baseman, also was recruited and was Taylor's leader on the field,

Kathryn Rogan. She married Wilber Rogan in 1921. Kathryn was known as an outdoors person, with fishing high on her list of activities. She and Wilber purchased a second home in the Ozarks, where the fish always seemed to be biting.

The Detroit Stars, 1920. Top row (L to R): Bill Holland, Edgar Wesley, Bruce Petway, Charlie Harper, William Gatewood, Unknown, Unknown. Middle row: Buck Hewitt, Pete Hill, Tenny Blount (owner), Jimmie Lyons, Andy Cooper. Bottom row: Unknown, William Force, Orville Riggins, Unknown. In 1923, Holland, a native of Indianapolis, led all pitchers in the Cuban Winter League with a 10-2 record, which earned him the $500 bonus that was awarded to the league's top hurler.

Fans poured onto the field; fights broke out everywhere. A small regiment of eighteen cops wielding billy-clubs was needed to quell the riot. DeMoss and Charleston were charged with assault and battery and carted off to jail. The gentlemanly C.I. Taylor found the incident deplorable. Taylor, whose ABCs began a journey to Cuba immediately after the game, sent a wire to the Indianapolis *Freeman*, condemning the actions of his two rabble-rousers:

"That was a very unwarranted and cowardly act on the part of our center-fielder. There can be no reason given that will justify it . . . . I want to ask that the people do not condemn the ABC baseball club nor my people for the ugly and unsportsmanlike conduct of two thoughtless hotheads."

Bond was posted for Charleston and DeMoss, and the two made their way to Cuba in time for the ABCs twenty-game series with Almendares and Havana. Upon returning to Indianapolis, DeMoss and Charleston were immediately arrested for missing their scheduled court appearance. According to the Indianapolis *Star*, when they were

arrested for the second time, the police department announced that it would no longer allow games between black and white teams. The newspaper quoted a police captain as saying, "It occurs to me that it is time to call a halt in baseball playing between whites and blacks when two teams of mixed colors can no longer play without trouble."

Despite their late-season difficulty, the ABCs remained for many years an upper-echelon team, respected every bit as much as the Chicago American Giants or the Lincoln Giants. In October of 1916 the ABCs squared off with Rube Foster's American Giants in what the *Freeman* billed as the World Series. It turned into a highly controversial nine-game set (eight, according to Foster), with the Indianapolis team winning five for the championship.

After splitting the first two games, the ABCs held a 1-0 lead in game three when the trouble started. Foster was coaching first when he picked up his first baseman's glove, which was lying nearby. (It was customary then for players to leave their gloves in the field when batting.) Ben Taylor, the ABCs'

The Kansas City Monarchs, 1920. Standing (L to R): John Donaldson, Sam Crawford, Rube Currie, Rodrigues, Zack Forman, Unknown, George Carr, Wilber Rogan. Front row: Jose Mendez, Unknown, Bartolo Portuando, Walter Moore, Otto Ray, Hurley McNair. In 1915, Mendez, who possessed one of the game's better fastballs, killed teammate Jose Rigarola when he hit him in the chest with a pitch during batting practice. Forman, a right-handed pitcher, had attended Langston University, Langston, Oklahoma. His life ended tragically when he was shot while leaving a party in Oklahoma.

The Hilldale Athletic Club, 1921. Back row (L to R): Ed Bolden, George Johnson, Chaney White, Richard Whitworth, Jim York, Cornelius (Broadway) Rector, Louis Santop, "Pud" Flournoy, Toussaint Allen, Byrd (stockholder). Front row: Otto Briggs, McKinley (Bunny) Downs, Jake Stephens, Flammer, Dobbins, Bill Francis (captain), Napoleon Cummings, Phil Cockrell. Hilldale, which finished the '21 season with a 105-41-3 record, featured four twenty-game winners: Rector (22-8), Whitworth (22-10), Cockrell (23-12) and Flournoy (23-6). George Johnson, a center-fielder, was a native of San Marcos, Texas, who broke into the professional ranks with the Fort Worth Wonders in 1909. He later played with the Kansas City (Kansas) Giants and Brooklyn Royal Giants before signing with Hilldale in 1918. Johnson batted .391 with 31 home runs in 1922, and .413 with 22 homers in 1923.

The Chicago American Giants, 1920. Standing (L to R): Christobel Torrienti, Tom Johnson, Unknown, Unknown, Rube Foster, Elwood (Bingo) DeMoss, Leroy Grant, Tom Williams, Jack Marshall. Kneeling: Jim Brown, Otis Starks, George Dixon, Dave Malarcher, Dave Brown, Unknown, John Reese. The entertaining DeMoss always played second base with a toothpick in his mouth. Leroy Grant, a first baseman, later was incarcerated at a prison in Michigan, where he was stabbed to death. Dave Malarcher was a graduate of New Orleans University.

first baseman, asked the umpire to tell Foster to take off the glove. The umpire did so, but Rube refused to comply, saying he was not in violation of any rule. The parties argued back and forth before the umpire finally ejected the recalcitrant Foster. The Giants' skipper departed, but took his team with him. The result? Victory by forfeit for the home team.

Foster, intensely competitive, was extremely bitter and refused to concede defeat even after losing the series. The locals, meanwhile, were the toast of Indianapolis. Their triumph was heralded by the *Freeman* in its biggest and boldest type: "ABCs Win World Series." The *Freeman* reporter seemed to take particular joy in the fact that the ABCs' victim was Rube Foster. "It was a pitiful sight to look on Mr. Foster as he slowly withdrew from the field," the reporter wrote. "He smiled, but it was not a good smile. He lectured his men severely, but it was not their fault. The best team won . . . ."

The paper also printed a column called "Notes of the Game." One item described Foster's anguish: "As the train pulled out of the Union Station Sunday night that bore the American Giants to Chicago, the mighty Rube locked himself in his stateroom and said, 'Don't anyone bother me until we get to Chicago' . . . . with that he went to bed and thought over the incidents of the past week. It's hard but it's fair, Rube."

There was another team that fared well in the

Below and next page: These five photographs are of White Sox Park in Los Angeles. During the 1920s, non-white baseball teams were banned from using any of the Pacific Coast League stadiums. Thus, a special park was designed for the Negro clubs. Joe Pirrone, who was the driving force behind the California Winter Leagues, had the park built specifically for the black teams. Located at 38th Street and Hopper Avenue, it opened in 1925. "We built White Sox Park for the Negro clubs," Pirrone proclamed, "and it will always be for the Negro clubs."

George Sweatt (standing, second from left). He was both an infielder and outfielder for the Kansas City Monarchs, the Chicago Giants and the Chicago American Giants from 1920 to 1927. Pictured here with the Pittsburg (Kansas) Manual College basketball team, he also received varsity letters in track and football.

summer of 1916, beating on occasion both the champion ABCs and Foster's Giants. The All Nations team, which was created in 1912 by J. Leslie Wilkinson, was comprised of blacks, whites, Indians, Mexicans, Cubans and Asians. It was a traveling team, with its own custom-made railroad car, like that of the Page Fence Giants. In contrast to the Page Fence team, though, the All Nations club shared their accomodations with a group of wrest-

lers and a musical band with which some of the ballplayers moonlighted. Their white manager Wilkinson, himself a former player and manager of several semipro teams in Iowa, was of the belief that you couldn't have **TOO** much entertainment.

By 1916, Wilkinson, led by his two outstanding pitchers, John Donaldson and Jose Mendez, had assembled a fine team. He also had an excellent

Tom Baird (kneeling, third from right). He started in baseball as a player on local teams in Kansas City, Kansas. His playing career was cut short by a railroad accident in 1918 that left him with a permanent limp. Baird then organized the T.Y. Baird Club and won two city championships. In 1919, he went to work for J.L. Wilkinson, who became the owner of the Kansas City Monarchs one year later. Baird and Wilkinson's alliance lasted almost the entire span of the Negro leagues.

Fred Langford. He was a former catcher for the Kansas City (Kansas) Giants and the Parson (Kansas) Smart Set. In 1920, the first year of the Negro National League, Langford was sitting in the stands at a Chicago American Giants game when Jack Marshall, alluding to the growing prosperity of the league, yelled from the field, "Fred, you better join one of these clubs and get some of this easy money."

William Lowe. He attended A&M College in Huntsville, Alabama, where he was coached by George Harney, later an accomplished spitball pitcher for the Chicago American Giants. A member of Tennessee State's first graduating class in 1924, he was soon signed by the Detroit Stars, who paid him $180 per month. In 1926, while managing the Chattanooga Black Lookouts of the Negro Southern League, he signed Satchel Paige to his first professional contract.

The Peters Union Giants. Robert P. Gilkerson (standing, center) was a longtime owner who took his teams throughout the Upper Midwest. From 1926 to 1928 his team played more than 360 games and was shut out only once. Hurley McNair (kneeling, far left) played with Gilkerson's teams for several years.

Cuban outfielder in Christobel Torrienti, a lefty-swinging power-hitter, and a solid catcher in Clarence (Pops) Coleman. The All Nations swept the ABCs and won one of three games from the American Giants shortly before Indianapolis and Chicago met for the championship.

The *Chicago Defender*, a black newspaper, pointed to the All Nations team as an indicator that whites and blacks could share the diamond successfully. In an October issue it called on the lords of baseball to start opening the doors to men of color. "The All Nations baseball team," the *Defender* said, "besides playing the ABCs off their feet and winning one game from the champion American Giants, have demonstrated to the world one thing in particular — that it is possible for

Indianapolis *Freeman* cartoon, 1907. Well before the arrival of C.I. Taylor in Indianapolis, the Indianapolis ABCs had established a strong tradition as a baseball power. Nevertheless, it was under Taylor's guidance that they reached their zenith.

Oscar Charleston and friend. Sportswriter John Johnson of the *Kansas City Call* wrote that Charleston was so fast "he makes Ty Cobb look like a runner with a handicap." In 1921 the St. Louis Giants played the major league St. Louis Cardinals in a five-game exhibition series. The Cardinals won four of the five games. Charleston batted .304 and hit two home runs.

black and white to play professional baseball in harmony on one team." It went on to say that the Donaldsons, Lloyds, Petways, etc., surely would enhance the White Sox's or Cubs' chances of reaching the World Series.

The *Defender* also could have looked back to 1914 and wondered why no blacks were given a chance to play on the major league level. As the first shots of World War I were being fired in Eastern Europe, the American and National Leagues were under fire from an ambitious organization called the Federal League. Formerly a minor league, the Federal League tried to establish itself as a major league by signing several players from major league teams, among them such stalwarts as Edd Roush and Mordecai (Three Finger) Brown. The league operated for only two years before agreeing to bow out in return for compensation from the older leagues. Surely the Federal League would have stood a better chance of surviving if it had dared to break baseball's unwritten rule and signed the best black players of the day.

In concluding its story about the All Nations team, the *Defender* said baseball integration

The Louisville Giants were greatly reduced in weight by the little Davids (A. B. C's.)

Carroll (Dink) Mothell (left) and an unidentified player. In 1927, Negro League umpire Bert Gholston wrote of Mothell, "He is one of the best second basemen in the circuit. His fielding is the talk of the day throughout the league. He is an ideal running mate for any good shortstop. He can range far to the left or right with perfect ease and he is deadly on slow hit balls that require accurate fielding and a quick throw."

John Henry Lloyd. In 1924 Lloyd, then forty, collected eleven consecutive hits while playing for the Bacharach Giants of the Eastern Colored League.

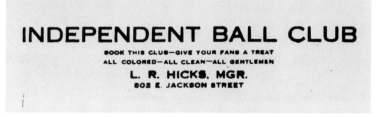

INDEPENDENT BALL CLUB
BOOK THIS CLUB—GIVE YOUR FANS A TREAT
ALL COLORED—ALL CLEAN—ALL GENTLEMEN
L. R. HICKS, MGR.
802 E. JACKSON STREET

L.R. Hicks. He had been a regular third baseman for the Browns Tennessee Rats for many years before trying his hand at the business end of baseball. As indicated by his letterhead, he was convinced that personal hygiene and gentlemanly behavior were essential to his promotion.

should be the responsibility of the "magnates, not the players, to give the public what they demand — a winning club, not a club of white men, but a club of all men like the All Nations, regardless of color or creed, a team with ability."

The *Defender's* hope notwithstanding, a color-blind national pastime was still in the distant future. What was on the horizon was a more organized approach to the game. As America plunged into World War I in April of 1917, many of the barnstorming teams, including the All Nations, disbanded after being decimated by the military draft. For the next eighteen months, not only the number of teams, but the level of play, dropped significantly. When the war ended in November of 1918, those players who returned, along with those who had remained behind, were ready for a new beginning. It was up to Rube Foster, the Father of the Negro leagues, to provide it.

Chapter 5

Since the early days of his professional career, Rube Foster had been having a recurring dream. In it the leaders of Negro baseball, putting aside parochial differences, came together and built a grand stage for their game, one that provided their players a proper setting for their considerable talents. Attendance grew steadily, especially as the pennant races heated up, and the World Series established a true champion at season's end. The newspapers satisfied their readers' craving for information by providing total coverage, from game stories and columns to the standings and box scores. In Rube's fantasy owners and players alike prospered — in the Negro leagues.

For many years, Foster, along with several black sportswriters, had written of the need for a more organized approach. In 1913, the game's most well-known and respected figure penned a state-of-the-game analysis for the *Indianapolis Freeman*. It was published under the headline, *What the Greatest Pitcher of his Time Thinks of the Baseball Situation* and in a segment on the game's future, Foster wrote:

"Organization is its only hope. With the proper organization, patterned after the men who have made baseball a success, we will, in three years, be rated as other leagues are rated. We have the players and it could not be a failure, as the same territory is traveled now by all the clubs, with no organization or money. It would give us a rating and standing in the daily papers which would create an interest and we could then let the best clubs in our organization play for the world's championship with other clubs, champions of their leagues."

Foster called on blacks to take advantage of baseball's increasing popularity. "It would be a crime," he wrote, "for the Negro who has such an abundance of talent in such a progressive age, to sit idly by and see his race forever doomed to America's greatest and foremost sport."

In closing, Foster stated that any organization would have to be "for the welfare of all . . . . and can only be successful on the same basis as a big league is formed."

In October of 1916 the Chicago American Giants visited Kansas City to play a three-game series against J.L. Wilkinson's All Nations team. While there, Foster and his American Giants were honored with a banquet at the Chase Cafe. With many of Kansas City's political and civic leaders in attendance, the tribute quickly turned into a campaign, led by Foster, to form a Negro baseball league. Though little progress was made, Foster, throughout his travels, was beginning to gather support for his grand plan.

As the decade closed and the '20s began to roar, Foster had made believers of other influential owners in the Midwest. All had grown weary of the independent ways of their game. It was time to start restraining greedy players who jumped teams at the drop of a dollar. It was time to rid the sport of the powerful white booking agents, who exerted an economic choke hold on the game and who could cripple a franchise by denying it access to the major ballparks. It was time to bring an end to their

The Los Angeles Royal Giants, 1929. Standing (L to R): Lonnie Goodwin, Andy Cooper, Crush Holloway, Neil Pullen, L.D. Livingston, T.J. Young, Raleigh (Biz) Mackey. Kneeling: Carroll Mothell, Wilber Rogan, Unknown, Newt Allen, Newt Joseph. Livingston played for the Monarchs in the late 1920s when they beat the Houston Buffalos in a "world series" of Western teams. Afterward, he went to visit relatives in Dallas. While waiting for a cab, he was approached by two white policeman who wanted to know what he was doing. When Livingston explained that he was a member of the Monarchs, one of the cops said, "You're one of those Northern boys who beat the Houston club in that series." Ushered off to jail, Livingston was subsequently fined $20. When he asked the desk sergeant what the charge was, he was told, "Hell, boy, you're in Texas."

William Perkins. A catcher, he was a member of the Pittsburgh Crawfords with Satchel Paige and Josh Gibson in the '30s. Although Perkins was a better defensive catcher than Gibson, he was relegated to bench duty because of Gibson's powerful bat. When he did get to play, Perkins sometimes would get mad at Paige for throwing so hard, and would often fire the ball back to the mound almost as hard as it came in.

nomadic existence and maximize their economic potential. It was time for the Negro leagues.

On February 14, 1920, a historic two-day meeting, presided over by Foster, was convened at the YMCA in Kansas City. Other owners in attendance included John (Tenny) Blount of the Detroit Stars, Joe Green of the Chicago Giants, J.L. Wilkinson of the All Nations and C.I. Taylor of the Indianapolis ABCs. John Matthews, owner of the Dayton Marcos, was unable to attend because of illness but pledged his cooperation. Team secretary Lorenzo Cobb represented the St. Louis Giants, while Foster handled the affairs of the American Giants and the Cuban Stars. Other invitees included sportswriters David Wyatt and A.D. Williams of the *Indianapolis Ledger,* Elwood C. Knox of the *Indianapolis Freeman,* Gary Lewis of the *Chicago Defender* and C.A. Franklin of the *Kansas City Call.* Elisha Scott, an attorney, was there to assist in legal matters.

The sportswriters spent the evening drafting a constitution, and it was approved the following day. There would be an eight team "experimental" league called the Negro National League, consisting of the Chicago American Giants, the Chicago Giants, the Dayton Marcos, the Detroit Stars, the Indianapolis ABCs, the Kansas City Monarchs, the St. Louis Giants and the Cuban Stars. Wilkinson, the only white owner in the league, would operate the Monarchs, while maintaining the All Nations as an independent. All owners paid a $1,000 binder, and

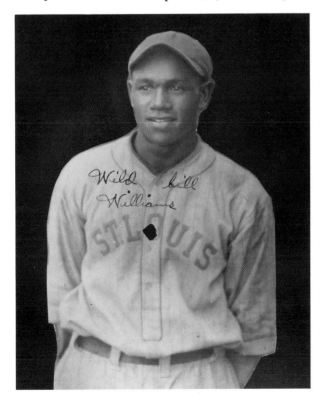

Robert (left) and George Mitchell. Opponents of the St. Louis Stars in 1924 might have thought they were seeing double when they stepped into the batter's box and saw Robert behind the plate and his identical twin brother, George, on the mound.

John Williams, 1928. According to James (Cool Papa) Bell, Williams, a right-hander, was an outstanding pitcher and a fine utility outfielder.

Maurice Wiggins (left) and William (Big) Mitchell. During the depression in 1933, Wiggins played in 131 games for the Gilkerson Union Giants. When he returned to Chicago at season's end, he had a grand total of $19 to show for his efforts. Mitchell was a hard-throwing pitcher who never played in the Negro National League because he refused to leave his job in the Chicago stockyards. He spent his entire career playing semipro baseball in the Chicago area.

Frank Duncan. In 1939 he played the last half of the season with the Palmer House Hotel team in Chicago. During one game he was hit in the temple with a pitch. According to teammate Maurice Wiggins, "Duncan dropped like a rock," and had to spend three days in a hospital.

agreed to honor each other's player contracts. Rube Foster, naturally, was elected league president.

The magnates also established an overall governing body called the National Association of Colored Professional Baseball Clubs. By joining, a team could be assured that its players were safe from the advances of other teams in the organization.

As president, one of Foster's first duties was to return players who had jumped in recent years to their previous teams. Oscar Charleston, for example, was sent from Chicago back to Indianapolis. Jose Mendez, Sam Crawford and John Donaldson, formerly of the All Nations, were ordered to leave the Detroit Stars and join Wilkinson's Monarchs.

The league opened May 2 in Indianapolis, where the host ABCs defeated the Chicago Giants, 4-2. By the time it ended in September, most of the franchises had seen a major improvement in

attendance over the preleague years. In Chicago and Kansas City, more than 200,000 showed up during the course of the season to root on the American Giants and Monarchs. Although the league did not release financial records after the first season, a story in the *St. Louis Argus* indicated that the St. Louis Giants enjoyed a profitable year. St. Louis, formally known as the St. Louis Giants Baseball and Amusement Association, was the only team that wasn't individually owned. "During their January 15, 1921, annual meeting," the story in the *Argus* stated, "the stockholders of the St. Louis Giants were paid a 14 per cent dividend on their first season's investment in organized baseball. The team also set aside a fund to send the players to the South for spring training." Team president Charles Mills remarked, "Baseball in St. Louis has now been placed upon a sound foundation, not only as a sport, but as a safe business proposition. The company has established itself in the confidence of the people and everybody is pulling for

On the road with the Kansas City Monarchs. This photograph, taken in 1928, shows (L to R) Newt Allen, Newt Joseph, L.D. (Goo Goo) Livingston and owner J.L. Wilkinson as they help a farmer with his automobile. Evidently Joseph, with goggles, was driving the Monarch bus.

Cool Papa Bell and wife Clara. The Bells were married in 1928 and spent their honeymoon in Cuba, where Cool Papa made his debut in the Cuban Winter League, leading the circuit in runs scored (44), home runs (5) and stolen bases (17).

Chaney White. He played for Hilldale, the Bacharach Giants and several other East Coast teams. White was known as a player who wasn't afraid to "take one for the team," that is, allow himself to get hit by a pitch to get on base. Once there, he was always a threat to steal. According to Judy Johnson, "White had speed to burn."

Otto (Jay Bird) Ray (left) and Mule Knight. In 1919, Ray was a sergeant in the 805th Infantry. He was also the catcher on the regiment's baseball team, which was called the Bearcats. The team was undefeated during 1919.

Eddie Dwight. In 1929 Dizzy Dismukes wrote, "In Dwight, an outfielder, the Kansas City Monarchs have just about the fastest thing on foot in baseball. J. [Cool Papa] Bell on the St. Louis Stars, too, is somewhat of a hoofer, which brings about a general discussion as to who is the faster."

The Hilldale Club, 1929. Team owner Edward Bolden was once asked to name the greatest player ever to suit up for Hilldale. "Many an athlete of superb ability has come and gone since we entered the game," Bolden said. "To single out any man and say that he surpassed all others would be impossible. In fact, I would not attempt to pick out the best man for each position of the club. While it would be easy for some spots like first base, what would I do when I got to the outfield and had to consider Chaney White, Jess Barber, Oscar Charleston, Clint Thomas, Otto Briggs, George Johnson and other high-class men?"

the home team. I predict big things for the Giants.''

Despite that first year's success, there were obstacles that had to be overcome, though they were not as devastating as those surfacing in the major leagues. The 1920 major league season was played under the cloud of an investigation into the Chicago White Sox, several of whose members, it was revealed, had conspired with gamblers to throw the 1919 World Series against the Cincinnati Reds. The Negro National League was untarnished by scandal but did have its share of problems. Among them:

● Newspaper coverage remained incomplete. In general, papers continued to cover their team's home games, while ignoring out-of-town games and the rest of the league. The 1920 season concluded with no final standings published, though the Chicago American Giants were awarded the pennant.

● Unstable franchises weakened the league during the first few years. Many lasted only a year; some folded in midseason. The Dayton Marcos dropped out after 1920 and were replaced by the Columbus Buckeyes, who lasted a year before folding. The Chicago Giants resumed playing independent baseball after the '21 season. In 1922, the Buckeyes and the Giants were replaced by the Pittsburgh Keystones and Cleveland Tate Stars, both of whom collapsed and were replaced by the Toledo Tigers and the Milwaukee Bears in 1923. Both of those teams then dropped out of the league in midseason.

● There was a great disparity in the number of games the teams played. According to final standings published in 1921, the American Giants again won the pennant, winning forty-one out of sixty-two games for a .661 winning percentage. Coming in second were the Kansas City Monarchs, who played eighty-one games, winning fifty (.617). A similar imbalance occurred the following year when the pennant-winning American Giants played fifty-nine games, while the runner-up ABCs played

Cool Papa Bell (left) and Jim (Candy) Taylor. Taylor dedicated his life to baseball. He used to tell his ballplayers, "Do anything you want to do because I don't care if you hit standing on your head, as long as you hit." Bell said of Taylor: "He kept his ballplayers loose, and you loved to play for him."

Kansas City Monarchs letterhead. When J.L. Wilkinson owned the team, he operated the club from Kansas City, Missouri. When Tom Baird purchased the team from Wilkinson in 1947, he operated from Kansas City, Kansas.

The Kansas City Monarchs, 1928. Manager Bullet Rogan would do anything to get his players to the practice field. Playing along are (top row, L to R) Newt Allen, T.J. Young, L.D. Livingston, Carroll (Dink) Mothell. Seated: Newt Joseph, Leroy Taylor, Frank Duncan. Standing (front row): Hallie Harding, Alfred (Army) Cooper and Rogan.

Left: Carl (Lefty) Glass, 1929. The *Kansas City Call* wrote of Glass, the Memphis Red Sox manager, "Glass is a splendid coach, a close student of baseball, clever and original. He inspires the team with the spirit of true sportsmanship and fair play along with the aggressiveness that wins."

Center: Dave Malarcher. In 1928 Bert Gholston, Negro league umpire, was asked about Malarcher, manager of the Chicago American Giants. "[He] is a product of the Rube Foster school," Gholston said. "His foundation is of the best, and his ability in developing young players has made him a distinct success."

Right: George Giles. In 1927, as a rookie, he shared the Monarchs' first base job with Lemuel Hawkins. As part of his indoctrination that year, manager Bullet Rogan wouldn't allow Giles to drink water during practice or games. The next year, owner J.L. Wilkinson called Giles and said, "We have let Hawkins go. The first base job is yours." When spring training opened, Giles went to his manager and said, "Hey, Rogan! I'm going to drink water this year."

sixty-nine. The fifth place St. Louis Stars, formerly the Giants, played only forty-six games.

A St. Louis sportswriter named J.M. Batchman complained about the scheduling in September of 1922, noting that teams playing fewer league games were forced to rely heavily on independently scheduled contests. Batchman lamented that as of early September, the American Giants, the league's biggest draw, had not visited St. Louis. "The cry in this city," Batchman wrote, "is for a game with Mr. Foster's American Giants, yet St. Louis, one of the best-backed teams in the circuit, has at this writing been denied the sight of Rube's warriors. No one knows how good or bad they are."

● Players jumping from team to team within the league was not a problem, but clubs always had to be on the lookout for the marauding Eastern teams.

The Negro National League was powerless to stop a player from joining any team outside of the National Association. When the Eastern Colored League started up in 1923, competition for talent between East and West grew even more intense.

Despite the difficulties, the league still was able to provide a sorely needed legitimacy that had been lacking before 1920. A series of games against an opponent took on added meaning with a league championship at stake. Barnstorming games remained an important source of revenue for all teams, but league contests were of greater significance.

The league also served to boost attendance. The fans of Negro baseball had been thirsting for a league, too. In 1920, the Monarchs drew 15,000 to Association Park for a Sunday game with the American Giants. Later in the year, 11,000 turned

Jose Mendez. In 1928 umpire Bert Gholston paid tribute to Mendez, who had died recently, by saying: "He was a superman of baseball. As a pitcher he was skillful, wily, lionhearted, courageous and showed a wonderful change of pace and control. The stage has but one Bert Williams, the ring has seen but one Joe Gans and baseball has but one Jose Mendez. There will never be another. May his soul rest in peace."

out to see the Monarchs tangle with the Dayton Marcos. Similar numbers were common at many of the parks.

For the players, the increased attendance meant not only an increase in their paychecks, but greater security, as well. Unlike earlier days, player payrolls almost always were met, even if it took an infusion of money from the league office. According to Foster, many of his players were making as much as $175 a month in the early '20s.

It was no doubt the success of the Negro National League that spurred team owners in the East to establish the Eastern Colored League in 1923. Two teams from the East, Hilldale of Philadelphia and the Bacharach Giants of Atlantic City, had been affiliated with the Negro National League through the National Association of Colored

Professional Baseball Clubs. Hilldale's Ed Bolden and Nat Strong, owner of the Brooklyn Royal Giants, were the guiding forces behind the Eastern circuit, establishing a six-team league comprised of Hilldale, the Royal Giants, the Bacharach Giants, the Lincoln Giants, the Cuban Stars (East) and the Baltimore Black Sox. Having seen the error of the NNL's ways, the ECL vowed that all teams would play a uniform number of games.

In their first year, the Easterners didn't fare much better than their counterparts in the West. Plagued by many of the same problems, the league sputtered through their first season, with teams playing anywhere from thirty-six to forty-nine games. Hilldale posted a 32-17 record to beat out the Cuban Stars, who finished 23-17. In the Negro National League, the Kansas City Monarchs ended the American Giants' three-year reign, winning the pennant with a 57-33 record.

The Eastern teams, with an attractive package to offer, stepped up their raiding of Western talent the

Moses Miller. He was an outfielder for the Okmulgee (Oklahoma) Drillers, who played "outlaw ball," a term reserved for independent teams that didn't belong to a league.

Raleigh (Biz) Mackey. A first-rate catcher, he also was used as a utility infielder. In 1927 Mackey, a switch-hitter, hit the first home run in Japan's newly built Jingu Stadium. The *Japan Times* wrote of Mackey's clout: "His homer whistled through the air and landed without a drop in the center-field bleachers and then rolled out of sight some hundred feet into a clump of trees."

season and were replaced by Robert Lewis's Memphis Red Sox, the second Southern team to join the Negro National League (Birmingham was the first).

The main event of 1924 came at season's end when the leagues' two pennant winners — the Kansas City Monarchs and the Hilldale Club — squared off in the inaugural Negro league World Series. The Monarchs finished with a 55-22 record to beat out the Chicago American Giants (49-24), while Hilldale concluded with a 47-22 mark, well ahead of the second place Baltimore Black Sox (30-19). Between feuds over player raids, Rube Foster and ECL President Ed Bolden had managed to hammer out details during the season for the World Series, deciding on a best-of-nine series, with the sites rotating among the cities of the top two teams in each league.

Due to Foster's lobbying, Chicago's Schorling Park, owned by Rube's partner, John Schorling, was

following year. Besides paying more money, the Eastern league also offered the added enticement of far less travel. Teams in the West were spread out from Kansas City to Cleveland. In the East, the league teams were located between Baltimore and New York, all within 200 miles of each other. No team was hit harder by the easterners' raids than the Indianapolis ABCs, who lost ten players, including player/manager Dizzy Dismukes. The ABCs had already been weakened by the death of C.I. Taylor at age fifty in 1922. Taylor, who also served as vice-president of the league, was a revered figure in Indianapolis. The *Chicago Whip*, in its obituary of Taylor, stated: "He fought for baseball. He lived for baseball. He died for baseball. A lasting monument to his memory is the ABC baseball club." The ABCs, wracked by the defections, folded soon after the opening of the '24

Chet Brewer. During a 1928 winter league game, Brewer hit major leaguer Eddie Pick with a pitch. Pick went to first base and eventually advanced to third, where he began yelling at Brewer. The pitcher said nothing until Pick blurted out, "You black blankety blank! You hit me purposely." Brewer threw down the ball and charged at Pick. When the fists stopped flying, Pick had a badly bruised left eye.

penciled in as the site for the final two games. Under the original set-up, three games were to be played in Kansas City, though none on Sunday, when crowds were largest. Those maneuvers sparked an outcry from the *Kansas City Call*, which railed against Foster for including Chicago and Baltimore in the October fest and depriving the locals of a Sunday game. Under the headline, *Hilldale and Chicago get the World Series Apple; We get the Core — If There is One!*, the *Call* wondered, "Whose World Series is this, anyway?" Foster came under attack for "trying to aid Chicago, a noncontestant, rather than Kansas City." The story went on to say that if Foster, "in his zeal to get games for Schorling Park," excludes K.C. from a Sunday date, then he "will be the most unpopular man who ever walked out on the Union Station Plaza."

Foster evidently was swayed somewhat by the furor in the press. Game six was played Sunday, October 12, in Kansas City. The final three games, however, were played at Schorling Park.

Despite the scheduling problems, the Series did bring together some of the great players of the era. The Monarchs had player/manager Jose Mendez, pitchers Wilber (Bullet) Rogan and William Drake, infielders Newt Allen, Newt Joseph and Walter (Dobie) Moore, and outfielder Hurley McNair. For the Hilldale Club, there was catcher Louis Santop, catcher/infielder Raleigh (Biz) Mackey, infielder

William (Judy) Johnson, outfielder Clint Thomas and pitchers Rube Currie and Jesse (Nip) Winters.

Games one and two took place at Shibe Park, home of the Philadelphia A's. Rogan, widely regarded as the game's finest pitcher, hurled K.C. to a 6-2 victory in the opener on Friday, October 3. Hilldale came back the next day and, with left-hander Nip Winters pitching, drubbed the Monarchs, 11-0. Crowds of 5,366 and 8,661 attended the first two games.

The Series moved to Baltimore for games three and four. The third game was a thirteen-inning marathon that was halted by darkness with the score even at six. Game four was tightly contested until the ninth, when second baseman Newt Allen's bases-loaded throwing error allowed Judy Johnson to score the winning run. Rube Currie, who'd jumped to Hilldale from the Monarchs in '23, was the winning pitcher. The batting star was Bullet Rogan, a regular in the outfield when not on the mound. Rogan had two hits and two RBIs in the losing effort. From an attendance standpoint, the Baltimore games were a disaster. Game three drew 5,503, a disappointing turnout for a Sunday, though there was some competition in the area for the fans' attention — on the same day the Washington Senators and the New York Giants were playing game two of the major league World Series. Game four of the Negro Series, played on a Monday, drew

The Baltimore Black Sox, 1929. Top row (L to R): Eggie Clark, Pud Flournoy, Holsey (Scrip) Lee, Oliver Marcelle, Jesse Hubbard, Merven (Red) Ryan, Pete Washington, Bill Force. Bottom row: Herbert (Rap) Dixon, Cook, Gomez, Frank Warfield, Jud Wilson, Dick Lundy, Laymon Yokely. During a game in Cuba in 1928, Marcelle, running from first, successfully broke up a double play but lost two teeth when shortstop Willie Wells' relay to first hit him in the mouth.

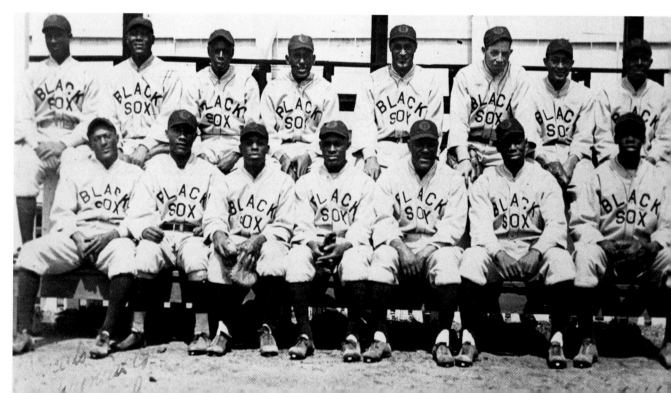

The Cienfuegos championship team, 1930. Standing (L to R): Unknown, Willie Wells, Unknown, Frank Duncan, Unknown, Unknown. Middle row: All Unknown. Front row: Unknown, James (Cool Papa) Bell, Newt Joseph, Unknown, Unknown, Unknown. Bell stole 17 bases during the Cuban Winter League season and once hit three home runs in one game. In 1934 sportswriter Nat Trammell wrote of Bell: "He is the fastest player anywhere. That's right, I know what you are thinking, but go get your [track stars Ralph] Metcalf and [Eddie] Tolan, put them in uniform and start them around the base path, and put your year's salary down and I'll take Bell for the winner."

only 584.

For the fifth, sixth and seventh games, the Series shifted to Kansas City, where the locals were eagerly awaiting the return of their heroes. When the Monarchs' train pulled into Union Station, they were met by a fifty-piece band and a crowd numbering in the thousands. In game five, Rogan and Winters engaged in a classic pitching duel. The

Monarchs scored twice in the first inning but were stymied the rest of the way. Hilldale managed to nick Rogan for a run in the fourth, but continued to trail as the game entered the ninth. After a pair of Monarch errors allowed the tying run to score, Judy Johnson stepped in against Rogan with two men on base and promptly blasted a home run over center-fielder George Sweatt's head, giving the Easterners a 5-2 victory and a 3-1 Series lead.

Kansas City bounced back in the sixth and seventh games, deadlocking the Series with a pair of one-run triumphs. The seventh game went twelve innings before Rogan's infield hit drove in Sweatt with the winning run. For their coveted Sunday encounter, game six, the Monarchs drew 8,885, the largest crowd of the Series.

Now it was on to Chicago for the deciding games. The Monarchs won a thriller in the eighth game, scoring three runs in the bottom of the ninth for a 3-2 victory. Frank Duncan delivered the key blow, a two-out, bases-loaded single that drove in two runs and brought K.C. to the doorstep of the

Maurice (Doolittle) Young. In 1929, he was a member of the Negro House of David. The team featured such players as John Donaldson, Art and Charlie Hancock, and Jack Potts. Like the white House of David, the team's games were booked by Ray L. Doan of Muscatine, Iowa, and its players let their beards grow. His brother, T.J. Young, was a member of the Kansas City Monarchs.

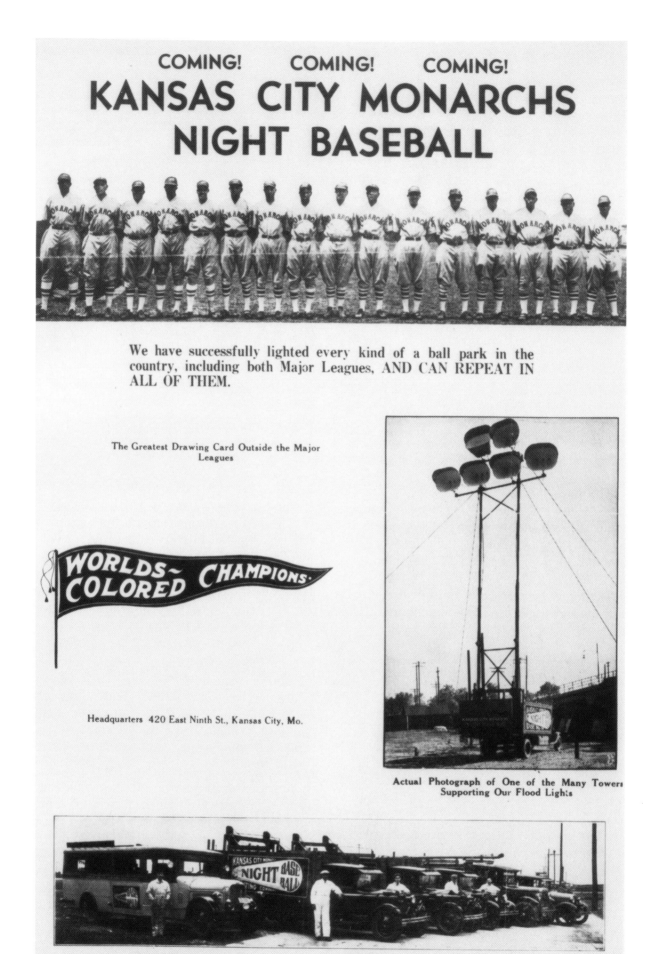

COMING!   COMING!   COMING!

KANSAS CITY MONARCHS
NIGHT BASEBALL

We have successfully lighted every kind of a ball park in the country, including both Major Leagues, AND CAN REPEAT IN ALL OF THEM.

The Greatest Drawing Card Outside the Major Leagues

WORLDS- COLORED CHAMPIONS.

Headquarters 420 East Ninth St., Kansas City, Mo.

Actual Photograph of One of the Many Towers Supporting Our Flood Lights

Actual Photograph of Trucks Used to Transport the Monarch Lighting Plant and Towers

Left: Pioneering night baseball. J.L. Wilkinson, owner of the Kansas City Monarchs, proclaimed, "Night baseball will be to baseball what talkies were to movies." When the Monarchs first started playing under lights, their attendance increased dramatically.

championship. But Hilldale wasn't through yet. The Eastern champs rebounded the next day with some ninth-inning magic of their own. Before a Sunday crowd of 6,271, Hilldale, taking advantage of some sloppy fielding by the Monarchs, scored two in the ninth and held on for a 5-3 win. The Series was down to one game, winner take all.

On the day of the tenth game, Monarch owner J.L. Wilkinson, noticing that pitchers Rogan, Drake and William Bell all had been used for the previous two games, asked Mendez, his manager, who would be doing the pitching. "Joe Mendez," was the quick reply. Wilkinson was taken aback, since Mendez had undergone surgery recently and was

under doctor's orders to stay off the mound for the rest of the season. After collecting himself, the owner warned Mendez that he could be making an unhealthy mistake. "I don't care," Mendez retorted. "I want to win today."

October 20 was a chilly day in Chicago. According to a game report, "fur coats predominated in the stands." Though it was the deciding game, a crowd of only 1,549 was on hand at Schorling Park. (Even with a championship at stake, Monday was a bad day for baseball.) Those who did show up were treated to a brilliant display by an aging, but clever, pitching legend. Though possessing nothing close to the velocity he once had, Mendez,

The Chicago American Giants, 1927. Top row (L to R): John Hines, George Harney, Charles Williams, George Gurley, James Brown, Kobek. Middle row: George Sweatt, Willie Foster, Sam Crawford, Rube Currie, Walter (Steel Arm) Davis, Webster McDonald. Seated: Nat Rogers, Larry Brown, Dave Malarcher, Willie Powell, James Miller, Edward Miller. James Brown was nicknamed "Bad Blood" for his habit of physically abusing umpires. He was the manager of the American Giants in 1929 and 1930.

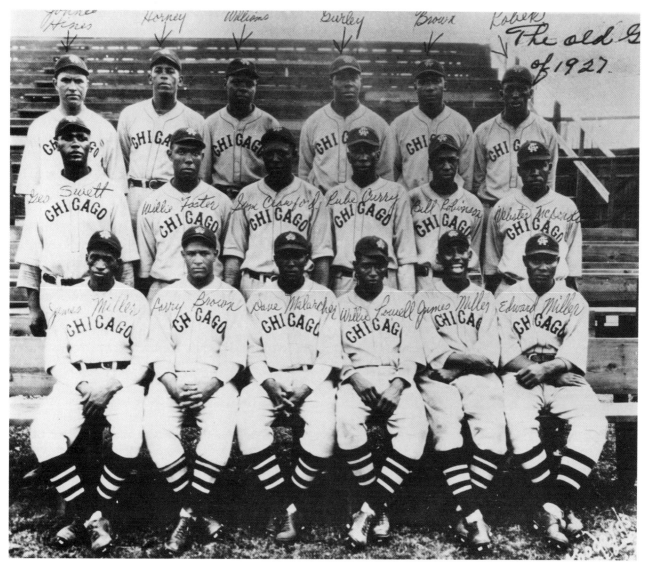

thirty-six, baffled the Hilldale batters with perfect control and an assortment of curves and changes. He had to be almost perfect; Holsey (Scrip) Lee matched him zero for zero for seven innings. Lee, in fact, allowed only one hit in those seven innings. In the eighth, however, the Monarchs erupted for five runs on four hits. Outfielder Oscar Johnson delivered the only run Mendez would need, a double that scored shortstop Dobie Moore. Mendez shut out Hilldale the final two innings, finishing with a three-hitter that included two strikeouts and one walk. Jose Mendez, nicknamed "the Pearl of the Antilles," had made the World Series his oyster and delivered Kansas City their first world championship.

With two leagues operating, fan interest on the rise, and players and owners both doing well financially, the Negro leagues were on relatively solid ground in the mid-'20s. The World Series had provided credibility to both fledgling leagues, and there certainly was no shortage of talent. Many of the all-time great players came into prominence

Carroll (Dink) Mothell. In 1931, sportswriter A.D. Williams wrote: "When Mothell first entered the big show some eleven years ago we found him to be a player of remarkable ability. Through all these years we have watched his work, checked him at every turn and find him to have a record hard to beat. His career in the NNL is one that any player should feel proud to claim. Men like Dink are not found every day."

during what has often been referred to as America's Golden Age of Sport. While mainstream sports fans were paying homage to such legends as Babe Ruth, Red Grange, Jack Dempsey, Bobby Jones and Bill Tilden, followers of the Negro leagues had their own heroes to glorify.

Three of the top outfielders were Martin Dihigo, James (Cool Papa) Bell and Norman (Turkey) Stearnes. Dihigo, a native of Cuba who debuted in the United States in 1923, made his name as a versatile player for Alex Pompez' Cuban Stars (New York). A great hitter, he could play any position, including pitcher. Bell, a switch-hitter who consistently batted well over .300, was the fastest man in either league. When he started in 1922 with the St. Louis Stars, he, too, was a pitcher. Stearnes started with the Negro Southern League's Montgomery (Alabama) Grey Sox in 1921. Known for his prodigious slugging, he reached the Negro major leagues in 1923 when he was signed by the Detroit Stars.

As for third basemen, there weren't many better than Jud Wilson and Judy Johnson. Wilson, a lefty hitter, began his career with the Baltimore Black Sox in 1924. A feared clutch-hitter, he twice won the batting championship of the Cuban Winter League with averages of .430 and .424. Johnson was an important contributor to the powerful Hilldale team, which he joined in 1920. He consistently hit well over .300 and was a smooth fielder with a

Smoky Joe Williams (left) and Cannonball Dick Redding. The two terrific righthanded pitchers, who were teammates at one time with the Lincoln Giants, later became great rivals, with Redding, according to the *New York Age*, making "no secret of his belief that he was Joe Williams' master." After a 1920 game at Ebbetts field in which Redding outdueled Williams, a representative from the *New York Age* tried to get the pitchers to pose while shaking hands. Neither complied. "I'll stand beside him," Redding said. "I don't want to shake his hand," said Williams.

strong arm.

Shortstops John Beckwith and Willie Wells also came into prominence in the '20s. Beckwith played for the Chicago American Giants from 1921 to 1923 before moving east to play for several teams. He was an average fielder but well above the norm when it came to hitting the long ball. Beckwith was one of only a few players to hit a ball over the left-field fence at Cincinnati's Redland Field. Wells and Walter (Dobie) Moore of the Kansas City Monarchs were the best fielding shortstops of the era. Wells was with the St. Louis Stars from 1924 to 1931, and though he hit well, it was his work with the glove that built his reputation.

At second base, Newt Allen, who joined the Kansas City Monarchs in 1922, was widely regarded as the successor to Bingo DeMoss as the top performer at his position. He was a right-handed hitter who had exceptional range in the field.

The first baseman who had the loudest impact was George (Mule) Suttles. He wasn't strong defensively and he didn't hit for a high average, but he was renowned for his thunderous home runs with the St. Louis Stars.

Behind the plate, Frank Duncan of the Monarchs and Larry Brown of the Memphis Red Sox began having an impact. Brown and Duncan, though not great hitters, possessed excellent arms and were the top defensive catchers.

There were many outstanding pitchers during this era, but none were better than right-hander Wilber (Bullet) Rogan of the Kansas City Monarchs, left-hander Jesse (Nip) Winters of Hilldale, left-hander Andy Cooper of the Detroit Stars and lefties Willie Foster and Dave Brown of the Chicago American Giants.

The talent was there, and the structure, though a little shaky, was in place, but there were still some nagging problems plaguing the Negro National League. One of the most persistent centered on

The Manhattan Cafe. Located in Mexico City, it was owned by a black man and was one of the city's finest restaurants. Whenever black players were in Mexico City, they frequented this establishment.

(L to R) Robert (Bubber) Lewis, Lilla Lewis, Epsia Freeman, Anita Walton, Mattie Bell and Mae Bently pose in 1916. Lewis became the owner of the Memphis Red Sox of the Negro Southern League and Negro National League. He also owned a baseball park (named Lewis Park) and an undertaking establishment in Memphis. Lewis once borrowed money from Dr. J.B. and Dr. B.B. Martin, using his park as collateral. After a series of rainouts resulted in several missed payments, the Martin brothers foreclosed on Lewis, taking first his field and then his team.

Grave site of Andrew (Rube) Foster. Sportswriter Rollo Wilson wrote of Foster, who died on December 9, 1930: "When the big game shall have become history, there will stalk across the pages of the record a massive figure and its name will be Andrew Foster. A loud-voiced man with a smelly pipe who kids his opponents and makes them like it. The dominant power of the commission and of the league. The master of the show who moves the figures on his checkerboard at will. The smooth-toned counselor of infinite wisdom and sober thought. The king who, to suit his purpose, assumes the robes of his jester. Always the center of any crowd, the magnet attracting both the brains and the froth of humanity. Cold in refusals, warm in assent. Known to everybody, knows everybody. That's Rube."

Rube Foster, the omnipotent one. Foster, in addition to being league president, was the league's booking agent and secretary, hired all umpires and was responsible for settling all disputes, all while continuing as co-owner and manager of the Chicago American Giants.

Right off the bat, there was much resentment to his grabbing five percent — his cut for booking the games — off the top of every league game. According to W.S. Ferrance, team secretary of the St. Louis Giants, Foster netted himself $11,220 in 1920 alone from booking games. "Now, mind you," Ferrance wrote in a February 9, 1923, article for the *Kansas City Call*, "there was not a man connected [with the league] that was not in position to book his own club and had been doing so for years."

He went on to take Foster to task for pulling his American Giants off the field during disputes in games against Kansas City, Indianapolis and St. Louis in 1921. Opposing managers were powerless to fight him in these situations. "Why?" Ferrance wrote. "Because each manager would have to file a complaint against Manager Foster, mail it to Secretary Foster and then President Foster would have to decide."

Later in the year, the *Call* asked Foster to relinquish his role as field manager. "It doesn't

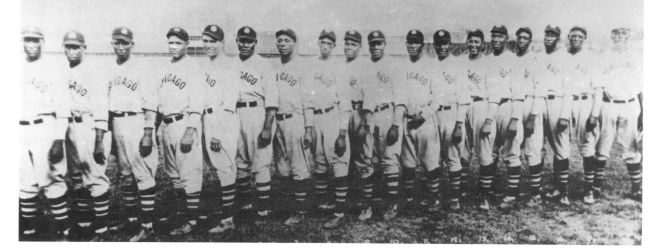

The Chicago American Giants, 1926. (L to R) Dave Malarcher, Sanford Jackson, Ernest Powell, Larry Brown, John Hines, Eddie Miller, James Bray, William Rogers, Charles Williams, George Gurley, James Brown, Webster McDonald, George Harney, Willie Foster, Walter (Steel Arm) Davis, Rube Currie, Sam Crawford, George Sweatt. Sportswriter A.D. Williams once said of manager Crawford: "He was always a stickler for strict training rules obeyance. He never let up in a game even though the game might seem safely tucked away in the win column. He was something after the old C.I. Taylor and the Andrew Foster style, the go-get-'em type."

read well in accounts of games played," the newspaper stated, "that protests were made of contests participated in by the Giants, directed from the field by Foster. It would be hard to convince the fans that the decision rendered later by the president would be fair."

It was generally recognized that Foster's Giants could get away with a more aggressive brand of ball than other teams. His players were known for sliding with their spikes high, a tactic which often led to fights on the field. Umpires, fearing Rube's

wrath, were reluctant to take any measures to prevent the rough stuff. There was leaguewide sentiment that Foster's intimidation of the umps was compromising their judgment in games involving the American Giants. After the '23 season, the league established a rule that prohibited the league president from firing umpires. According to a story by Carl Beckwith in the *Kansas City Call* on July 11, 1924, the rule had little effect on Foster's bullying tactics. "There are more ways of getting rid of undesirable umpires than discharging them and Rube knew it," Beckwith wrote. "Where is Debow,

The Chicago American Giants pitching staff, 1926. (L to R) Webster McDonald, George Harney, Willie Foster, Rube Currie, Edward Miller and Willie Powell. Harney was one of the great spitball pitchers. According to Maurice Wiggins, "On occasions his spitball would dance so much that the catcher could only stop it by letting it hit his chest protector." As a member of the Little Falls, Minnesota team from 1928 through 1931, McDonald posted a record of 61-9, including fifteen shutouts.

Dayton Marcos players. (L to R) Unknown, C. Shepard, "Dink" King. The Marcos, who were owned by John (Big) Matthews, began playing in the early 1900's and were the only nonwhite team in the Ohio-Indiana League for several seasons.

one of the best umpires in the game? Rube didn't fire him — he made his work so disagreeable to him that he quit!"

Beckwith asked the league either to form an appellate committee to handle all league disputes, or to oust Foster as president. "We realize,"

Beckwith wrote, "that Foster can make his living outside the league and it's our opinion that it would be better for the league if he were urgently requested to do so!"

Foster would have none of it. This was his creation, and he was committed to nurturing it to maturity. He had big plans for the league. He could see the day coming when Negro baseball would be just as highly regarded as the white major leagues. He could see a day when there would be one genuine World Series, the Negro League champs against the major league champs.

If he was a heavy-handed administrator, it was because he had lived through the free-wheeling early days when there was no league, no World Series, no discipline, nothing but independent teams playing randomly against each other. He occasionally abused the power of his office, but those abuses usually came on the field, when his vision of a great league became blurred by his intense competitiveness. His role as the booking agent may have been a sweetheart deal, but it was granted in lieu of a salary. Also, he often injected his own money into floundering franchises that were struggling to meet payrolls and other expenses. Even his detractors recognized that without Rube's dictatorial leadership, the league stood little chance of surviving.

"We are the ship, all else the sea" was the slogan

Francis Moore and Wilber Rogan, Jr. Francis was the wife of famed Kansas City Monarchs shortstop Dobie Moore. In 1926 Dobie's career came to a sudden halt when he was shot in the leg. Although doctors assured him that he would never play again, Moore continued for years to make promises in the local press that he had recovered and planned to make a comeback.

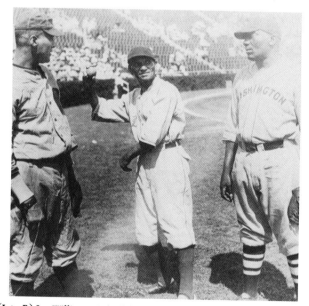

(L to R) Joe Williams, Sol White and Dick Redding. Redding is said to have thrown twenty-seven no-hitters during his career. One came in Cuba against pitcher George Mullin and the Detroit Tigers. In 1912 he threw a no-hitter and struck out nineteen in a game against Jersey City of the Eastern League (a minor league). Playing for Jersey City were former major leaguers Mike Donlin and James (Ducky) Holmes.

on the letterhead of the NNL. Another line could have been added: "Rube is the captain, all others the deckhands." Despite the grumblings, there would be no mutiny on his ship.

Both the Negro National League and Eastern Colored League continued to operate with few changes through the 1927 season. Strong teams such as Kansas City, St. Louis and Chicago in the West, and Hilldale, the Bacharach Giants and Brooklyn in the East, had built up loyal followings and prospered. Weaker franchises like the Dayton Marcos, the Cleveland Elites, the Washington Potomacs and the Newark Stars made cameo appearances, some lasting a full season, others dropping out midway through the summer months.

The World Series was held every year, but never captured the fan interest that league executives anticipated. In 1924, the first year it was held, attendance for the ten games was 45,857. It never improved. Even the players were ambivalent. Whether they reached the Series or not, they knew they'd be playing somewhere in October. They also knew they could make just as much money or more by barnstorming against major league all-star teams.

In 1925 the Negro National League inaugurated a new format, splitting the season into two halves to maintain fan interest throughout the summer. The Monarchs, winners of the first half, beat the St. Louis Stars in a seven-game series for the pennant, setting up a rematch of the '24 Series. Hilldale avenged their loss by winning five of six games. Hoping to avoid the previous year's mistakes, the Series was held entirely in Kansas City (four games) and Philadelphia (two games). It made little difference; attendance remained about the same.

Rube Foster's American Giants ascended the throne in 1926 by beating the Bacharach Giants of Atlantic City. For Rube, it should have been one of the highlights of his career. To get to the Series, the Giants, trailing the Monarchs four games to three in the pennant playoff, had to sweep a doubleheader, which they did with Rube's half-brother, Willie, outdueling Bullet Rogan in both games. The younger Foster, a southpaw who began his career in 1923 with the Memphis Red Sox, was equally effective in the World Series. He won the sixth

Chet Brewer. He traveled to Cuba for the first time in 1930, but the league ceased operations after only a month because of poor weather. Along with several Monarch teammates, Brewer headed to the West Coast to play in the California Winter League.

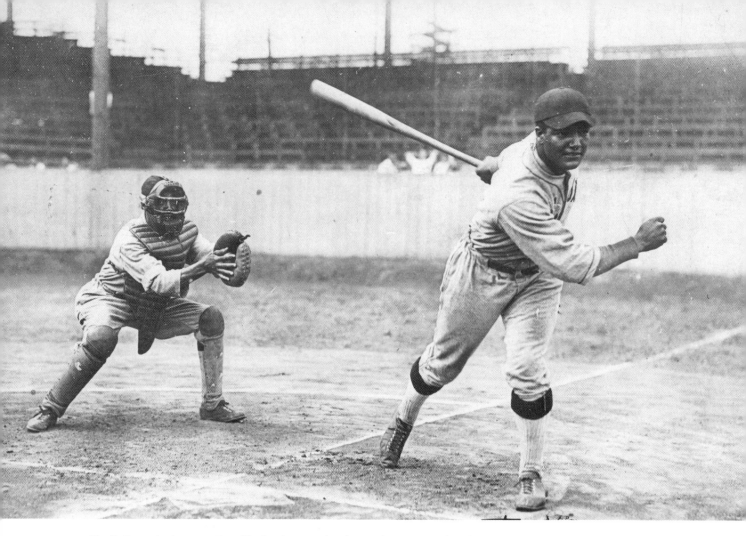

Charlie Hancock takes a cut. He and his brother, Art, played more than 25 years of professional baseball. Neither ever played with any Negro league teams, choosing instead to play with independents such as the Colored House of David, the Van Dykes, and mixed teams in Jamestown, North Dakota.

game and was sent to the Schorling Park mound for the eighth game, with the American Giants holding a 4-3 lead in the Series.

Allowing ten hits and escaping trouble almost every inning, Foster was unhittable when he had to be, and the American Giants emerged with a 1-0 victory and the championship. Chicago's lone run came in the bottom of the ninth, when Floyd (Jelly) Gardner singled, went to second on a sacrifice by Dave Malarcher and scored on Sandy Thompson's single to center. It was a vintage Rube Foster game — strong pitching, good defense and a manufactured run. Unfortunately, Rube wasn't there to see it; he was in a mental institution in Kankakee, Illinois.

In May of 1925 Foster was in Indianapolis for a series against the ABCs, who had reorganized after breaking up in 1924. He was alone in his hotel room one morning when a gas pipe ruptured. Foster became asphyxiated and was lying on the floor near death when one of his players stopped by to visit. The player, who had heard the sound of running water, broke down the door after his knocks went unanswered. Foster, after a brief stay in a hospital, returned home to Chicago to recuperate.

He managed to return later in the year to supervise the affairs of both the American Giants and the NNL. However, the pressures of his administrative duties and the aftereffects of his near-fatal accident were beginning to take a toll. In midsummer of 1926, on the advice of friends, he left Chicago for what was supposed to be a long and restful vacation. He couldn't stay away, however. Shortly after returning from his trip, he suffered a nervous breakdown, and after an eight-day examination in a local hospital he was declared mentally irresponsible and sent to the institution in Kankakee. Rube Foster remained hospitalized until his death on December 9, 1930.

The passing of the Father of the Negro leagues from the baseball scene was a crippling blow. Until 1926, Rube was there to solve all problems. He wasn't loved, or even liked, by all; opinion was

Willie Foster. In a 1930 exhibition game against a barnstorming major league team, Heinie Manush blasted a drive off Foster that looked as if it would be a sure triple. Cool Papa Bell, playing shallow, raced back to deep center-field, reached up and made a "snow cone" catch before falling to the ground. Manush told Foster's catcher, Ted Radcliffe, "I sure am glad you colored players aren't in our league; I wouldn't ever hit .300."

sharply divided on his domineering style of management, but all agreed that without Rube there would not have been any Negro leagues. Now, without his commanding presence, it remained to be seen what would happen to his creation.

The Eastern Colored League was the first to fall. In April of 1928, Ed Bolden of Hilldale, citing uneven scheduling and depleted finances, decided he'd had enough of "organized baseball."

"I am always in favor of a league," Bolden said. "I sponsored it and still believe it is the right idea, [but] when one team plays forty home games and another four, then it is time for a halt.

"Hilldale made plenty of money in the days of independent baseball and that is the reason we have gone back to our old methods.... last year the club dropped $18,000. I still am ready to join a real league, which I hope will be in existence someday."

Gilkerson Union Giants scorecard, 1930. Their outfielders — Hurley McNair, Christobel Torrienti and Eddie Dwight — all were former Negro National League players.

Sarah Foster. The wife of Rube Foster, she is standing in front of a shop that is advertising a Homestead Grays-Chicago American Giants game. Throughout the black business community, shopkeepers posted signs in their windows to keep fans informed of upcoming games.

The advent of the Negro leagues had not come at the expense of independent baseball teams. Ed Bolden's decision to go "back to our old methods" was one that enabled him to maintain a competitive schedule and still keep the team in operation. There were many teams during this era that chose to play "outlaw ball," the term used for clubs unaffiliated with a league. Two of the best were the Homestead Grays, who played out of Pittsburgh, Pennsylvania, and the Gilkerson Union Giants, who were based in Spring Valley, Illinois but spent most of the summer months traveling throughout the Midwest. Both teams were capable of giving any of the league teams a tough battle. Robert Gilkerson, a native of Pittsburgh, bought the Union Giants from W.S. Peters in 1917 and continued to operate the team throughout the '20s and most of the '30s. Gilkerson's club was an important source of talent for the leagues, as were most of the independents. Players such as Chet Brewer, T.J. Young, Christobel Torrienti, Richard (Subby) Byas, George Giles and Eddie Dwight all wore the Union Giants' uniform at some point during their careers.

In the late spring of 1928, shortly after Hilldale dropped out, the Eastern Colored League disbanded entirely. In 1929 another attempt to organize was made in the East when the American

The Kansas City Santa Fe Railroad team, 1927. Most integrated businesses had segregated sports teams and, generally, the teams didn't play against each other.

At the start of the 1926 season, the Kansas City Monarchs became the first team to travel exclusively by bus. Owner J.L. Wilkinson, seeking a more economical mode of transportation than trains, bought an eighteen-seater that had specially constructed cushions with reclining seats. America's expanding highway system made travel by bus just as quick as by train and less expensive.

Colored League was formed. Most of the teams from the ECL returned, but it went the way of its predecessor, failing to answer the bell for the 1930 season.

In the West the burden of directing the Negro National League fell on Judge W.C. Hueston, a Gary, Indiana, attorney who was named president in 1927. Hueston, originally from Kansas City, was a longtime supporter of Negro baseball. He had attended the 1916 meeting in Kansas City, where Rube Foster had laid out his plans for the Negro

National League. He had no allegiances to any team, which was an important qualification after the years of complaints about Foster's conflicts of interests. The Eastern Colored League, which was administrated by Ed Bolden and Nat Strong of the Brooklyn Royal Giants, took a similar tact when it elected Isaac Nutter, an Atlantic City lawyer, as the league's president in 1927. Both Hueston and Nutter tried to make strong first impressions in the early days of their tenures. When Frank Duncan of the K.C. Monarchs, Andy Cooper of the Detroit

Tom Baird. Working for the House of David, he signed female Olympic track and field star Babe Didrikson and Grover Cleveland Alexander to contracts and offered Babe Ruth $20,000 after he retired in 1935. Baird was always reminding sportswriters that "all the stars are not in the major leagues."

(L to R) Wilber Rogan, Unknown, Crush Holloway. Clint Thomas once said of Holloway: "He was what could be classified as a crazy ball player. You could never defense him well or pitch certain kinds of pitches because he was so unpredictable. If you were nine runs down, Holloway might try to steal home if he thought it might help to motivate the team in their comeback effort."

Mr. and Mrs. Bill Robinson. In 1926, Robinson, the famed tap dancer and entertainer, came to Los Angeles' White Sox Park during the California Winter League and proclaimed, "I will give $5 to any man who hits a home run during any game this season." When the White Sox, a team of Negro leaguers, started hitting the ball out of the park too regularly, Robinson reduced the offer to $1 per home run. He finally stopped giving money altogether when Norman (Turkey) Stearnes hit four home runs in one game. Robinson stated: "It's time for me to stop handing out money; you fellows are breaking me."

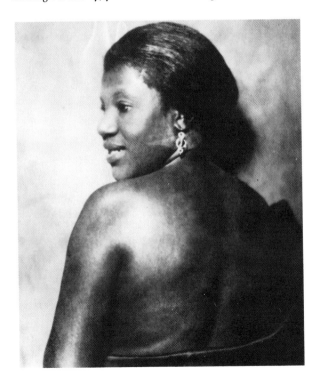

Clara Smith. She was the wife of Charles (Two Sides) Wesley, a second baseman for the Birmingham Black Barons and later manager of the 1929 Memphis Red Sox. Smith was a blues singer and recording artist with Columbia Records. She recorded such blues hits as "Mean Papa Turn in Your Key," "Don't Advertise Your Man," "Papa I Don't Need You Now," "Alley Rat Blues," and "Salty Dog."

J.E. Miller. He was the official photographer for the Negro leagues from 1920 to 1931. His prints appeared in newspapers all over the country.

Stars, Raleigh (Biz) Mackey of Hilldale and Herbert (Rap) Dixon of the Harrisburg Giants broke their contracts at the start of the 1927 season by joining promoter Lonnie Goodwin on an exhibition tour of Japan, Hueston and Nutter announced that the players would be suspended for five years. It was the sort of action that could have sent a strong message, one that would have told players and owners alike that the leagues would not tolerate such casual regard for contracts. However, when the players returned later in the summer after compiling a 23-1 record against Japan's top teams, the league presidents quickly backed down and reduced the players' penalties to a $50 fine.

Though Hueston lacked Foster's charisma and

The Denver White Elephants, 1930. Back row (L to R): Bill Carey, "Lefty" Banks, Robert Clay, Pete Albright, Ed Steward, Reginald Cooper, Fleming Von Dickerson. Middle row: A.H.W. Ross (owner), Red Threets, "Boogie-Woogie" Pardue, Logan Harper, "Little Johnny" (scorekeeper), George Walker. Front row: Ike Bell, Willard Stevenson, bat boy, Joe Tucker, Theodore Johnson. The only non-white team in the Denver City League, the Elephants won the championship behind the pitching of Albright, who struck out eleven in the title game.

Ed Rile (far left) and Wade Johnston (far right). On July 11, 1927, Rile, pitching for the Detroit Stars, beat the Kansas City Monarchs in both ends of a doubleheader, firing a three-hit shutout in the opener and allowing eight hits in the second game. At 6'6", he was the tallest man in Negro baseball during the 1920s.

Members of the Dayton Marcos. (L to R) Howard Kelso, Unknown, Red Radcliffe, Chester Blanchard. The Marcos, who dropped out of the Negro National League in 1921, were reinstated in 1925. Their second attempt in the NNL was as unsuccessful as their first, as they again withdrew in mid-season.

leadership abilities, he did manage to hold the league together for the next three seasons while confronting the same obstacles that Rube had faced.

More and more those obstacles were threatening the league's existence. In January of 1930, Candy Jim Taylor, then managing the Memphis Red Sox, wrote a story for the *Kansas City Call* in which he underlined the reasons for the league's declining appeal. Taylor spared no one, taking to task incapable owners, poorly conditioned players, incompetent umpires and inconsistent press cover-

age. For the latter he blamed the teams, noting that the newspapers often weren't given the necessary information.

By the early '30s, Hueston and the Negro National League were in serious trouble. The stock market crash in October of 1929 and the ensuing Great Depression took a heavy toll on the beleaguered circuit. For the ticket-buying public, there was little money in the budget for frivolities such as baseball.

The league suffered another important setback shortly before the 1931 season, when the Kansas

Howard University reunion, 1924. The university took pride in its contribution to baseball. John Shackleford (kneeling, third from right) played for the Lincoln Giants, and Frank (Doc) Sykes (kneeling, second from right) played for the Baltimore Black Sox. Bill Wiley, a catcher for the Lincoln Giants in 1918, was also a Howard graduate.

The St. Louis Stars, 1928. Standing (L to R): Jim Taylor, Clarence Palms, Theodore Trent, George (Mule) Suttles, James Williams, Eggie Hensley, Willie Wells, Henry Williams, Dewey Creacy. Seated: bat boy, James Russell, Cool Papa Bell, Branch Russell, Richard Cannon, Roosevelt Davis, Wilson Redus, Luther (Old Soul) McDonald. Suttles, whom the Stars purchased from Birmingham, reputedly hit sixty-nine home runs in 1929. In 1933 he appeared in the movie "I'm No Angel," which starred Mae West. Redus was from Muskogee, Oklahoma, the hometown of fellow Negro leaguers Henry Williams, Newt Joseph and Nelson Dean. Davis, a native of Bartlesville, Oklahoma, was renowned for throwing a scuffed ball. After a victory in the 1941 *Denver Post* tournament, he remarked, "I throw the kind of pitching that if you could hit it, you would be in the big leagues."

City Monarchs, one of the league's most stable franchises, decided to reclaim their independent status. The Monarchs, who had won four pennants, were a good draw both at home and on the road, but their owner, J.L. Wilkinson, had discovered a more profitable approach to the game — night baseball. Five years before the major leagues discovered electricity, the Kansas City Monarchs became the first team to play regularly under the lights.

It was not the conventional lighting that is seen atop stadiums today. These lights were placed on retractable poles and powered by a portable generator. The motor and generator were contained in a twenty-eight seat bus, which enabled the Monarchs to take their nocturnal show on the road with them. The novelty proved to be a great

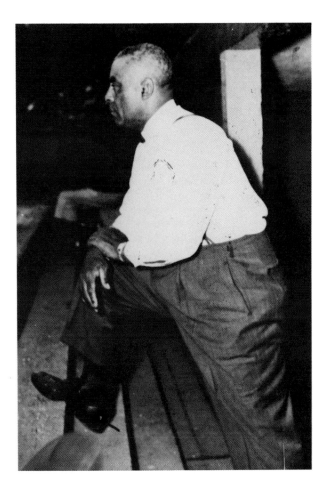

Oscar Charleston. Former player and manager Dave Malarcher selected Charleston, Jimmie Lyons, Pete Hill and Christobel Torrienti as the four all-time best outfielders. "They were greater than Ty Cobb and Babe Ruth," Malarcher said, "because they were all good defensive as well as offensive players. They had speed, could bunt, throw and run." Later in his career, Charleston played first base.

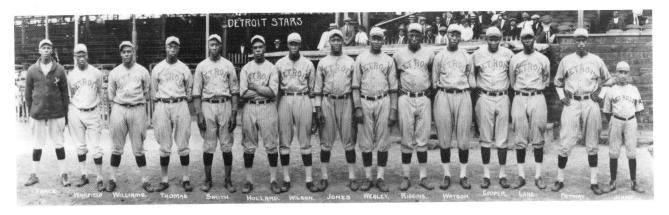

The Detroit Stars, 1922. (L to R) Bill Force, Frank Warfield, Poindexter Williams, Clint Thomas, Clarence Smith, Bill Holland, Wilson, John Jones, Edgar Wesley, Orville Riggins, Watson, Andy Cooper, I.S. Lane, Bruce Petway, Johnnie (mascot). Though he weighed only 155 pounds, Petway was arguably the greatest catcher ever to play in the Negro leagues. The smallest player in league history was Edward (Boots) McClain, a third baseman who played for Detroit, Toledo and Dayton in the '20s. McClain stood all of 5'2' and weighed 137 pounds.

Frank Duncan. In 1930, he managed Cienfuegos to the Cuban Winter League championship. In Latin America, black players were respected for their knowledge of the game and leadership abilities. Although Duncan was a successful manager in Cuba, he was unable to land a skipper's job at home until 1941 because there was an abundance of qualified managers in the organized leagues.

Tom Wilson. The son of two prominent Nashville doctors, he used his family wealth to start the Nashville Elite Giants and build Wilson Park in the 1920s. The park became home to both the Elite Giants professional baseball and football teams. He later moved his baseball team to Baltimore, turning the park into a dog track. When the dog track failed to return enough of a profit, Wilson demolished it and built a nightclub, the famous Paradise Ballroom.

Clara Thompson Bell. She married Cool Papa Bell in September of 1928, and they honeymooned in Cuba, where Cool Papa played in the winter league.

attraction. With fans eagerly awaiting their first look at night baseball, the Monarchs, with their portable power plant and lights in tow, had a very busy season in 1930. They continued to play in the NNL, but the large and curious crowds which were coming to see them convinced Wilkinson that there were greater profits to be made without the constraints of a league.

Wilkinson was no stranger to innovations. When the Negro National League first started, he had used his All Nations club as a farm team, bringing the better players to the Monarchs, while using the All Nations to develop talent. He was one of the first owners to use promotional days — Ladies' Day,

Kids' Day, Tennessee Day, Alabama Day, etc. — to inflate the gate. As the country began to develop its highways in the 1920s, Wilkinson was the first to abandon the trains for buses, a more thrifty mode of transportation.

Wilkinson's financial gain from night baseball proved to be a serious loss for the Negro National League in 1931. The Cuban Stars, another charter member, also departed the same year, along with the Birmingham Black Barons, who had joined in 1924. That left only six teams: the Chicago American Giants, the St. Louis Stars, the Detroit Stars and the Indianapolis ABCs, plus two newcomers, the Louisville White Sox and the Cleveland Cubs.

The country's financial crisis, which had put millions on the unemployment line, severely weakened or destroyed once-solid franchises and ultimately caused the demise of the Negro National League in 1932. The Negro Southern League, which had started up in the early '20s, continued to

Charles Zomphier. A native of St. Louis, he played the infield for six different Negro league teams beginning with the St. Louis Stars in 1926.

operate, but that was considered a minor league, a stepping-stone to either the Negro National League or a strong independent Northern team. Two teams from the NNL, the American Giants and ABCs, joined the Southern circuit in '32, with the Chicago team winning the pennant. The rest of the Negro National League teams either disbanded or returned to the barnstorming trail.

Rube Foster's ship, after a sometimes stormy, sometimes glorious twelve years on the high seas, had sunk.

Chapter 6

There were two likely candidates to pick up the pieces of Rube Foster's Negro National League. One was J.L. Wilkinson, the well-respected owner of the Kansas City Monarchs; the other was Cumberland Posey of the Homestead (Pennsylvania) Grays. Wilkinson was recognized as one of the game's top promoters and businessmen. It was through his creative efforts that the Monarchs had become one of the most successful franchises.

Night baseball had enabled the Monarchs to increase the number of games they played, thus improving their financial situation. Doubleheaders were commonplace, and they even played triple-headers on rare occasions. Between regular junkets to Canada and Mexico, the Monarchs stayed busy playing a full complement of games against other independents and minor league teams and by entering several semipro tournaments. And when the major league season ended, Wilkinson booked games against barnstorming teams such as the Dizzy Dean All-Stars.

By reorganizing or rejoining a league, Wilkinson would have had to sacrifice some games to meet league commitments. The Monarch owner was not about to shorten his schedule — and reduce revenues — for the sake of a league, at least not during the heart of the depression.

Homestead, Pennsylvania, is located a few miles southeast of Pittsburgh by the banks of the Monongahela River. For much of the 1900s, it thrived under the smoke that spewed from the stacks of its steel mills. The Grays, originally known as the Murdock Grays, were first organized in the

early 1900s as a team of steelworkers who played weekend games against area semipro teams. Cumberland Willis Posey, an all-around athlete who played both basketball and baseball at Penn State and Duquesne Universities, joined the Grays as an outfielder in 1911. Five years later he was named manager and began building the Grays into an Eastern powerhouse.

Posey, like Rube Foster, was devoted to the game and knowledgeable in all areas, from the field to the front office. The success that the Grays achieved under his reign, which lasted until his death in 1946, was directly attributable to his skills as a talent scout, manager and businessman. By 1931, he had several outstanding players wearing the Grays' uniform, among them an aging Smoky Joe Williams, Oscar Charleston, Judy Johnson, Jud Wilson, Vic Harris, Ted Page, Sam Streeter and Josh Gibson. There weren't too many teams that could compete with that lineup.

Except for 1929, when the Grays were members of the short-lived American Negro League, Posey had remained partial to "outlaw ball." By 1932, however, with his collection of superstars, he was ready for another crack at league play. Under his direction, the East-West League was formed and consisted of the Grays, Hilldale, the Cuban Stars, the Baltimore Black Sox, the Newark Browns, the Washington Pilots, the Cleveland Stars and the Detroit Wolves, who also were owned by Posey. Great expectations accompanied the league's opening in April. The press, as always eager to cooperate, began paying attention immediately.

The Pittsburgh Crawfords. Manager Oscar Charleston addresses (L to R) Herbert (Rap) Dixon, Josh Gibson, Judy Johnson and Jud Wilson. Dixon not only was among the best right-fielders in the game, but he was also a superior hitter. His career was cut short when he injured his back while sliding during a winter league game in Venezuela.

regularly printing the standings, along with the pitching and batting leaders. The comprehensive coverage didn't help at the gate, though; the league was finished by late June, another victim of the grim economic situation. While several teams disbanded, unable to meet payrolls, the Grays and the Cuban Stars remained intact and returned to barnstorming.

Syd Pollock, the Stars' owner, saw no reason for optimism until "the baseball fans go back to work at regular wages." In a July 1 story in the *Kansas City Call*, Pollock wrote of the hard times encountered by teams that tried to survive the depression. "The Cuban Stars, like everyone else, lost money and plenty of it in attempting to establish a real colored league in the wrong year," Pollock wrote. "It's tough scraping by this year, many miles of travel, many grinding overnight jumps." Nevertheless, Pollock remained hopeful. "Something is bound to happen on the political horizon real soon to bring some changes for a weary, but courageous, world to go on to secure a better foothold and lease on

life," Pollock wrote. "Let's hope for future seasons which will bring a better fare to baseball, which is now undergoing a severe strain."

With one of the potential successors to Rube Foster unwilling and the other unable, it was left to the unlikeliest of candidates to resuscitate the Negro leagues.

Just a few miles from Homestead, on the north side of Pittsburgh, is an area known as the Hill District, home to the city's black community. At the corner of Crawford and Wylie Avenues stood the Crawford Grille, which was owned by a man named W.A. (Gus) Greenlee. He had little in common with Rube Foster, or any other baseball leader for that matter.

Baseball had been Foster's life. The son of a United Methodist Bishop, Foster was a religious man who didn't drink, didn't carouse and was as dedicated to his family as the game allowed him to be. His unwavering devotion transformed the original Negro National League from concept to reality. Gus Greenlee not only shared few of

Foster's clean-living principles, but he had no baseball background, either. If anything, when it came to reviving the Negro major leagues, he had to be considered more of a suspect than a successor.

A veteran of World War I, Greenlee moved from Marion, North Carolina, to Pittsburgh in 1920. Several years later he opened the Grille, a two-story restaurant and dance hall that on any given night might have featured the swingin' sounds of Duke Ellington or Count Basie or any of the era's top jazzmen. It provided a legitimate front for Greenlee's real business, an illegitimate but wildly profitable venture that was as easy as 1-2-3. Greenlee was the numbers king of Pittsburgh — pick a three-digit number, plunk down your penny, nickel or dime and you stood a 1000-to-1 chance of winning a 600-to-1 payoff. The long odds weren't much of a deterrent when a small fortune could be made from such a small investment. Greenlee also capitalized on the Eighteenth Amendment, which had been ratified in 1919 and made the sale of alcoholic beverages illegal. Gus, a bootlegger to boot, was only too willing to do his part to ease the pain of Prohibition.

As proprietor of one of the city's hottest night spots, Greenlee became acquainted with many of the ballplayers who passed through Pittsburgh to play the Grays. Wherever they were when the day's work was done, many players gravitated to the

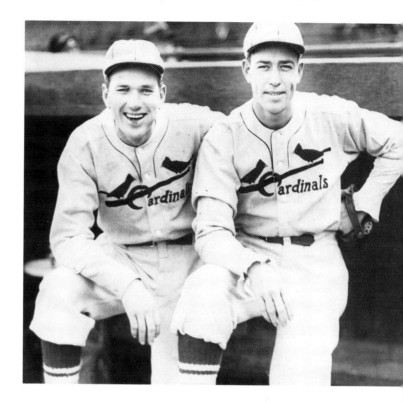

The Dean brothers. In 1934, Dizzy (left) and Daffy won two games apiece to lead the St. Louis Cardinals over the Detroit Tigers in the World Series. Following the final game, they went to Oklahoma City with a barnstorming team of major leaguers to meet the Kansas City Monarchs. Fifteen thousand people stormed a park built for 7,500 and saw Daffy get ripped for eight hits in three innings. Dizzy allowed two hits in two innings. The game was called after the fifth inning when the fans could no longer be controlled. Every Monarch in the lineup had a hit that day.

The Cincinnati Tigers, 1937. Top row (L to R): Virgil (School Boy) Harris, Josh Johnson. Middle row: Jess Houston, Neil Robinson, Porter Moss. Front row: Tennie Edwards, Olan (Jelly) Taylor, Marlin Carter, Harvey Peterson. Moss was a hard-throwing, submarine-style pitcher. Tiger manager Ted (Double Duty) Radcliffe spotted Moss playing softball on a Cincinnati playground and signed him that same day.

Josh Gibson. According to Clyde McNeal, a shortstop for the American Giants, Gibson had a strong following south of the border. "Everywhere I went in Mexico," McNeal said, "someone wanted to show you where Josh Gibson had hit a tape measure home run."

LeRoy (Satchel) Paige, 1935. He is pictured in a Bismarck hat and Kansas City Monarch uniform shortly after signing his first contract with K.C. Paige had led his Bismarck team to a tournament championship in Wichita, Kansas, striking out a tournament record sixty batters in winning four games. He then came to Kansas City and defeated the Monarchs, recording another fifteen strikeouts. Two weeks later he signed with the Monarchs and defeated a team of major leaguers that included Charlie Gehringer, "Schoolboy" Rowe and Tommy Bridges.

nightlife. In New York, that meant a swing through the clubs of Harlem, while in Chicago, the South Side was the hot spot. Kansas City had its Vine Street and Memphis its Beale Street. And in Pittsburgh, there was the Hill District, and more often than not, the Crawford Grille.

Greenlee had no involvement in baseball until 1930, when he began sponsoring the Crawford Colored Giants, a local semipro team. Whether he was bitten by the baseball bug or merely seeking shelter for his cash isn't certain, but in 1931 Greenlee decided to move up in class. He became determined to field a team that could compete with the Grays.

Greenlee, who named his team the Pittsburgh Crawfords, was not the type to scrimp; he had plenty of cash and didn't mind flaunting it. Needing

transportation for his team, Greenlee plunked down $10,000 for a brand-new, twenty-two seat bus. His next order of business was to find a first-class facility. When they first started out, the Crawfords, like the Grays, played many of their games at Forbes Field, home of the Pittsburgh Pirates. It was a fine stadium, but there were two drawbacks: the hefty rental fee and the Jim Crow locker rooms (players were forced to dress before coming to the park and were denied the luxury of a postgame shower). Greenlee took care of the situation by building his own stadium. Known as Greenlee Field, it was located on Bedford Avenue in the Hill District and seated 6,000. The cost of construction was $100,000 — a princely sum in the heart of the depression even for the king of numbers.

The next item on the agenda was to put together a team worthy of such lavishness. As might be expected, Greenlee spared no expense. In 1931, the Cleveland Cubs of the Negro National League disbanded in midsummer. The ace of their staff was a native of Mobile, Alabama, named LeRoy (Satchel) Paige. Paige had begun his professional career in 1926 under manager William Lowe with the Chattanooga Black Lookouts of the Negro Southern League. By the time he finally retired in 1965, he was as well known as anyone who ever played the game. Greenlee jumped at the opportunity to sign this budding legend for $250 a month.

In Paige, the "Craws" not only had one of the game's greatest pitchers, but also one of its biggest gate attractions. Greenlee, however, was just getting warmed up. Over the course of the next year, he pulled off a series of raids that would make any commando proud. Focusing his attack on the neighboring Grays, Greenlee transformed his team into a powerhouse (and decimated the Grays) by signing Oscar Charleston, Judy Johnson, Johnny Russell, Jake Stephens, Jud Wilson, Ted Page and Josh Gibson. Posey was outraged, but, of course,

(L to R) Eddie Dwight, Clarence (Pops) Coleman and Walter (Steel Arm) Davis enjoy a break from baseball. In 1934, while a member of a team in Jamestown, North Dakota, Davis hit two home runs and a double against a team of major leaguers managed by Connie Mack's son, Earle. Tommy Thomas and Doc Cramer allowed the home runs, while Rip Sewell surrendered the double. According to Subby Byas, "Davis used to hit major league pitchers like they were schoolboys."

The East-West Game, 1937. Standing (L to R): Elwood (Bingo) DeMoss, Walter Ball, Nat Rogers, Frank Duncan, Willie Foster, Ted Trent, Ted Strong, Jim (Candy) Taylor, Norman (Turkey) Stearnes, Andy Cooper, Porter Moss, Alex Radcliffe, Willard Brown, Willie (Sug) Cornelius. Kneeling: Richard (Subby) Byas, Jess Houston, bat boy, Henry Milton, Ted (Double Duty) Radcliffe, Newt Allen, Eldridge Mayweather, Wilson (Frog) Redus, Lloyd (Ducky) Davenport, Paul Hardy, Timothy Bond. Sitting: Howard Easterling, Rainey Bibbs, Henry (Dimps) Miller, bat boy, Wilber (Bullet) Rogan, John Markham, Hilton Smith. Dick Pieper, a sportswriter, wrote, "The majors tapped a gold mine when the color line was broken."

Above: The Kansas City Monarchs entered the newly formed Negro American League in 1937 and won the pennant in a playoff with the Chicago American Giants.

Below: Satchel Paige and Bob Feller. In 1939, Joe DiMaggio stated that Paige is "unquestionably the greatest pitcher I've ever faced in my life."

powerless to stop it. The resulting bad blood became the basis for one of Negro baseball's greatest rivalries, as intense as the Monarchs-American Giants and ABCs-American Giants in the Midwest.

Greenlee showed no interest in joining Posey's East-West League in 1932. With his large payroll, he felt he needed to play as many games as possible. The Craws began their season in Monroe, Louisiana, on March 25, and by the time they finished in late September, they had won ninety-nine out of 135 games, losing only two series, one to the New York Black Yankees and the other to the Grays. Their on-field success failed to carry over to the box office, however; Greenlee lost $16,000.

In 1933, in hopes of cutting his losses, he decided to try his hand at organized baseball. Spearheading the movement, Greenlee brought together the owners of the American Giants, the

Homestead Grays, the Indianapolis ABCs, the Detroit Stars and the Columbus Blue Birds, and formed the second Negro National League. Like Foster's original effort, the group established an organization called the National Organization of Professional Baseball Clubs, which guaranteed its members that they would not be raided by other

member clubs. Greenlee was named league chairman.

It didn't take long for some familiar problems to arise. In an effort to refurbish his lineup after Greenlee's search-and-destroy mission in 1933, Cum Posey snatched two players from the Detroit Stars. Chairman Greenlee, who now frowned on

The *Kansas City Call* heralds the arrival of Satchel Paige in 1935. Said Dizzy Dean of Paige: "You know, my fastball looks like a change of pace alongside that little pistol bullet ol' Satch shoots up to the plate."

such practices, kicked the Grays out of the league. Indianapolis, unable to meet expenses, also made a speedy departure. These teams were replaced by the Nashville Elite Giants and the Baltimore Black Sox.

Cole's American Giants (the original Chicago club had been bought by a mortuary owner named Robert Cole) won the first half of the split season, posting a 21-7 record to nose out the Crawfords (20-8). The second-half schedule was not completed, but the American Giants, on the strength of their first-half performance, staked a claim to the pennant. But this was Gus Greenlee's league, and, months after the season ended, the chairman decided that his Crawfords were the true pennant winners. It was the sort of high-handed maneuver that had generated so much grumbling about Rube Foster in the '20s. It was also the reason the league moved quickly in 1934 to name Rollo Wilson, a

sportswriter for the *Pittsburgh Courier*, commissioner of the league, though Greenlee remained chairman of the board.

All went smoothly for the new commissioner until he disallowed a protest by Robert Cole during the pennant playoff between the American Giants and the Philadelphia Stars. Philadelphia eventually won the battle for the pennant, 4-3, but Cole, the league's treasurer, won the war with Wilson by withholding his paycheck until several months after the season. By the following season, Wilson had resigned and was replaced by Ferdinand Morton, a civil service employee from New York whose main task was to attend league meetings.

Another of Greenlee's important contributions to Negro baseball was the East-West Game. Like the major league All-Star Game, which also debuted in 1933, the East-West Game was a celebration of the sport, both for the players and fans. The idea was

James (Cool Papa) Bell (right), Andy Porter, and two Mexican fishermen display their catch. In 1933 Pittsburgh Pirate standout Paul Waner said, "The fastest man I have ever seen on the baseball diamond was [Cool Papa]. He was on first base and the next batter hit a single to center. This fellow Bell by that time was rounding second base and watching me as he ran. He never stopped. I made a motion, thinking to get him at third. As I started the throw I saw I was going to be too late. So I stopped . . . but he didn't. He kept on for home plate. By the time I could get the ball away he had slid in there, was dusting himself off and walking calmly away."

"Dink" Mothell jokingly holds a shotgun on Hallie Harding as the Monarch bus driver looks on during a trip in 1930. Harding was called a "football tramp" because he played quarterback for Wiley, Fisk, Knox and Wilberforce Colleges. Not known for his modesty, when he joined the Fisk team he announced, "Boys, you had a fine team last year, but you'll have a better one now that I am a member of the varsity. I am going to serve as captain for the team until you have time to elect me and then I am going to make several changes in the lineup."

The Pittsburgh Crawfords at spring training in Hot Springs, Arkansas, 1935. Top row (L to R): Olan Taylor, Judy Johnson, Leroy Matlock, Unknown, Josh Gibson, Hood Witter (trainer). Middle row: "Cool Papa" Bell, Sam Bankhead, Oscar Charleston, Clarence Palm, Jimmie Crutchfield, Ernest (Spoon) Carter, William Perkins. Front row: Timothy Bond, Howard, Bertrum Hunter, Sam Streeter, Harry Kincannon and Duro Davis. Kincannon was the product of a mixed marriage. Since he could "pass" as a Caucasian, he used to go into "whites only" ice cream shops, order a float, then sit by the window and smile as his teammates walked by.

the brainchild of Roy Sparrow, a Greenlee associate who worked for the *Pittsburgh Sun-Telegram*. The two men had discussed the idea in 1932 but were unable to arrange a convenient site or date. Greenlee remained enamored of the concept, though, and worked diligently at implementing it the following year. Given the shaky foundation upon which their league was operating, the vision of a nearly full big league stadium came clearly into focus for Greenlee. Of course, he wasn't solely concerned with the greater good of the league —as promoter, he stood to haul 10 percent of the gate back to Pittsburgh.

Once the site and date were established in '33, coinciding with the Chicago World's Fair, Greenlee and Sparrow took the game to the fans, who were charged with choosing the teams. Voting was

Reuben Jones. In 1933, he was manager of the Little Rock Black Travelers. According to Marlin Carter, one of his players, "Jones didn't abuse his ball players like some managers. He was a down-to-earth sort of person. Late one night, a member of our pitching staff complained of a sore arm. I remember Jones got up in the middle of the night and worked for several hours on the player's arm." Jones played for the Detroit Stars and San Antonio Black Indians and managed the Memphis Red Sox and Birmingham Black Barons during his career.

administered by black newspapers such as the *Pittsburgh Courier,* the *Chicago Defender* and the *Kansas City Call* (even though the Monarchs were not in the league). Though the deck was stacked in favor of the big-city players, Greenlee had succeeded in baiting his hook — and the fans were biting.

The inaugural game drew 20,000 to Comiskey Park, which became the permanent home to the stars. The rosters read like those for a Crawfords-American Giants game. For the East, there were seven Craws in the lineup: Cool Papa Bell, Oscar Charleston, Josh Gibson, Judy Johnson, John Russell, Sam Streeter and Bertrum Hunter. The Philadelphia Stars managed to place four, the Grays two and the New York Black Yankees one. For the West, which used just nine players, there were only two players not from Cole's American Giants: Leroy Morney of the Cleveland Giants and Sam Bankhead of the Nashville Elite Giants. The rest of the team consisted of Norman (Turkey) Stearnes, Willie

Quincy J. Gilmore. He was the business manager of the Kansas City Monarchs. Of the team's visit to Mexico in 1932, Gilmore said, "We shall never forget the fine treatment that we have received here. While standing in front of the hotel, I saw a young colored lady coming down the street on the arm of a young Mexican student. This same student was just as white as any white student in the States and this young woman was about the color of myself."

T.J. Young, Kansas City Monarchs catcher. When the Monarchs beat Dizzy and Daffy Dean, 7-0, in 1934, Young banged out four hits in five trips to the plate, including a triple off Daffy and a double off Dizzy. After the game Young said, "I think Dizzy Dean is a great pitcher. I also think we have a great bunch of hitters. I got a big kick out of hitting Dean tonight because all my life it has been one of my ambitions to hit the best hurlers in the majors. So now I figure that maybe I'm not so bad with the bat."

Wells, Walter Davis, Alex Radcliffe, George (Mule) Suttles, Larry Brown and Willie Foster.

Under a steady drizzle, Foster pitched all nine innings and Suttles cracked the game's only home run in an 11-7 West triumph. The partisan Chicago crowd loved it, and the spinning turnstiles made it joyfully clear to Greenlee that Sparrow's idea would fly. The windfall from the East-West Game also helped Gus get over the news that Prohibition, along with his bootlegging business, was about to end.

The success of the Chicago game prompted league officials to stage a second annual all-star game. Billed as the North-South Game, it was played in the fall, usually in either Memphis or New Orleans, and soon became the biggest baseball event in the South.

Although that first East-West game was considered a commercial success, some members of the press gave it a hearty thumbs down. In the weeks before the '34 game, Frank A. Young of the *Kansas City Call* took Greenlee to task for billing the game as an East-West game when there was

Clockwise from top left: Edward (Pep) Young, Norman (Turkey) Stearnes, Alex Radcliffe and Richard (Subby) Byas. In the 1932-33 California Winter League, Alex Radcliffe led the all-black Nashville Giants to the championship. In addition to the Nashville nine, the league was composed of two white teams and one Mexican team. Radcliffe won the batting title with a .381 average. Satchel Paige led all pitchers with a 9-0 record and 79 strikeouts. Young was a native of St. Louis who began his professional career with the Titanium Pigment Company in 1937.

only one league, and the West was represented almost exclusively by Cole's American Giants. Wrote Young:

"The East vs. West Negro All-Star baseball game of last year was won by the Chicago American Giants with the help of two other players, Bankhead and Morney . . . . In the meantime, in cities where teams have made names for themselves, fans are asking why Negro players who stood high in the voting did not take part. These fans also are asking why all but two of the players were Chicago men . . . . Fans are asking why Newt Allen, crack second sacker of the Kansas City Monarchs; George Giles, first baseman of the same club; Charlie Beverly and Chet Brewer, Rogan and Duncan, all of the same club, never appeared in the game . . . . Newt Allen's name appeared in the daily papers among the chosen players who would take part in the game while most of the players knew that the Monarch players were not in Chicago but were in Wichita, Kansas, to play as a team . . . . In other words, there·is going to be another exhibition game again this year and it will be dubbed the 'second annual East vs. West All-Star Negro game.' Hooey!"

Hooey or not, the East-West game was here to stay. For the players, who never were paid much, if at all, for their participation, it was a formal stamp of

recognition, a message from the fans that said, "You're one of the best." For the owners, who shared in the profits, it sometimes provided the difference between insolvency and survival. For the fans, who flocked to Chicago from all over to see and be seen, it was a grand affair, a big-time show in every sense. And for the sportswriters, who trumpeted the game for weeks in advance, it gave them an opportunity to show off their skills to their readers, who were eager to absorb all that was written about the contest.

Throughout most of the 1930s, the game drew between 20,000 and 30,000. It became **THE** event of the season, with anticipation running high for weeks before fans converged on Comiskey. The '34 game drew 30,000 and featured a brilliant display of pitching by both teams, which again were heavily stocked with Crawfords and American Giants. Slim Jones (Philadelphia Stars), Harry Kincannon and Satchel Paige (both of the Craws) combined for a seven-hit, 1-0 victory over the West's pitching trio of Ted Trent (American Giants), Chet Brewer (Kansas City Monarchs) and Willie Foster (American Giants). The lone run came off Foster in the eighth, when Cool Papa Bell walked, stole second and scored on Jud Wilson's single up the middle. Paige, the winning pitcher, entered the game in the seventh after Willie Wells' (American Giants) leadoff double.

Chester Washington of the *Pittsburgh Courier*

Sam Bankhead in Mexico (circa 1940). He was one of the game's most versatile players. Roy Welmaker, a teammate of Bankhead's with the Homestead Grays, said, "He could play anywhere and was as good as anyone I have ever seen at shortstop."

Hittin' the road. By the late 1930s every major club had its own bus. In their travels, teams sometimes had to use the bus for sleeping quarters when stopping in a town that refused to accomodate a group of fifteen to twenty black men. On one occasion, according to Lorenzo (Piper) Davis, the Omaha Tigers had to spend a night in jail because local officials "didn't want us on the streets."

described Satchel's entrance as follows:

"Pandemonium reigned in the West's cheering sections. An instant later a hush fell upon the crowd as the mighty Satchel Paige, prize 'money' pitcher for the East, leisurely ambled across the field toward the pitcher's box. It was a dramatic moment. Displaying his picturesque double wind-up and nonchalant manner, Satchel started shooting 'em across the plate, and in five tosses fanned [Alex] Radcliffe. The East's supporters breathed a sigh of relief. Turkey Stearnes flied out to Vic Harris and Mule Suttles' bat dropped another fly ball into the accurate hands of Harris. This sounded taps for the West because from then on Sir Satchel was the

master of the situation."

The 1935 game may have been the greatest of them all. Greenlee, responding to criticism that the East was overstocked with talent, shifted the representatives of the Crawfords and Grays, who were back in the league, to the West. It turned out to be a fortuitous move. With 25,000 in attendance, the teams battled to a 4-4 tie through nine innings. In the top of the tenth, the East struck for four runs off Bob Griffith of the Columbus Elite Giants. The West came right back in their half, scoring four times off Luis Tiant and Martin Dihigo, both of the New York Cubans.

The East threatened in the eleventh when Jud

The Cincinnati Tigers, 1935. Standing (L to R): Marlin Carter, Robert Smith, Olan Taylor, Neil Robinson, Miller, Josh Johnson, Jerry Gibson, Maddox, Ewing Russell, Sonny (Sweets) Harris, Wolf, Virgil Harris, Harvey Peterson, Jesse Houston, Porter Moss, Willie Simms. Kneeling: manager Jim Glass. The team was owned by the great track runner and Olympic gold medalist, D. Hart Hubbard. Uniforms were provided by the Cincinnati Reds of the National League and the two teams looked identical on the field, except for the color of the players. In 1937 they joined the newly formed Negro American League.

Wilson walked and went to second on a groundout. Biz Mackey then stroked a liner to left that Suttles charged and grabbed off his shoe tops. Another groundout stranded Wilson. In the bottom of the eleventh, Cool Papa Bell led off with a walk and was sacrificed to second. Dihigo then struck out Chester Williams of the Crawfords for the second out. That brought to the plate the game's number one slugger, Josh Gibson, who already had four hits, including two doubles. Webster McDonald, the East's manager, paid Gibson the hitter's compliment and ordered an intentional walk. Next up was Mule Suttles, an eighteen-year veteran who was one of the outstanding home-run hitters in the first Negro National League.

Courier sportswriter Walter Nunn, who along with Frank Young of the *Kansas City Call* were the official scorers, captured the drama that unfolded as Suttles took his final swing:

"Once again came [Dihigo's] smooth motion, that reflex action of the arm, and then! — a blur seeming to catapult towards the plate.

"Suttles threw his mighty body into motion. His foot moved forward. His huge shoulder muscles bunched. Came a swish through the air, a crack as of a rifle, and like a projectile hurled from a cannon, the ball started its meteoric flight. On a line it went. It was headed towards right-center. Bell and Gibson were away with the crack of the bat. But so was [Paul] Arnold, center-fielder of the East team and [Alejandro] Oms, dependable and dangerous Cuban star, who patrolled the right

Norman (Turkey) Stearnes in Mexico, 1932. He first made a name for himself as an outstanding hitter with the Detroit Stars in the 1920s. Former player and manager Ted Radcliffe once said, "Give me Ducky Davenport, Willard Brown and Turkey Stearnes in the outfield and I wouldn't lose a ball game." Cool Papa Bell was similarly impressed. "If Turkey Stearnes isn't in the Hall of Fame," Bell said, "I don't know what I'm doing there."

The Homestead Grays, 1940. Back row (L to R): Unknown, J.C. Hamilton, Josh Johnson, Robert Gaston, Unknown, Jud Wilson, Eugene Hicks, Jerry Benjamin, Howard Easterling, Edsell Walker, Unknown. Front row: Buck Leonard, Ray Brown, Matthew Carlisle, Norman (Jelly) Jackson, Rocky Ellis, Vic Harris, Willie Ferrell. Ray Brown was an All-State center in basketball in Alger, Ohio. He started his baseball career with the Detroit Wolves in 1930. One of many good hitting pitchers, he was as adept in the outfield as he was on the mound. After the war, he no-hit the New York Yankees in an exhibition game in Puerto Rico.

Roy Partlow and his mother, Rosa. After graduation from Stowe High School in Cincinnati, Ohio, in the mid 1930s, Partlow became the star pitcher of the Cincinnati Tigers second team. The two teams squared off one day after players from the second unit boasted that, with Partlow pitching, they could beat the first team. Before the game started, Partlow had the bat boy tell leadoff hitter Marlin Carter: "I know you can't hit a curveball." Carter drilled the first curve he saw right back to Partlow. The ball deflected off his glove and hit him in the eye, forcing him to leave the game. The second team eventually lost, 19-1.

garden. No one thought the ball could carry to the stands.

"Headed as it was, it took a drive of better than 450 feet to clear the fence.

"The ball continued on its course and the packed stands rose to their feet. Was it going to be caught?! Was it going to hit the stands?!

"No, folks! That ball, ticketed by Mule Suttles, CLEARED the distant fence in far away right center, landing 475 feet from home plate. It was a Herculean swat. One of the greatest in baseball. As cheering momentarily hushed in the greatest tribute an athlete can ever receive, we in the press box heard it strike the back of a seat with a resounding thud, and then go bounding merrily on its way.

"And then . . . . Pandemonium broke loose. Suttles completed his trip home, the third-base line filled with playmates anxious to draw him to their breasts. Over the stands came a surging mass of humanity."

The Pittsburgh Crawfords, 1932. Standing (L to R): Gus Greenlee, Jones, L.D. Livingston, LeRoy (Satchel) Paige, Josh Gibson, R. Williams, Rev. Canady, William Perkins, Oscar Charleston, John Clark (secretary). Kneeling: Sam Streeter, Chester Williams, Harry Williams, Harry Kincannon, Clyde Spearman, Jimmie Crutchfield, Bobby Williams, Ted Radcliffe. In a game against St. Louis, Sam Streeter had a no-hitter broken up with two outs in the ninth inning when manager Jim Taylor put himself in the game as a pinch-hitter and stroked a single up the middle.

The Chicago American Giants, 1931. Top row (L to R): Nat Rogers, Kermit Dial, Walter Davis, Willie Foster, "Turkey" Stearnes, Alex Radcliffe. Middle row: "Pops" Turner, Clarence Palm, Sandy Thompson, Manager Dave Malarcher, Johnny Hines, F.B. Dixon, Walter Harper. Front row: Norman Cross, Jack Marshall, Willie Powell, Melvin Powell, Jimmie Lyons, Luther McDonald. In 1912 Lyons was considered the fastest man in baseball, prompting these words from a Chicago sportswriter: "He steals bases as easy as he gets on a street car."

Kansas City Call reporter Frank Young wrote that the West's 11-8 victory "may go down in the record books as the game of games from a ball fan's point of view.

"Not since the celebration following the news that the armistice had been signed ending the bloody conflict known as the World War has Chicago seen its citizenry go stark mad for a few minutes. Score cards were torn up and hurled into the air. Men tossed away their summer straw hats and women screamed."

And when the screaming died down, the players stepped out of the national glare and returned to the routine business of league play. For the six Crawfords who played in the '35 East-West Game, the team they were rejoining may have been equally as good as the one they'd just left.

The Pittsburgh lineup included Josh Gibson (catcher), Oscar Charleston (manager/first base), Pat Patterson (second base), Chester Williams (shortstop), Judy Johnson (third base), Sam

Bankhead (left-field), Cool Papa Bell (center-field) and Jimmie Crutchfield (right-field). The pitching staff was comprised of Leroy Matlock, Sam Streeter, Roosevelt Davis and Bert Hunter. It was a perfect blend of youth and experience.

The Craws easily won the first half of the season, posting a 26-6 record to finish seven games in front of the second-place Columbus Elite Giants. They lost the second half to the New York Cubans, which set up a seven-game series for the pennant. The Cubans, who were owned by Alex Pompez, were a solid team that featured Americans David (Showboat) Thomas (first base), ex-Monarch Frank Duncan (catcher), Herbert (Rap) Dixon (outfielder) and Dick Lundy (shortstop), along with Cuban pitchers Luis (Lefty) Tiant, Alejandro Oms and Martin Dihigo, who also managed and played the outfield. Defensively, the Cubans were just as strong as the Crawfords. Duncan was a better receiver than Gibson, while Lundy, though getting on in years, was regarded as one of the best shortstops of the era. Rap Dixon, a feared power-hitter, also was a stalwart defensively.

The Craws started slowly in the series, falling behind 3-1. They won game five and rallied on home runs by Charleston and Gibson to win game six. In the finale, which was played at Philadelphia's Thirty-Fifth Street Park, the Cubans carried a 7-4 lead into the ninth inning. Pompez, according to Jimmie Crutchfield, phoned New York and advised friends to "let the celebration begin." The Crawfords, with men on first and second, were down to their last out when Judy Johnson stepped in against Dihigo, the Cubans' ace right-hander who had been summoned from center-field to get the last out. Johnson, a seventeen-year vet, kept the Craws alive when he beat out a slow roller to the right side. That set the stage for Oscar Charleston, a renowned clutch-hitter who was in his twenty-first year as a professional. Charleston, as intense a competitor as there ever was, took a swipe at Dihigo's first pitch and drilled it over the left center-field fence for a dramatic grand slam that won the pennant for the Crawfords.

As awesome as the Crawfords were in 1935, they might have been downright unbeatable if they'd had the ace of their '34 staff. Satchel Paige had jumped ship after the 1934 season after a salary dispute with Greenlee. Seems Satch had married recently and found that the dollar wasn't going quite as far as it once did. Greenlee, who had just signed Paige to a two-year contract, refused his request and Satchel refused to pitch.

It was the move of a confident man to turn his back on $250 a month in 1934. But Satchel Paige was the game's top drawing card, and he wasn't afraid to play it for all it was worth. After leaving the Craws, he accepted a deal to pitch for Bismarck, N.D., a mixed independent team. Before the '35 season, Greenlee, who was livid, issued Paige an ultimatum: return to the Crawfords or be banned from the Negro National League. Paige opted for the latter and headed to North Dakota.

The local press joined the Pittsburgh owner in vilifying Paige. Under the headline *Contracts or Scraps of Paper,* Chester Williams (no relation to the Crawfords' infielder) of the *Pittsburgh Courier* wrote:

"No player is bigger than a baseball club and no player is certainly more important than the National Association of Negro Baseball clubs. And this goes for Satchell [*sic*] Paige, too.

"Satchell was a great pitcher and he may be missed as thousands cheer in the East-West and the New York four-game doubleheaders. But the issue would have arisen sooner or later. The league means business. The owners have invested their money in the game and they don't intend to 'play around' with the players.

"Heroes come and heroes go. The champ of today may be the chump of tomorrow. So it may be with Paige. The league helped to make him and now the league may be the medium to break him.

The Brooklyn Eagles, 1935. Standing (L to R): Ben Taylor, C.B. Griffin, Ted Page, Lamon Yokely, Unknown, George Giles, Unknown, Harry Williams, Ted Radcliffe. Front row: Bobby Williams, Unknown, Tex Burnett, Dennis Gilcrest, Ward, Leon Day. In the winter of 1934-35, Ben Taylor traveled all over the country assembling this team. When the season opened at Ebbets Field, the Homestead Grays crushed them. Giles complained to owner Abe Manley that Taylor "was playing old-time baseball, that one-run-at-a-time stuff." Manley fired Taylor and hired Giles as the manager.

The Lone Rock (Iowa) All-Stars, 1932. Teams such as these served as minor leagues for Negro players. Fred Langford, who used to travel with independent clubs of this type, once said, "You would leave home, play ball on the road for thirty days, four to five games a week, only to find that when you returned home again, you had less money than you had previous to leaving."

"Satchell apparently made the mistake of regarding his contract as a 'scrap of paper' and now he must pay the penalty."

In truth, the players were bigger than the game. And no one was bigger than Satchel. Despite the bluster in the press, Greenlee would have welcomed Paige back with open arms. Not only was he a draw for the Crawfords, but Greenlee had further tapped Paige's earning power by renting his star's services to semipro teams. Nothing guaranteed a boost at the gate like Satchel's presence, and both he and Greenlee capitalized on it.

In Bismarck, Paige and his wife, Janet, found that life in Pittsburgh wasn't so bad after all. Following a long and fruitless search for housing, team owner Neil Churchill situated them in an old railroad car that had been converted to house work gangs. On the field, with Paige as the star of a team that included such black standouts as Hilton Smith, Quincy Trouppe and Ted (Double Duty) Radcliffe, Bismarck won a national semipro tournament in Wichita and was much in demand throughout the Midwest.

Semipro tournaments, such as the one in Wichita

The Nashville Elite Giants, 1935. Standing (L to R): Sammy T. Hughes, Andy Porter, B. Wright, Hoss Walker, Robert Griffith, Samuel Thompson, R. Wright, Tom Glover, Jim West. Kneeling: William Byrd, Jim Willis, Leroy Morney, Paul Hardy, Jim Taylor, Zollie Wright, Felton Snow, Nish Williams, Red Parnell. In 1940, Al Moses of the Associated Negro Press wrote these words about two great first basemen: "Buck Leonard [Grays] is a greater first baseman than [Babe] Dahlgren of the New York Yankees or [Dolph] Camilli of the Brooklyn Dodgers. Showboat Jim West of the Philly Stars would be worth the admission price for the exhibition he puts on, the greatest since Rabbit Maranville put his spikes and gloves in mothballs."

(L to R) Jim (Candy) Taylor, Dave Malarcher and Larry Brown. After a game, preparations for travel had to be made quickly. Taylor would tell his players the exact time the bus was to depart, and if one of them was late, he would be left behind. Taylor was once quoted as saying, "I wouldn't wait for my own mother; this is business, so take it seriously."

(L to R) Clinton Thomas, Clarence (Fats) Jenkins and Clyde Spearman. During a four-team doubleheader in Yankee Stadium on September 9, 1934, Thomas cracked a 450-foot home run off Ted Trent to defeat the Chicago American Giants, 4-3, before a crowd of 30,000.

and the *Denver Post* tournament (the most prestigious) became important events to black baseball teams — that is, once the tourneys dropped their color barrier. Paige first played in the *Denver Post* tournament in 1934, when Greenlee "loaned" his ace, along with catcher Bill Perkins, to the House of David team, a highly successful independent team that toured the United States. The House of David, a religious movement centered in Benton Harbor, Michigan, sought to publicize its word through its baseball team, whose players were distinguished by their long hair and beards. As good as they were (several refused major league offers), they reached out to Paige to carry them through the tournament.

It was in 1934 that the Denver tourney first opened its doors to all-black teams. The Kansas City Monarchs made their debut that year and if not for Paige's presence would have won the double-elimination tournament. The Monarchs' two losses were to the House of David, which went undefeated. Satchel, the "Chocolate Whizbang," as he was called by the *Denver Post,* struck out forty-four in twenty-eight innings and was named the "Outstanding Pitcher," a distinction that earned him a coffee percolator. Norman (Turkey) Stearnes, an outfielder with the Monarchs, was voted the "Outstanding Player" of the tournament. For winning the championship, the House of David collected $5,000.

After finishing his season in Bismarck in '35,

John McGraw (left) and Christy Mathewson. When he managed Baltimore in the early 1900s, McGraw once tried to put a black player on his roster. A 1912 story in the *Philadelphia Tribune* called that McGraw had said he "would give anything in the world if Rube Foster was a white man; it was too bad that Walter Ball was colored; that it is a shame that [John Henry] Lloyd could not show the public what he could do; that if he had [Bruce] Petway no money cold buy him; that the world was robbed of seeing a most sensational player on account of [Bill] Monroe's color." By 1933, though, he had changed his outlook, telling *New York Daily News* columnist Jimmy Powers that it would not be a good idea to allow blacks in the major leagues. Powers reported that "Branch Rickey, Jacob Ruppert of the Yankees, Frankie Frisch, Herb Pennock and Lou Gehrig all displayed a refreshing open-mindedness" toward admitting blacks.

Paige was off to the West Coast, where he formed Satchel Paige's All-Stars, an all-black team that competed in the California Winter League. In 1936, he returned to the Crawfords (all was forgiven) and helped them win the second half of the split season. (The Washington Elite Giants had won the first half, but no playoff was held.) He was back with Pittsburgh the following year, but only briefly.

While in New Orleans for spring training, Paige was approached by an emissary from President Rafael L. Trujillo of the Dominican Republic. Trujillo, a dictator who had seized control of the country in 1930, was annoyed with a foe of his regime whose popularity seemed to be growing with the success of his baseball team. Trujillo's team, meanwhile, was doing poorly, and in a country where *beisbol* was king, that didn't bode well for el Presidente. Trujillo sent his representatives to lure Paige with an offer of $30,000 to be split among Paige and eight teammates. That averaged out to about $3,000 per man, Satchel figured, "even if I didn't skim some off for

managing the whole thing." It was too much to refuse; Satchel and friends soon were on a plane to Santo Domingo.

Among those joining Stachel on the excursion to the West Indies were pitchers Leroy Matlock and Robert (Schoolboy) Griffith, catcher Josh Gibson, shortstop Sam Bankhead, third baseman Chester Williams and outfielder Cool Papa Bell. Most were Paige's teammates on the Crawfords, though Gibson, who had been traded, then was playing for the Homestead Grays.

The action of the players brought swift condemnation from the league. In an official statement Greenlee announced, "The men who have sacrificed their time and money to develop Negro baseball will not allow any one player or any group of players to wreck the league. These men must realize that the league is far larger and more powerful than they are. They left without notice after they had been signed to contracts to play with league clubs.

"If they fail to report to their clubs by Saturday,

Above: House of David team photograph.

Below: John R. Tucker. He was a regular for the House of David team for more than twenty years. According to teammate Tom Dewhirst, "Over 250,000 people visited the House of David religious colony [Benton Harbor, Michigan] annually during the peak years of the organization."

Above: George Anderson.

Below: House of David infield.

Above: King Ben. His real name was Benjamin Purnell and he was the founder of the House of David movement. In a 1924 story in the *Kansas City Times,* it was stated that "Purnell is about fifty-five years old and he weighs nearly two hundred pounds. He also is about 5'6" tall. Rewards totaling approximately $3,000 have been offered for his arrest. Warrants charging statutory offenses are out against him, sworn to by Gladys Bamford Rubel and Ruth Bamford Reed, sisters, who charged seduction while they were members of the colony."

Right: Babe Didrikson. Known as the Girl Marvel, she won two gold medals in track at the 1932 Olympic Games. She traveled with the House of David baseball team during the summers of 1932 and 1933. Didrikson was called the "greatest female all-around athlete of all time." She died of cancer in 1956 at age forty-two.

Below: The House of David operated several teams at once. One club worked the East, another the Midwest and Upper Northwest, and still another remained home in Benton Harbor, Michigan. A junior club also played games in the Benton Harbor area.

Miniature trains were a popular attraction in Benton Harbor, where the House of David eventually organized a resort. The cult was also well known for their pioneering of frozen foods and their ice cream parlors.

May 15, they will be barred from organized baseball for one year and fined."

Trujillo's renegades, unfazed by Greenlee's threats, managed to win the championship, and that, according to Satchel, may have been the most important victory of their careers. In his auto-biography, *Maybe I'll Pitch Forever,* Paige wrote:

"By the seventh inning we were a run behind and you could see Trujillo lining up his army. They began to look like a firing squad. In the last of the seventh we scored two runs.... You never saw Ol' Satch throw harder than that. I shut them out the last two innings and we'd won. I hustled back to our hotel and the next morning we blowed out of there in a hurry. We never did see Trujillo again. I ain't sorry."

Upon returning to the States, they picked up catcher William Perkins, infielder Pat Patterson, outfielder Roy (Red) Parnell and pitcher Chet Brewer and enjoyed a successful tour as the Trujillo All-Stars. The team won the *Denver Post* tournament with a 6-1 record, as their pitching staff compiled an ERA of 1.00 while limiting the opposition to a .166 batting average. Red Parnell, who had joined the team from the Washington Elite Giants, led the offensive onslaught with fifteen hits in thirty-six at-bats for a .417 average.

The Negro National League, meanwhile, was struggling. Low salaries, always a problem, were causing players to seek employment elsewhere. More and more, Dominican, Cuban, Puerto Rican and Mexican leagues were becoming viable alter-natives, and not only because the money was better. Longtime Negro League shortstop Willie Wells explained to *Courier* sportswriter Wendell Smith that in Mexico, "we live in the best hotels, we eat in the best restaurants and can go anyplace we care to .... we don't enjoy such privileges in the United States."

Nobody was hit harder by the Latin lure in 1937 than Greenlee, who not only lost players to the Dominican Republic but to Cuba, as well. Greenlee's once-dominating team was going the way of his financial empire. His bootlegging business had been destroyed by the Twenty-first Amendment, and when he lost some friends in local government, Pittsburgh's finest suddenly

The House of David built its colony around religious activities.

began raiding his numbers operation. With diminished revenues came diminished salaries — and unhappy ballplayers. The Craws quickly lost their reputation as the league's classiest team, as players fled in search of a bigger paycheck. The loss of talent dropped them to fifth place in the first half of the '37 season. They had sent nine players to the East-West Game in 1936 but managed to place just

A bumper sticker from the House of David Resort, 1933.

three on the East's roster the following year.

Even tougher for Greenlee to take was the ascendency of the archrival Grays to the Negro National League throne. With Gibson, first baseman Buck Leonard, outfielder Vic Harris and pitcher Willie (Lefty) Gisentaner leading their attack, the Grays won the first half and were declared league champs at season's end.

Although problems abounded within the NNL — player defections, weak franchises, erratic scheduling, etc. — there was a positive development in 1937: the formation of the Negro American League. The league, which was several years in the making, was organized by H.G. Hall, who had bought the American Giants from Robert Cole. At a February meeting in Chicago, which brought together eight team owners from the Midwest and South, details were worked out for a league with franchises in Chicago, Kansas City, Detroit, Indianapolis, Cincinnati, St. Louis, Memphis and Birmingham.

As was the case in the first Negro National League, Wilkinson's Monarchs became one of the key franchises. Since their withdrawal from the

ST. LOUIS CARDINALS vs. KANSAS CITY MONARCHS
Six Thousand People Attended this Game at Oxford, Nebraska, October 4, 1933

This game was not against the entire Cardinal team. Only Dizzy Dean and Pepper Martin were in the lineup that night. The rest were minor leaguers.

original Negro National League in 1931, they had played almost exclusively on the road, where there was still some money to be made. They made annual trips to Mexico and Canada and embarked on frequent tours with the House of David. In 1933 they played only six games in Kansas City, but as the decade wore on through the unrelenting depression, the Monarchs, like most independents, found it difficult to maintain a full schedule.

Nevertheless, the Monarchs could always count on Wilkinson to come through on payday; throughout his tenure as team owner he never missed one. When the original NNL tried to cut costs by imposing a salary cap, Wilkinson earned his players' gratitude by reducing the roster rather than the paychecks. He once had the opportunity to buy the Kansas City Blues of the American Association, an opportunity he rejected in favor of remaining with

The Memphis Red Sox and Birmingham Black Barons, 1935. The Red Sox played in Martin Park, one of only a few black-owned baseball parks. Others included Bugle Field in Baltimore, Wilson Park in Nashville and Greenlee Field in Pittsburgh.

T. J. Young (left) and Chet Brewer. Young and Brewer became friends in 1924 and remained close throughout their careers. Their real names, Thomas Jefferson Young and Chester Arthur Brewer, reflected the black custom of naming children after famous Americans.

the Monarchs. His devotion to the team wasn't lost on his players, some of whom called him "Dad." During good times he was quick with a bonus, and he was always willing to help a player in need. When Eddie Dwight, a Monarch outfielder, wanted to open an ice cream shop and needed $30,000, it was Wilkinson, along with team booking agent Tom Beard, who arranged for the loan through a Kansas City bank.

"He was a considerate man," said Newt Allen, a longtime Monarch second baseman. "He understood, he knew people. Your face could be as black as tar; he treated everyone alike. He traveled right along with us."

Added pitcher Lefty Bryant: "Wilkie was a heck of a man. You couldn't ask for a better person to work for. He was just a fine fellow, that's all."

The love and respect he earned from his players stemmed from the sensitivity with which he treated them. Over the years, Wilkinson had learned which towns were hostile and which were hospitable, and if food or lodging couldn't be found in or near a particular town, then it was off the itinerary for future trips. He stood up for his players in their encounters with Jim Crow hotels and restaurants, and they appreciated it. On one occasion, a hotel clerk tried to bunch four and five players in a room. According to Monarch pitcher Chet Brewer, Wilkinson told the man, "My players aren't a bunch of dogs. Either you give us decent accommodations or I'll take my business somewhere else." Which is just what he did.

When Wilkinson entered his Monarchs in the Negro American League, the move was greeted with great enthusiasm in Kansas City. The ticket buyers realized they'd be getting more for their money with a pennant at stake. Not only that, but they'd also be getting more home games. The team's booster club, upon hearing the good news, immediately began preparing for the home opener against the Chicago American Giants. Saturday, May

Elmer Dean and father. Dizzy and Paul Dean were the stars of the family, but brother Elmer and their father were players, too, traveling with the House of David team during the mid-1930s.

15, was the big day, and the community turned out en masse for an all-day celebration.

The festivities started with a noontime parade through the city, with league officials, the teams, local dignitaries and two fifty-piece bands marching to Muehlebach Field. Local businesses offered various prizes for the player who hit the first home run or triple, made the first putout or error, drew the first walk, etc. Prizes ranged from a pair of silk pajamas to a jar of spaghetti. More than 12,000 people plunked down their 40 cents (general admission) or 25 cents (bleachers) and saw Willie Foster of the American Giants shut out their beloved Monarchs, 2-0. The loss may have dimmed the celebration, but it didn't prevent the party from carrying on through the evening's homecoming dance.

The Monarchs, as usual, had a strong team in '37. Veterans Newt Allen, Frank Duncan (catcher) and Eddie Dwight (center-fielder) combined with youngsters Hilton Smith (pitcher), Willard Brown

The Kansas City Monarchs, 1934. Standing (L to R): Willie Foster, George Giles, T.J. Young, Turkey Stearnes, Chet Brewer, Sam Crawford, John Donaldson, Curtis Harris, Andy Cooper. Front row: Frank Duncan, Wilber Rogan, Carroll (Dink) Mothell, Sam Bankhead, bat boy, Newt Allen, Newt Joseph, Eddie Dwight. Photograph was taken at the *Denver Post* baseball tournament, which was established to determine the best semipro team in the West. In 1933, Young, Giles, Allen and Brewer were entered into the balloting for the East-West Game, and all, with the exception of Brewer, who finished second, were the top vote-getters at their positions. However, on game day, all were in Wichita, playing with the Monarchs.

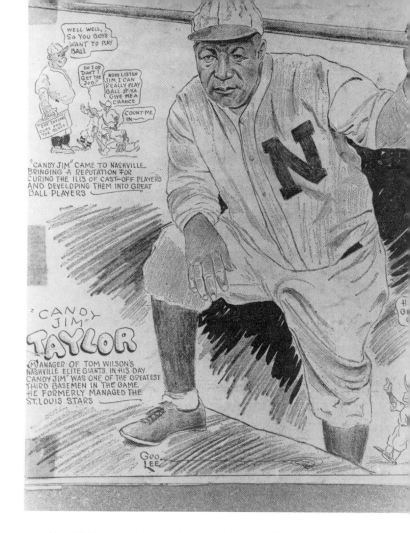

After the 1932 regular season, the Monarchs took a tour of Mexico. Quincy Gilmore, team secretary, sent this report back to Kansas City: "We have been told that the Monarchs are the best-behaved baseball club that has ever visited the Republic of Mexico. While most of the visiting ball clubs spend their time in the fine saloons of the great city, the Monarchs are the only club that has gone to the parks every day, even when not playing a regular game."

Jim (Candy) Taylor. George Lee sketched all the great players and events which were happening in black sports. His drawings appeared in the *Chicago Defender* and the *Pittsburgh Courier*.

(shortstop) and Henry Milton (outfielder) to lead Kansas City to the pennant. The Monarchs won the first half of the split season with a record of 19-8, edging the American Giants (18-8) by a half game. In the second half, final standings were not published, though the American Giants were declared the winners. The Monarchs then beat the Giants four out of five games to win the championship.

That Kansas City was awarded first place after having played one more game was indicative of the league's casual regard for even scheduling. That final standings for the second half were not published was not surprising. It happened frequently in the leagues — they started strong, with newspapers providing complete coverage. By the second half of the season, after some games were canceled and others went unreported, newspapers were unable to offer accurate standings, leaving first place to be decided by mandate of the league office.

Joe Greene (back row, second from right) was a member of this local men's club in Stone Mountain, Georgia. It was not uncommon to find players involved in community activities off the field.

Leroy Morney. He began playing professionally as a shortstop with the Monroe (Louisiana) Monarchs in 1932 and went on to play for more than ten teams in a twelve-year career.

Nevertheless, a pennant is a pennant, and no two teams were as dominant in the '30s and '40s as the Kansas City Monarchs and the Homestead Grays. The Grays, who began playing part of their schedule in Washington, D.C., in 1937, won eight out of nine pennants from 1937 to 1945. Cum Posey, who had struggled to stay afloat after Greenlee's raid in 1932, put the Grays back on course in 1935, when he found a money man named "Sonnyman." Rufus (Sonnyman) Jackson moved in behind the scenes, supplying Posey with the capital he needed to revive the franchise. Like Greenlee, Jackson was in the numbers business and also operated a few gambling houses in Pittsburgh.

Greenlee and Jackson weren't the only policy men who became enamored of baseball in the

(L to R) Webster McDonald, Joe Hall and Oscar Charleston. McDonald was the manager of the Philadelphia Stars and Charleston the manager of the Pittsburgh Crawfords when this picture was taken in the 1930s. McDonald's Stars beat Cole's American Giants to win the Negro National League pennant in 1934. In 1945, Branch Rickey organized the United States Baseball League and announced that Joe Hall had been given the Ebbets Field lease for all Negro games.

Advertisement depicting black baseball. As can be seen, it was a negative image that was usually presented.

Oscar Charleston. According to William Dismukes, writing in the *St. Louis Argus,* "Charleston hit one of Slim Jones' offerings out of Greenlee Field for a home run which won the ball game for the Crawfords, and as Jones watched his opponent round the bases, he started to shed real tears."

'30s. Team owners Abe Manley (Newark Eagles), Alex Pompez (New York Cubans) and Ed Semler (New York Black Yankees) also supported their baseball interests with their rackets. Teams were losing so much money that, were it not for the numbers men, who could afford the losses, many teams in the East and surely the NNL itself would have folded.

It also should be noted that the numbers men weren't regarded as criminals in the communities where they provided their customers with a daily dream. They were entrepreneurs; businessmen who dressed and drove in style, and were admired, like the athletes and the musicians, for having risen above their impoverished environment.

It was the infusion of Jackson's capital that enabled Posey to acquire such players as Buck Leonard, Josh Gibson, Cool Papa Bell, Jud Wilson, Howard Easterling, Sam Bankhead, and Vic Harris. The Grays became the team everyone loved to beat, but seldom could. Greenlee, in fact, gave up trying after the '38 season, leaving the team to devote his sporting attention to his boxing stable, which included the light heavyweight champion John Henry Lewis.

The Monarchs, meanwhile, won five of the first six Negro American League pennants. Their status was further enhanced in 1939 by the signing of

Ted Page (left) and Josh Gibson. As a member of the 1932 Pittsburgh Crawfords, Gibson led his team with a .380 batting average. His other totals included 123 games, 490 at-bats, 114 runs, 186 hits, 45 doubles, 16 triples and 34 home runs. His 16 three-baggers were second behind Oscar Charleston's 19.

Stuart (Slim) Jones. At 6'6", Jones and Ed Rile were the tallest pitchers in Negro baseball history. Jones was the ace of the 1934 Philadelphia Stars, winners of the Negro National League pennant. He was also one of the hardest throwing left-handers in the game, reputed to be faster than Satchel Paige. On September 9, 1934, Jones and Paige, then pitching for the Pittsburgh Crawfords, dueled in Yankee Stadium before a crowd of 30,000. Jones tossed a three-hitter and struck out nine, including both Cool Papa Bell and Josh Gibson twice. Paige struck out twelve and allowed six hits in the game, which was called because of darkness in the ninth inning with the score 1-1.

The Cincinnati Tigers, 1936. Standing (L to R): Porter Moss, Provens Bradley, Neil Robinson, Willie Jefferson, Eugene Bremer, Marlin Carter, J. Payne, Lloyd (Ducky) Davenport. Seated: Olan (Jelly) Taylor, Howard Easterling, Junius (Rainey) Bibbs, Ted (Double Duty) Radcliffe, Sonny (Sweets) Harris, Jess Houston, Josh Johnson. The Tigers were led by their hard-hitting infielders. Taylor finished the season with a .285 average, while Easterling batted .326 and Carter .387. Bibbs led the team with a .404 average.

Paige, who had left the Crawfords in '38 after another salary war with Greenlee. The Crawford owner finally became so fed up with his star that he sold him to Abe Manley and his wife, Effa, owners of the Newark Eagles, for $3,000. The Manleys, though, were left holding the bag when Satchel failed to report, opting instead to pursue the peso in the Mexican League.

"Everybody's been fussing over Satchel and telling him how good he is — that's why he's acting up," said Effa Manley, who operated the legitimate portion of her husband's businesses. "There are other pitchers around that can toss even with him."

That may have been true, but none could fill the seats like Satchel.

While in Mexico, Paige, who'd never suffered a serious injury, developed a sore arm that forced him to cut short his season. He returned home, fearing the worst — that at thirty-two years old, he'd never pitch again. Over the winter he made several

The Bismarck (North Dakota) Baseball Club, 1935. Standing (L to R): Hilton Smith, Red Haley, Barney Morris, Satchel Paige, Moose Johnson, Quincy Trouppe, Ted (Double Duty) Radcliffe. Front row: Joe Desiderato, Leary, Neil Churchill, Oberholzer, Hendee. This team was the winner of the first National Baseball Congress Tournament, which was held in Wichita, Kansas. The all-black Claybrook (Arkansas) Tigers finished second.

Junius A. (Rainey) Bibbs. He was a star fullback for Indiana State University in 1935. Bibbs once remarked, "Many times my own teammates would not block for me and got a kick from seeing me get hit." Bibbs recalled, "Once Evansville, the opposing team, did everything imaginable to me, and by the half I was bleeding from both ears, beaten and bruised all over. Wally Marks, our coach, asked me if I wanted to play the second half. I told him the biggest lie ever — I said, 'Yes.' " Bibbs, an infielder, played for several teams during his ten-year Negro league career.

calls to prospective employers, none of whom were in need of a broken-down, contract-jumping pitcher. None even expressed interest in hiring him as a manager or coach, which wasn't surprising since Satchel hadn't exactly endeared himself to management along the way. While contemplating his sorry fate one day, he received a phone call from J.L. Wilkinson, who expressed interest in his services.

Paige jumped at the opportunity and reported to Kansas City the following week. He didn't mind being relegated to the Monarchs' second team, a barnstorming outfit that toured the Upper Midwest. Wilkinson's plan was to use Satchel's magical name to attract the crowds, while having him pitch only a couple of innings. It was the same formula Wilkinson and booking agent Tom Baird had used in promoting Monarch games against major leaguers Dizzy Dean and Grover Cleveland Alexander, a 373-game winner in the major leagues who pitched for several years with the House of David. It had worked in the past and, with a name like Satchel Paige, it would work again.

According to Paige, however, Wilkinson's motivation in signing him wasn't strictly commercial. As Paige wrote in his autobiography, *Maybe I'll Pitch Forever*:

"If you were down and needed a hand, [Wilkinson] would give you one. He was all the time hiring ballplayers that'd been great and were on their way downhill.

" 'They can still do some good,' he used to say. 'And they've done a lot for the Negro leagues and

The Columbus Blue Birds, 1933. Standing (L to R): Dennis Gilcrest, Ameal Brooks, Dewey Creacy, Joe Scott, Bill McClain, Leroy Morney, Roosevelt Davis, Wilson Redus. Front row: C.B. Griffin, Jarman, William Byrd, manager William Dismukes, Kermit Dial, Alphonso Lattimore, Roy Williams. This team, which lasted only one season, played its games at Neil Park on Cleveland Ave.

Josh Gibson at bat, Baltimore's Robert Clark catching, and Fred McCreary umpiring. During a Homestead Grays-Kansas City Monarchs game, Jesse Williams, Monarchs' shortstop, picked a broken bat out of the Grays bat rack and asked, "Is this your old bat, Josh?" Gibson replied, "I don't break bats, I wear 'em out."

made us all some money so I'm just trying to pay them back a little.'

"And even if you weren't going down, just having a bad time, Mr. Wilkinson was a mighty patient man. He'd give you plenty of time to come back.

"That's what he was doing for me back that day when he offered me a job with the traveling squad."

Wilkinson's benevolence was rewarded one late summer day when Paige's arm misery disappeared as mysteriously as it had appeared. While warming up, Paige, who'd been getting roughed up by teams he once dominated, felt no pain. Suddenly Satchel, who'd been trading on his name, again had the goods to go with it. The Legend was alive.

Under orders from Wilkinson, Paige finished out the '38 season with the second team, gradually regaining his famed fastball. In 1939, he split time with both teams and helped the Monarchs win their second Negro American League pennant. (The Memphis Red Sox and Atlanta Black Crackers had won the two split seasons in 1938.) With Satchel anchoring the staff, the Monarchs continued to win NAL pennants from 1940 to 1942.

But Paige wasn't their only weapon. The Monarchs also had a powerful gun in right-hander Hilton Smith, who in the eyes of many was just as good as his more publicized colleague. It was

simply a fact of life for Paige's teammates that no matter how good they were, the ink belonged to Satchel. And no one knew it better than Smith, a native of Giddings, Texas, who came out of the Texas Negro League and joined the Monarchs in 1937 after playing a year with Paige in Bismarck. Smith, who threw a no-hitter against the Chicago American Giants in 1938, was voted to the East-West Game six straight years starting in 1937. Nevertheless, throughout the Monarchs' travels, their arrival was always heralded with the announcement that "the great Satchel Paige is in town." It was the case even when Paige and Josh Gibson were teammates on the Pittsburgh Crawfords. Even a great slugger like Gibson, who was a threat to blast a home run every time he stepped to the plate, was overshadowed by Satchel.

What was it about Satchel Paige that forced all others into the background?

Start with his nickname. LeRoy Paige was born July 7, 1906, in Mobile, Alabama. The nickname came from a childhood job in which he hauled bags at a railroad station for ten cents apiece. To maximize his earnings, he developed a system in which he put a pole across his shoulders that allowed him to carry several bags at once. In his autobiography, he wrote that his friends told him, "You look like a walking satchel tree." So long, LeRoy; hello, Satchel.

Then there was his incredible ability. He had a

The Trujillo (Dominican Republic) pitching staff, 1937. (L to R): LeRoy (Satchel) Paige, Robert Griffith, Rudolfo Fernandez, Leroy Matlock. "Griffith had every pitch mastered, except a knuckleball," said Cool Papa Bell. That same year, Griffith struck out Rogers Hornsby three times en route to a 12-0 victory over the Denver Bay Refiners in the *Denver Post* tournament. Matlock, like Jimmie Crutchfield, was a native of Moberly, Missouri. Both began their professional careers in 1928 with Bill Gatewood's Gatewood Browns, who played out of Moberly.

James (Cool Papa) Bell. His outstanding play in the 1936 and 1937 *Denver Post* tournaments prompted C.I. Parsons, sports editor of the *Denver Post,* to write, "All these years I've been looking for a player who could steal first base. I've found my man; his name is Cool Papa Bell." In thirteen tournament games, Bell batted .450, with two doubles, three triples and eleven stolen bases.

Tom Wilson. Along with the Martin brothers of Memphis, Wilson was one of the most prominent baseball men in the South. He served as president of the Negro Southern League and Negro National League. As the owner of the Nashville (later Baltimore) Elite Giants, he showed a keen eye for talent, signing Sammy T. Hughes, Sam Bankhead, Roy Campanella and Junior Gilliam to their first professional contracts.

Hallie Harding. He was an all-around athlete who played college football and later became an outstanding shortstop for the Detroit Stars and Kansas City Monarchs. Harding once tried unsuccessfully to arrange a boxing match against Art Shires, a Chicago White Sox infielder who fought professionally in the off-season. A.D. Williams, sportswriter for the *Kansas City Call*, wrote, "If Harding likes to scrap in the ring as much as he does on the ball field, it would have been one great battle."

high-octane fastball that was so unhittable he didn't start throwing a curve until the mid-'30s. Even then, he relied almost exclusively on the "bee ball" or "Long Tom," as he referred to his fastball. It didn't matter who he was facing, Negro leaguers or major leaguers; they were all overmatched. Roy Campanella, who broke in with the Baltimore Elite Giants in 1937, was once asked how he hit against Paige. "I didn't," Campanella said. Dizzy Dean, who pitched against Paige in more than thirty barnstorming duels, was awed by Paige's talent. Writing a regular column for a Chicago newspaper in 1938, Dean, using his own personal English dialect, offered this glowing assessment of Satchel's ability:

"A bunch of the fellows get in a barber session the other day and they start to argufy about who's the best pitcher they ever see and some says Lefty Grove and Lefty Gomez and old Pete Alexander and Dazzy Vance .... But I see all them fellows .... and I know who's the best pitcher I ever see and it's old Satchel Paige, that lanky colored boy. Say old Diz is pretty fast back in 1933 and 1934, and you know my fast ball looks like a change of pace alongside that little pistol bullet old Satchel shoots up to the plate . . . . That skinny old Satchel Paige, with those long arms, is my idea of the pitcher with the greatest stuff ever I see."

Jud Wilson. He was a feared line-drive hitter who led the 1925-26 Cuban Winter League with a .430 average. He was also fearsome off the field. Once, after the Grays lost to Baltimore, Wilson confronted umpire Pete Cockrell, who was about to step into the shower. Accusing him of costing the Grays the game, Wilson picked up the terrified ump by the skin of his chest and berated him for his incompetence.

Curtis Harris. A slick-fielding first baseman, Harris, who was from Texas, spent a season with the Houston Buffalos before going to the Kansas City Monarchs in 1931. Harris had two nicknames that he went by: in the West he was known as Moochie, while in the East he was called Popsicle.

He had the colorful name, and he had the extraordinary ability, but he also possessed one trait that separated him from all other big-name talents in the Negro leagues: he was a natural showman. Dean touched on an important point in describing him as "skinny old Satchel Paige, with those long arms." At 6′3½″, 180 pounds, he was reed-thin and looked like anything but a power-pitcher. For the fans, seeing this unimpressive physical specimen saunter out to the mound and throw his fastball past some of the best hitters in the game was an impressive sight. They could also see and hear him continuously talking to his opponents, telling them what he was going to do and what they weren't going to do. He once had two strikes on the great Josh Gibson and told him, "I'm not gonna throw any smoke around your yoke. I'm gonna throw a pea on your knee." Josh struck out looking.

There developed somewhat of a love-hate relationship between Satchel and the press. Sportswriters were quick to criticize him for his casual regard for contracts, but they were just as quick to applaud his talent and personality. Whether they

Grover Cleveland Alexander clowns around with four-legged friend. He retired from the major leagues in 1930 and soon joined the House of David. Advance promoter Tom Baird tried to attract other well-known players. He also offered $350 a month to Edwin (Alabama) Pitts, an outstanding athlete who was about to be released from Sing Sing penitentiary in Ossining, New York.

Above: Grandstand for first night game at Kansas City's Muehlebach Field, 1930. The Monarchs defeated the Nashville Elite Giants, 15-8, before a crowd of 12,000.
Below: Temporary lighting system set up at Battle Creek, Michigan. The portable lighting system, the first of its kind, was owned by the Monarchs' J.L. Wilkinson, who leased it to the House of David for parts of the 1932 and 1933 seasons.

Spencer Williams and Tim Moore. Many entertainers, such as Williams and Moore, who were comedians and stars on the "Amos 'n Andy Show," were baseball fans and became close friends of the ball players.

came to praise him or bury him, it didn't matter to Satchel; the publicity, good and bad, helped make him the highest-paid player in the game.

There wasn't much competition for Paige on payday. The average salary in the Negro leagues during the late '30s and early '40s was in the range of $200-300 a month. Paige was making four or five times that. A few others, such as Gibson and Buck Leonard, the Grays' two superstars, also were paid well above the norm, though far less than Satchel.

As with any business, salaries were dictated by the employer's financial condition, which in the case of most teams meant shaky, at best. The Monarchs and Grays may have been operating at a profit, but they didn't have much company. Several clubs, like the Chicago American Giants, the Birmingham Black Barons, the Philadelphia Stars and the Memphis Red Sox managed to hover around the break-even point and plod on from year to year. Others, and there were many, made brief appearances, lasting only a year or two, sometimes not even that long. Into that category fell teams like the Columbus Blue Birds, Newark Dodgers,

Cleveland Red Sox, Washington Black Senators and Indianapolis Crawfords.

The low salaries, which were still significantly higher than those of their peers in the work force, made the leagues susceptible to the advances of the Mexican League. Jorge Pasquel, the wealthy liquor importer who founded the league, began stepping up his recruitment of American players in the late '30s. His timing was excellent; the Negro National League had voted to cut salaries in 1938. The players were only too willing to listen to Pasquel's pitch, and many, including stars such as Ray Dandridge, the great third baseman of the Newark Eagles, outfielder Vic Harris, shortstop Willie Wells and Josh Gibson, began flocking to Mexico.

The Negro leagues were on loose ground as they stumbled through the late '30s and early '40s. Rampant defections, coupled with the overall weak financial situation, offered team owners and players slim hope for a change in fortunes. Little did they know that World War II was on deck, and a big change was on the way.

Satchel Paige. During the 1939-40 Puerto Rican Winter League season, he proved to everyone that the arm problems which had been curtailing his effectiveness were behind him. Paige set a league mark with 208 strikeouts and posted a record of 19-3 to lead his team to the league championship.

(L to R) T.B. Watkins, Felix Payne and Quincy Gilmore. Payne was the king of the Kansas City policy racket and a staunch supporter of the Monarchs. He went to Chicago for the final game of the 1924 World Series and wagered $2,000 on the underdog Monarchs. When it was announced that Jose Mendez, Kansas City's aging manager, would be pitching against Hilldale, the odds went up and more money went down. Mendez won the game and Payne received a handsome payoff. To show his appreciation for their effort, Payne treated the Monarchs to a night on the town.

Chapter 7

Prosperity. It is not a word often associated with black baseball, but from 1942 through 1945 the Negro leagues enjoyed an unprecedented era of success. A dramatic rise in attendance not only stabilized franchises but also paved the way for much-improved salaries. The World Series, dormant since 1927, was revived, and the East-West All-Star Game, still the centerpiece of the season, drew about 50,000 spectators annually. Schedules were strictly followed, and complete statistics, the lifeblood of every baseball fan, were duly recorded and published regularly.

It was an era in which the major leagues, unable to overcome the loss of stars like Joe DiMaggio, Ted Williams, Hank Greenberg and Bob Feller to the draft, suffered a sharp decline at the gate (13 percent in 1943 alone). The Negro leagues, hit no less hard by the draft, nonetheless found fan interest swelling to new heights. Four-team double-headers in Yankee Stadium, Wrigley Field or Griffith Stadium could be expected to draw anywhere from 20,000 to 30,000. The Washington Homestead Grays, who leased the Washington Senators' Griffith Stadium for their home games, sometimes outdrew their landlords on days when both played. Throughout league cities, fans were flocking to the parks to see their beloved teams. And if Satchel Paige and the Monarchs were in town, well . . . .

"A Hollywood scenario writer could not have improved upon the factual script that the Washington Homestead Grays spun here at Griffith Stadium, Thursday night, before 28,000 stunned guests in outdueling the famous Kansas City Monarchs, Satchel Paige included, 2-1, in ten letter-perfect innings."

That's how Ric Roberts, sportswriter for the *Pittsburgh Courier*, described the Grays-Monarchs battle of August 13, 1942, when Paige and Hilton Smith matched zeroes with Roy Partlow for nine innings. K.C. scored a run in the top of the tenth, but the Grays answered with two in their half, the winner scoring on Partlow's triple.

"It took the mob fully twenty minutes to stop shrieking and screaming," Roberts wrote. "Partlow, the hero, was carried off the field on the shoulders of a hundred admirers; thousands swarmed onto the field to congratulate the champions of the West, the Kansas City Monarchs, and the champions of the East, the Homestead Grays, for the most beautifully contested baseball game ever seen on Griffith Stadium's sod. It was simply terrific."

What was simply terrific from the players' standpoint was the effect that crowds of 28,000 could have on a paycheck. By the mid-'40s, the average salary was approximately $500 a month, a significant improvement over the grim years of the Great Depression. Standouts like Josh Gibson and Buck Leonard commanded more than $1,000 a month. And as impressive as those numbers were, they didn't come anywhere near Satchel's yearly haul. According to the *1945 Negro Baseball Yearbook*, Paige was earning more than $40,000 a year, a figure that made him the sport's highest paid player. (Hank Greenberg of the Detroit Tigers had held that distinction until 1941 when he entered

Below: Wyman (Red) Longley. He was an all-around player in the mode of Sam Bankhead. As a young boy he used to shag balls for the Arkansas Travelers, a minor league team. He had a great arm and could reach home plate on the fly from deep center-field. He also played football for Shorter College in North Little Rock.

Above: Olan (Jelly) Taylor. A quick first baseman, he didn't hit especially well, but he was flashy in the field, always catching with one hand.

Right: Neil Robinson. He was one of the great long-ball hitters. In 1937, the Cincinnati Tigers played against their second team, the West End Tigers. Robinson hit one so far that the city changed the name of the park from West End Park to Neil Robinson Park.

the army and surrendered his $50,000 salary.)

Paige was virtually the only player to find fame outside of the close-knit community of black baseball. His flamboyant personality and celebrated barnstorming duels with Dizzy Dean and Bob Feller drew attention from national magazines such as the *Saturday Evening Post, Life,* and *Look,* all of which made him the subject of feature stories. In the view of sportswriter Ric Roberts, it was Paige's national exposure that was primarily responsible for the Negro leagues' surge in popularity.

Under an article headlined, *Negro Big League Baseball a Two-Million Dollar Business,* Roberts wrote, "The daily press and nationally circulated magazines have dramatized [Paige] in the same breath with Joe DiMaggio, Ted Williams or Marty Marion. Thus endorsed by the national publications, he has become a symbol of excellence within his own group and stepped up payrolls and box office figures with his presence." Roberts went on to mention, briefly, one other cause for "this box office renaissance," namely, World War II.

The bombs that were being dropped in Europe and the Pacific created a reverberating boom in the Negro leagues. As defense plants churned out the armaments for the United States' war effort, black

(L to R) Satchel Paige, Joe Greene and Hilton Smith, 1941. Hilton Smith was one of the all-time great pitchers. In 1938, he pitched a no-hitter against the Chicago American Giants. Connie Johnson, a teammate, said, "If I had to pick one pitcher to win one ball game, I would have to pick Hilton Smith. He had one of the best curveballs you ever wanted to see, and he looked like Bob Feller out there on the mound."

The Homestead Grays in action. Black baseball was built around speed and strategy. Major leaguers, who played a "slower" style, were often caught off guard by the Negro leaguers. According to Judy Johnson, one major league player was so amazed that "he asked me, 'Do you play this kind of baseball during the regular summer season?' "

Opening Day at Ruppert Stadium in Kansas City, 1940. The first home game was always a big event in Kansas City, with the dignitaries coming out in force. (L to R) Unknown, Dr. William Blount, Municipal Judge Edmund B. Smith, President J.B. Martin of the Negro American League, and Mayor J.B. Gage.

Satchel Paige. In 1941, the Monarchs were scheduled to play a July 4 game at St. Louis' Sportsman's Park, where blacks were not allowed to sit in the box seats. Paige complained loudly, saying "I will not pitch unless Negro baseball fans are allowed to sit in the box seats." A crowd of 19,178, the largest ever to witness a Negro baseball game in St. Louis, saw the Monarchs defeat the Chicago American Giants, 11-2.

workers found themselves with a new and improved status; suddenly, they were in demand. Wartime labor shortages afforded new opportunities for employment — at higher wages — and blacks worked alongside whites in the North on an equal basis, even gaining acceptance into labor unions. In 1941, Franklin Roosevelt, who was in the first year of his third term as president, issued an executive order which established the Fair Employment Practices Commission. The commission was authorized to investigate charges of discrimination based on race, color or creed. While its power was minimal, progress was made in its goal of preventing discrimination within government agencies and private firms with government contracts.

The employment opportunities in the North, where most of the industrial activity was concentrated, spawned another black migration from the South. There had been little movement in the previous decade because of the dreadful unemployment situation, but with the economy revived, more than a million blacks moved north during the '40s.

For the Negro leagues, the economic wellspring had an invigorating effect. Simply put, there were more fans with more money to spend on leisure-time activities such as baseball. Travel restrictions brought about by gas-rationing, also helped, keeping the local aficionados in the vicinity of the ballpark. The result was that teams no longer were locked in an annual fight for survival. From 1942 to 1948, the Negro National League lost only one franchise, the Harrisburg/St. Louis Stars. The Stars entered the league in 1943, played nine games and then left to go on a barnstorming tour with Dizzy Dean. Otherwise, the league consisted of the same six teams: the Baltimore Elite Giants, the Homestead Grays, the New York Black Yankees, the New York Cubans, the Newark Eagles and the Philadelphia Stars. The younger Negro American League was equally successful, losing only the Jacksonville (Florida) Red Caps once the era of prosperity started. From 1943 to 1948 the league was made up of the Birmingham Black Barons, the Chicago American Giants, the Cincinnati/Indianapolis Clowns, the Cleveland Buckeyes, the Kansas City Monarchs and the Memphis Red Sox.

The outlook was so bright in 1942 that the owners decided to resurrect the World Series. Not surprisingly, it was the Monarchs and the Grays, the leagues' perennial powers, who slugged it out for the championship just a few weeks before the St. Louis Cardinals beat the New York Yankees in five games in the major league World Series. The Grays had narrowly beaten the Baltimore Elite Giants by a half game for the NNL pennant. The Elite Giants, who were owned by longtime Negro league backer

Frank and Bertha Duncan. Duncan was in Cuba when former Monarch teammate Jose Mendez died in 1928. He later recalled the day his friend was put to rest: "His demise saddened our hearts as we stood before his casket in Havana and gazed upon him just before he was carried to his last resting place. Small wonder, indeed, that our heartstrings tightened a bit as we stood over his casket. He was our friend, our former leader and teammate, our buddy, our hero. Peace be with him!"

Tom Wilson, were a powerful team in their own right, with Roy Campanella catching, Thomas (Peewee) Butts at shortstop, Henry Kimbro in the outfield and Bill Byrd anchoring the pitching staff. But they weren't quite the match of Gibson, Leonard and Company. The Grays' supporting cast included shortstop Sam Bankhead, third baseman Howard Easterling, center-fielder Jerry Benjamin and pitchers Ray Brown, Roy Partlow, Roy Welmaker and John Wright.

The Monarchs were led by their outstanding pitching staff of Clifford (Connie) Johnson, Frank Bradley, Ford Smith and their two kings of the hill, Satchel Paige and Hilton Smith. The team's talent, however, was not confined to the mound. Catcher Joe Greene had a superb arm and was respected as a power-hitter. Greene, along with Ted Strong and Willard Brown, a couple of heavy-hitting out-fielders, and first baseman Buck O'Neil provided the punch for table-setters Jesse Williams (short-stop), Newt Allen (second base), Willie Simms (left-field) and Herb Souell (third base).

It was a formidable lineup that the Monarchs put on the field for game one at Griffith Stadium, but there was some doubt that the K.C. club was up to the challenge. *Kansas City Call* sports editor Sam

Francisco (Pancho) Coimbre. A native of Puerto Rico, he played in the United States as a member of the New York Cubans. At home he played for Ponce, winning winter league batting titles in 1943 and 1945 with averages of .342 and .425, respectively.

Andy Cooper (left) and Oscar Charleston shake hands at Comiskey Park in 1938. The two were the managers for the East-West Game. It was said that Charleston was so strong he could take a new ball in his massive hands and squeeze it until it became soft. Cooper became manager of the Kansas City Monarchs in 1935 and served in that capacity until his death of a stroke on June 3, 1941.

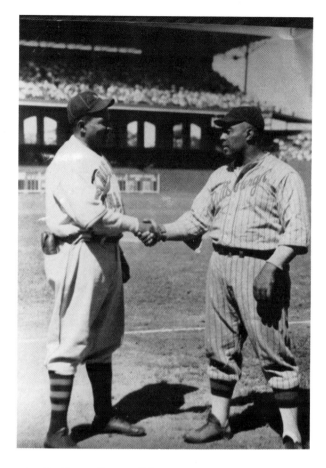

McKibben feared that the Grays' lefty pitchers, Partlow and Welmaker, would be the difference. "All of the Monarchs can hit some left-handed pitching some of the time," McKibben wrote, "but when the portsider has his stuff, the Monarch bats, with the exception of Joe Greene, Ted Strong and possibly Willard Brown, are silenced." McKibben went on to predict that "the Monarchs would win a game or so, but the Series would go to the Grays."

As was the case with the 1920s version, the best-of-seven Series was rotated among league cities. Griffith Stadium in Washington, D.C. was the first stop, and Satchel Paige made it clear right away that he was thoroughly unintimidated by the mighty Grays. The K.C. ace fired a two-hit shutout and was supported by a 14-hit attack that produced eight runs and made short work of Roy Welmaker. Games two and three, at Pittsburgh's Forbes Field and Yankee Stadium, respectively, produced similar results, with the supposedly weak-hitting Monarchs

Comiskey Park on the day of the East-West Game, 1938. In 1934, sportswriter Nat Trammell wrote: "The East-West Game is the greatest event that could be put over by anyone for the benefit of promoting interest in colored baseball. This game is an incentive to young ball players, as well as those who are already supposed to be made."

Left: Sarah Foster. Even after the death of her husband, Rube, she was treated as a celebrity in baseball circles. In 1956 A.S. (Doc) Young of the *Chicago Defender* noticed that twenty-six years after Rube's death, his name was still listed in the Chicago telephone directory, as sort of a memorial in print. "The telephone is just the same as he left it, BO 8-1351," said Sarah.

Below: Olan (Jelly) Taylor. When he first began his career in the East, Taylor was nicknamed "Satan," because it was said he could knock the devil out of a baseball. The name was changed because his mother refused to attend games and root for one so "evil".

Below: Buck Leonard. While with the Homestead Grays, he and Josh Gibson, who batted back-to-back in the lineup, were known as the "Heavenly Twins" because of their prowess both at the plate and in the field. Leonard was a line-drive, pull hitter. It was nearly impossible to get a fastball past him, so pitchers usually threw him off-speed stuff.

(L to R) Minnie Moore, Joan Byas, Richard (Subby) Byas and Marie Byas. Subby, whose I.Q. was 136, attended Crane Junior College before beginning his career with the Gilkerson Union Giants in 1930.

roughing up Roy Partlow and Ray Brown. Hilton Smith and Paige earned the victories as the Monarchs returned to Kansas City, site of game four, with a 3-0 lead.

With the Grays a game away from extinction, team owner Cum Posey decided that drastic measures were needed. To that end, the Grays' lineup for game four at Ruppert Stadium featured some new faces. Right-fielder Ed Stone, left-fielder Lennie Pearson and pitcher Leon Day, all of the Newark Eagles, and shortstop James (Buster) Clarkson of the Philadelphia Stars were summoned to Kansas City to help stop the bleeding. For that, all they really needed was Day, a mound surgeon who'd been operating successfully on Negro National League hitters since 1934.

By 1942, Leon Day, a native of Alexandria, Virginia, had established himself as one of the league's top pitchers, a hard-throwing right-hander with a good curve and superb control. Earlier in the season, before his "trade" to the Grays, he struck out eighteen in a one-hit victory over the Baltimore Elite Giants. His resume also included a victory in that year's East-West Game. With 48,000 looking on at Comiskey Park, Day, playing for the East, entered the game in the seventh inning with the score tied, 2-2, and struck out five of the seven batters he faced. The East rallied for three runs to make a loser of the West's late-inning reliever, Satchel Paige.

The two hurlers, probably the best in their respective leagues, squared off again in game four

Promotional events, such as this bathing beauty contest, became increasingly popular during the 1940s. The lovely ladies in the background here were one of the attractions at the Memphis Red Sox-Birmingham Black Barons game on July 14, 1940, at Martin Park in Memphis.

Richard (Subby) Byas. A switch-hitter, he earned his nickname as the backup catcher to Larry Brown of the Chicago American Giants during the 1933-34 season. While attending Wendell Phillips High School in Chicago, Byas became the first black to be named All-City in two sports, baseball and basketball.

of the Series. Once again the day belonged to Leon, who pitched his new teammates to a 4-1 victory to spare the Grays the embarrassment of a sweep. Or so they thought.

As could be expected, the Monarchs were outraged by Posey's unorthodox maneuver and filed a protest. Even the laissez-faire league officials agreed that the Grays were off base; the protest was upheld and the Series moved on to Philadelphia's Shibe Park for the "real" game four, which wasn't without its surprises either.

Paige was scheduled to start against Partlow in what the Monarchs hoped would be the finale. Problem was, at game time, Satchel was nowhere to be found. Manager Frank Duncan quickly had Jack Matchett warm up, and almost as quickly, he saw his team fall behind, 5-2. Paige ambled along as the game entered the fourth inning, explaining that he'd been arrested for speeding and fined $3 by the Lancaster (Pennsylvania) police. Duncan didn't ask many questions before sending his ace in to relieve Matchett. Satchel was virtually unhittable, shutting

Hilton Smith. In 1939, he received more votes than any other pitcher in the balloting for the East-West Game. Smith attended Prairie View A & M University in Prairie View, Texas.

Andy Cooper. As a member of the Monarchs in 1937, he pitched seventeen innings against the Chicago American Giants in a Negro American League playoff game. The game was tied, 2-2, when called because of darkness. Cooper allowed ten hits, three by Turkey Stearnes.

Larry Brown of the Memphis Red Sox slides past Kansas City Monarchs third baseman Herb Souell in New York City. Brown was not known for his hitting ability but was regarded as one of the all-time best catchers.

Quincy Trouppe. An all-around player who could catch, pitch or play the outfield, he also earned a reputation as an outstanding amateur boxer. In 1936, he was St. Louis' Golden Gloves heavyweight champ and also won the AAU title. Trouppe was called "one of the finest athletes ever developed in St. Louis," by the *St. Louis Globe Democrat.*

out the Grays the rest of the way, and the Monarch bats again came alive, strafing Partlow, John Wright and Welmaker for seven more runs and a 9-5 victory. Eighteen years after winning the first World Series, the Monarchs again were the certified champions of the world.

Their reign did not last long, however. The military draft started to take its toll on them the following year, when they slipped to fourth place. By 1944 they had tumbled all the way to the cellar. The loss of standouts Willard Brown, Buck O'Neil, Jesse Williams, Joe Greene, Connie Johnson and Ted Strong was too much to overcome.

Kansas City, of course, wasn't the only team to find itself in this predicament; from 1942 to 1945 more than fifty players either enlisted or were drafted. Along with the Monarch players, the names read like the rosters for an East-West Game: Howard Easterling, John Wright, and Roy Welmaker of the Grays, Larry Doby, Leon Day and Monte Irvin of the Newark Eagles, Dick Seay of the New York Black Yankees, Bill Perkins of the Philadelphia Stars and Dan Bankhead of the Birmingham Black Barons, to name a few. Some teams, such as the Philly Stars and the Newark Eagles, lost as many as thirteen players. And still the leagues thrived.

The sportswriters noted with pride that Negro baseball was "doing its part" in the war effort.

"Negro baseball, like every other institution, civic, social, political or athletic has made its full contribution in player personnel to the armed forces," wrote Art Carter, a war correspondent and former sports editor for the *Afro-American Newspapers.* "In fact, in every corner of the earth where the fighting is being done, somewhere among the fighting men may be found a member of the former flannel-clothed gang, which not so many months ago paraded his talents on the clay-smoothed diamonds of stadia in the East and West instead of crawling in the foxholes and ducking enemy shells."

Their contributions weren't limited to the battlefields. Back home, soldiers were admitted free to select games, while proceeds from others were used to buy war bonds or donated to the USO and Red Cross. It was only when the Office of Defense Transportation threatened to prohibit bus travel in early 1943 that the Negro leagues balked, and then only because their existence was threatened.

There was serious discussion in '43 about canceling professional baseball altogether. With the world at war, baseball seemed to some a frivolous

Above: (L to R) Cecil Travis, Dizzy Dean and Satchel Paige. Major leaguers like Travis and Dean often played against Negro leaguers after the regular season. In 1936, Paige was part of a black all-star team that participated in the *Denver Post* tournament. In one game, Paige fanned eighteen hitters, while teammate Robert Griffith struck out sixteen in another. Paige's team, which won $5,000 for winning the tournament, was called "the strongest club ever to play in the twenty-one year history of the tournament" by the *Denver Post.*

Right: Hilton Smith. He was the Monarchs' leading pitcher in 1937 and was almost unbeatable in Kansas City, where he posted a 9-1 league record.

Below: The Kansas City Monarchs, 1940. Manager Andy Cooper's Monarchs won both the first and second half pennant races. Seated (L to R): Floyd Kransen, Lionel DeCuir, Henry Milton, Junius (Rainey) Bibbs, Newt Allen, Hilton Smith, Dick Bradley. Standing: Quincy Gilmore (business manager), Andy Cooper, Joe Greene, Jesse Williams, Norman (Turkey) Stearnes, Jack Matchett, Leandy Young, John O'Neil. Bradley, a native of Benton, Louisiana, was one of the hardest throwers in the league.

Santurce, 1939-1940 Puerto Rican Winter League. Standing (L to R): Raul Acosta, Monchile Concepcion, Enrique Gonzalez, Wichie Calderon, Eduardo Nichols, Billy Byrd, Josh Gibson, Tingo Laviu, Luis Raul Cabreray, Dick Seay. Kneeling: Guillermo Angulo, Manolin Rosario, "El Indio" Ramirez, "El Brujo" Mangual, "Pookie Muniz" (mascot), Nenaco Vila, Liborio Ranirez, Mon Carrion, Fellito Concepcion. Gibson set the all-time Puerto Rican League batting record during the 1941-1942 season when he hit an incredible .480. Seay stole thirty-three bases as a member of Santurce in 1938-1939.

Dave Barnhill and Walter (Buck) Leonard. In 1941, Leonard, from Rocky Mount, North Carolina, hit a home run and had three RBIs to lead the East to an 8-3 victory in the East-West Game. In 1940-1941 Barnhill, then a member of Humacao led the Puerto Rico Winter League with 193 strike outs, while posting a record of 11-9.

activity, one the nation could do without during such perilous times. President Roosevelt, however, disagreed, deeming that the sport would provide a positive contribution to the country's morale. The show, both major league and Negro league, was allowed to go on. For Negro baseball, there was a downside to the president's decision. To cut down on gasoline use the ODT ordered all teams to use the railroads, which for the major leagues meant business as usual. For the Negro leagues, which had been relying on buses since the late '20s, it was a potentially crippling development, especially for the widespread Negro American League teams.

Besides being less expensive, travel by bus allowed teams to maintain a busy exhibition schedule while traveling between league cities. If, for example, the Monarchs were making the 700-mile trek to Birmingham, they could schedule several games along the way that would cover the cost of the trip. Since the railroads offered so much less flexibility, abandoning the buses would have negated an important source of revenue.

George Mitchell. Originally from Sparta, Illinois, he was a pitcher with a big round-house curve who broke in with the St. Louis Stars in 1924. He later became manager of the Stars and was chosen as the skipper for the West in the 1939 East-West game.

Upon hearing of the ODT's order, Monarch owners J.L. Wilkinson and Tom Baird, who had bought into the franchise during the depression, immediately began working to get an exemption. Enlisting the aid of C.A. Franklin, the editor of the *Kansas City Call*, they began circulating petitions, using both the local and national editions of the *Call* to appeal for public support. "If you have not sent your petition in, do it today," said one story. "Don't delay. Your name may help save Negro baseball." Telegrams were sent to Missouri senators Harry S. Truman and Bennett Champ Clark and Kansas senator Arthur Capper, requesting their help in the matter.

Syd Pollock, owner of the Cincinnati Clowns, also petitioned the representatives in his home state of New York, as did Dr. J.B. Martin, president of the Negro American League, in Illinois. Said Pollock, "Unless immediate action is taken, Negro baseball has been dealt a death blow."

San Juan, 1939-1940 Puerto Rican Winter League. Among the Negro leaguers on this team were Clarence Palms (standing, fourth from right), Ray Brown (standing, second from right), Roy Partlow (seated, far left), and Eugene Benson (seated, third from left). Brown was an outstanding athlete who led his Alger, Ohio, high school basketball team to the state championship. One of the game's best hitting pitchers, he batted .311 while winning twenty-one games in the 1936 Cuban Winter League.

Though they were prepared to comply with the order, the "death blow" never came; the ODT relented and granted the leagues their exemption, and the buses rolled.

While the '43 Monarchs found themselves in the unfamiliar role of also-rans, the Birmingham Black Barons took advantage of the situation and moved to the front of the pack in the Negro American League. The Black Barons, former members of the Negro Southern League and the original Negro National League, entered the NAL in 1937. They were partly owned by Abe Saperstein, a powerful booking agent/promoter in the South and Midwest. Like his counterparts in the East, Eddie Gottlieb and previously Nat Strong, Saperstein's power was based on his access to the parks that league teams rented. His fee for booking the games, including the East-West, ranged from five to ten percent of the gate.

Saperstein also was the founder and owner of the Harlem Globetrotters, the touring basketball team that began entertaining fans in 1926. During winter months, several Negro leaguers traded in their flannels for a basketball uniform and traveled with the Trotters, among them Reece (Goose) Tatum of the Indianapolis Clowns, Ted Strong of the Monarchs and Lorenzo (Piper) Davis of the

Above: Robert Bissant. In 1938 Charlie Henry of Louisville, Kentucky, formed the Zulu Cannibal Giants, who wore grass skirts and painted their faces. The idea generated from the war that was being fought in Ethiopia. Howard Easterling started with this novelty team in 1937 but quickly graduated to the Cincinnati Tigers of the Negro American League.

Right: Roy Partlow and unidentified fans. A versatile outfielder/pitcher, Partlow led the Puerto Rico Winter League with a .441 (122-54) average during the 1940-1941 season. He also topped league pitchers with a 1.49 ERA.

Chet Brewer (left) and Eugene Smith, 1947. In 1938 Smith, shown here with the Kansas City Royals of the California Winter League, pitched both ends of a doubleheader in Manitoba, Canada, throwing no-hitters in each game.

Black Barons. Jim Brown, a catcher with the Chicago American Giants, and Paul Hardy, a catcher with the Black Barons, found off-season work as bus drivers for the team.

In the late '30s the Black Barons were sold to Tom Hayes, the son of a successful mortuary owner in Memphis. Hayes named Winfield Welch manager in 1941. Welch, who also coached the Globetrotters, started his baseball career with the New

Right: McKinley (Bunny) Downs, 1942. Shown here as manager of the Ethiopian Clowns, the hustling infielder began his long career in 1913 as a member of the Nashville Giants. His playing days abruptly ended when he injured his arm in a game at Forbes Field in 1930. He etched his name in baseball history in 1952 when he signed cross-handed batting Hank Aaron to an Indianpolis Clowns contract.

Orleans Black Pelicans in 1926. Like most Negro league skippers, he was a disciple of the Rube Foster school of managing — scratch out a couple of runs and let your pitchers and defense carry you the rest of the way. It was a philosophy that the Black Barons rode to the World Series in both '43 and '44.

The Washington Homestead Grays took a different approach to the game. Of course, when you have a couple of high-powered weapons like Buck

Dan and Fred Bankhead. The Bankhead clan sent five brothers to the Negro leagues. Jim (Candy) Taylor signed Dan to play for Birmingham in 1940, while Fred began as a second baseman for the Memphis Red Sox under manager Ted (Double Duty) Radcliffe. Fred, who attended Daniel Payne College in Selma, Alabama, was a sure-handed infielder who could make the toughest of plays look easy.

Below: Marlin Carter. He began his career in 1931 with the San Antonio Black Indians of the Texas-Oklahoma-Louisiana League. While trying out, he impressed his manager and was named the team's starting third baseman. When he returned to the rooming house where the team stayed, Carter was astonished to find that the players who had been cut had stolen all of his clothing.

Right: Rufus Ligon. He was born in Hondo, Texas, and, like Marlin Carter, he broke in with the San Antonio Black Indians. He also played for the Memphis Red Sox in the '40s and later became their manager in the mid '50s.

Leonard and Josh Gibson batting back-to-back in your lineup, you tend to become more reliant on the long ball than the hit-and-run. It was the slugging of Leonard and Gibson, as well as the work of their solid pitching staff, that carried the Grays into two straight Series clashes with the Barons.

The two Series shaped up as intriguing battles of styles: the Barons' finesse versus the Grays' power. Birmingham's only hope rested with its fine pitching staff. If it could hold the Grays' sluggers in check — a longshot, at best — the Black Barons might be able to stage the improbable.

The scrappy Black Barons were outscored by a total of 41-23 in the '43 Series, but still managed to force a seventh game when John Markham out-dueled Roy Partlow, 1-0, in game six. In the finale, played in Montgomery, Alabama, the Grays plugged in the power again and jolted Baron pitchers for twelve hits in an 8-4 triumph.

Carta Blanca (Mexican League), 1941. Front row (L to R): Hector Leal, Sam Bankhead, bat boy, Preato, Cool Papa Bell, La Mala Torres, Ralph Caballero. Standing: Pedrozo, Leslie (Chin) Green, Barney Morris, Quincy Trouppe, Tom (Lefty) Glover, Chile Gomez, Galina, Daniel Rios, Willie Jefferson. A Coca-Cola salesman gave Ted Radcliffe a tip on a player who was doing time for theft in a Cleveland, Mississippi, prison. Radcliffe convinced the owner of the Claybrook (Arkansas) Tigers to pay the warden $300 to release the prisoner. The player was Willie Jefferson, who later became an outstanding pitcher for the Cleveland Buckeyes.

The following year the Series was decided as much on the highway as on the playing field. Negro baseball teams kept busy schedules that included many long hours on the roads. Overnight trips were not uncommon, nor were highway mishaps. The most tragic accident occurred on September 7, 1942, when two members of the Cleveland Buckeyes, Ulysses (Buster) Brown and Raymond (Smokey) Owens were killed when a truck rammed the back of the car in which they were riding. The team was returning from a game in Buffalo against the New York Black Yankees. Also injured in the crash were three other players, pitchers Eugene Bremmer, Herman (Lefty) Watts and Alonzo Boone, and business manager Wilbur Hayes.

Shortly before the '44 Series started, four Black Barons were involved in a car accident. There were no fatalities, but the good news ended there. Hard-hitting second baseman Tommy Sampson, catcher Lloyd (Pepper) Bassett and outfielder Leandy

The Baltimore Elite Giants of the California Winter League, 1939. Standing (L to R): Lloyd (Pepper) Basset, Terry, John Wright, Bill Hoskins, Unknown, Vernon Green, Unknown, Unknown, Lonnie Summers, Jim West, Mitchell. Front row: Marlin Carter, Jesse (Hoss) Walker, William Harvey, bat boy, Tom Blover, Jake Dunn, Terris McDuffie. This team won the California Winter League title.

Young missed the entire Series, while third baseman Johnny Britton played but was hampered by injuries. The outcome was predictable.

The tone was set in game one in Birmingham, Alabama, when Gibson broke up a 1-1 tie in the fourth inning with a long solo home run over the left-field fence. Leonard drilled a homer in the fifth for a 3-1 lead, and right-fielder Dave Hoskins made it 4-1 with a solo blast in the eighth. Cool Papa Bell's two-run triple added some icing to an 8-3 cakewalk. After a 6-1 victory in game two, left-hander Ray Brown fired a one-hit shutout in the third game that put the Black Barons on the brink. John Huber's three-hit shutout at Forbes Field in game four spared Birmingham a sweep, but it was a temporary reprieve. Left-hander Roy Welmaker outdueled Alfred Saylor, 4-2, in the fifth and final game to give the Grays their second straight championship.

They were hoping to make it three in a row in 1945 after winning both halves of the regular season for the third straight year. All that stood in their way were the Cleveland Buckeyes. Like the Black Barons, the Buckeyes relied on their talented pitching staff to carry them to the NAL pennant. As

Above: Webster McDonald, 1939. McDonald is signing a petition circulated by the Young Communist League, which was demanding that the major leagues drop the color barrier. The organization received 100,000 signatures.

Below: Kneeling (L to R): Jonas Gaines, Henry Kimbro, Tom Glover, Oscar (Red) Moore, Jesse (Hoss) Walker, Roy Campanella, Bill (Bojangles) Robinson, Chester Washington (a reporter for the *Pittsburgh Courier*), Bubber Hubert, Bill Byrd, Ace Adams, Boogie Wolf, Bill Wright, Thomas (Peewee) Butts. Standing: Bill Hoskins, Sammie T. Hughes, Vernon Green, Felton Snow, Doug Smith, Tom Wilson (Baltimore Elite owner), Ed Semler (New York Black Yankees owner), Alex Pompez (New York Cubans owner). This photograph was taken following a four-team playoff at Yankee Stadium to decide the Negro National League pennant in 1939. The Elite Giants ousted the Newark Eagles and then beat the Homestead Grays, who'd eliminated the Philadelphia Stars, to become the league champions.

The Tampico (Mexico) Tamps, 1939. This team featured four Negro leaguers in its lineup: T.J. Young (sixth from left), James (Cool Papa) Bell (seventh from left), Andy Porter (fourth from right) and Chet Brewer (third from right). In 1933, Bell, then thirty, was timed running the bases in 13.6 seconds.

in '43 and '44, there was no reason to think that the Grays wouldn't have their way with the Bucks, too.

The Buckeyes were formed in 1941 by Ernie Wright, a Cleveland numbers man who was granted a Negro American League franchise in 1942. They played in Cincinnati for a year before shifting their home base to Cleveland in '43. After finishing in third place their first three seasons, Wright and his

business manager, Wilbur Hayes, brought in Quincy Trouppe as a player/manager. Trouppe, primarily a catcher, and a good one at that, had begun his career in 1930 with the St. Louis Stars of the original Negro National League. Before coming to Cleveland, he'd played for six league teams, several semipro clubs and in the Mexican League. His experience proved to be just what the young

Clint (Hawk) Thomas (right) chats with players from the New York Black Yankees. Originally a second baseman, Thomas moved to center-field when his manager with the Detroit Stars, Bruce Petway, discovered that Jess Barber, his regular center-fielder, was drunk on the job. Thomas played six seasons in the Cuban Winter League, batting over .300 four times.

Above: Reuben Jones. As manager of the Memphis Red Sox in 1935, he was selected by the president of the Southern League to manage the South in the annual North-South Game. Jones' counterpart for the North was Oscar Charleston, manager of the Pittsburgh Crawfords.

Above left: (L to R) Ted (Double Duty) Radcliffe, Unknown, Jim (Candy) Taylor. Taylor was a superstitious manager who did not allow his players to eat peanuts in the dugout. To get his goat, visiting players would keep a pocket full of peanut shells and toss them into Taylor's dugout.

Left: Jesse Owens. He once raced against George Case, the Washington Senators outfielder who was supposedly the fastest player in the major leagues. Owens, wearing baseball spikes, made brief work of Case. However, on the occasions when Cool Papa Bell asked Jesse to race, the reply was always the same: "I don't have my track shoes, and I am not about to race you wearing some heavy baseball shoes."

Next page: Tetelo Vargas. He was an outfielder for the New York Cubans during the late '30s and early '40s.

Buckeyes needed.

Trouppe inherited a first-rate Cleveland pitching staff that he helped mold into the league's best in '45. Their ace was Willie Jefferson, who posted a 10-1 record and a league-leading 1.57 ERA. And they didn't lose much with their number two hurler, Willie's brother, George, who finished 11-1 with a 1.75 ERA. Frank Carswell (5-2, 2.14) and Eugene Bremer (8-4, 2.44) rounded out the starting rotation. Clearly, there wasn't much need for a bullpen with the Buckeyes.

As for their batting order, there wasn't a lot of power, but there were some top-notch hitters. First and foremost was center-fielder Sam Jethroe, who won the NAL batting crown in '45 with a .393 average. He also led the league in triples (ten) and stolen bases (twenty-one). His thirty-seven RBIs tied him with teammate Parnell Woods, a third baseman, for second most in the league. First baseman Archie Ware led the league with thirty-nine. In all, they had six players who hit better than .300, including pitcher George Jefferson.

Still, the awesome Grays had to be considered the favorite going into the Series. With Gibson and Leonard, along with Cool Papa Bell, Sam Bankhead, Jerry Benjamin and Jud Wilson, they had essentially the same team that had conquered the world the previous two years. What many failed to realize was that this was a team that Father Time was beginning to clutch in his powerful hands. Cool Papa, forty-two, could feel them, and so could the thirty-eight year old Leonard. Josh Gibson was thirty-four and showing signs of mortality. Third baseman Jud Wilson, who began his career in 1924, had been relegated to part-time duty. Shortstop Sam Bankhead and pitchers Ray Brown and Roy Welmaker, though still effective, all had begun playing professionally in the early '30s and were starting to show the effects of fifteen years in the leagues.

Despite the fact that the Grays were an aging team, no one expected them to show it as suddenly as they did in the World Series.

Beginning with Willie Jefferson in game one, the Buckeyes' starting pitchers thoroughly dominated the Series, throwing four complete games en route to a stunning sweep. The heavy-hitting Grays scored a grand total of three runs in the Series, getting one off Jefferson in the opener and two off Gene Bremmer in game two. George Jefferson and Frank Carswell fired four-hit shutouts in games three and four, respectively, to finish matters. The silence heard throughout the Series came from the

Frank Duncan, Jr. He joined his father on the Kansas City Monarchs in 1941, marking the first time in sports history a father and son had appeared professionally as active players on the same team.

Grays' bats, which produced no home runs or triples and only two doubles among their twenty-one hits.

The Buckeyes, meanwhile, didn't rip the cover off the ball, but then again they didn't have to with the job their pitchers did. Quincy Trouppe topped the hit parade with a .400 average, while Sam Jethroe (.333) and right-fielder Willie Grace (.316) also provided some punch.

It was an impressive victory for the Buckeyes, and when they returned home to Cleveland they were honored at City Hall in a ceremony befitting the new kings of Negro baseball. For Cum Posey's dethroned Grays, the decisive defeat served notice that their aura of invincibility was beginning to fade.

The World Series provided the leagues with a fitting conclusion to the season, but the baseball year continued to revolve around the annual gathering of All-Stars at Comiskey Park. During the '40s, East-West attendance was usually more than 40,000, and even cracked the 50,000 mark twice. In 1943, the year after Leon Day outdueled Paige in the late innings, 51,723 saw Paige blank the East in

a three-inning stint that earned him and the West a 2-1 victory.

It also earned him $800. Satchel, of course, was the only player who could command that kind of money. Though the game was wildly successful, you never would have known it from the players' take. Before the war, when many owners had to rely on the East-West proceeds to keep their franchises afloat, the stars of the show received $25 to $30, at most, plus expenses. But as the game's popularity took hold, so did the players' yearning for a larger piece of the pie. As Monarch first baseman Buck O'Neil told it: "One year there, [the players] wanted to strike. The ballplayers thought they were getting the short end of the stick, because [the owners] really weren't giving them as

(L to R) Booker McDaniel, William (Bonnie) Serrell and Jesse Williams, 1942. Both Serrell and Williams were natives of Texas. Serrell was nicknamed "El Gereo" (the cricket) by fans in the Mexican League. After baseball was integrated, all three were signed to play in the minor leagues.

The Kansas City Monarchs' bus. According to pitcher Jim LaMarque, the Monarchs' bus once was parked outside a baseball park in Houston when a policeman walked by and asked, "How much is the game?" The players replied, "Three dollars." The man thought for a moment, then remarked, "If I bring someone else that would make six dollars, and I ain't going to pay six dollars to see a nigger do nothing."

Monarch fishing trip, 1941. (L to R) Newt Allen, Joe Greene, Jack Matchett, Junius (Rainey) Bibbs. While riding on the highway the Monarchs noticed that the fish were jumping in a nearby stream. The bus driver pulled over and the players, armed with their bats, got out and started swinging at their prey.

much as they should have given them. You couldn't get in the ballpark — they were packing the place. This is why the guys were squawking."

Reluctantly, the owners upped the ante during the '40s to about $100 per man, a pittance compared to the owners' take, but not a bad payday for a few innings' work.

The East-West Game was the one event during the season that received any significant attention from the white press. The crowds that were swarming to Comiskey Park year after year made it increasingly difficult to ignore, especially in Chicago. The *Chicago Daily News* wrote a fourteen-inch story on the '43 game, which, naturally, focused on Paige. Under the headline, *Paige Hero as West All-Stars Beat East,* the unbylined story started:

"LeRoy 'Satchel' Paige, the pitching wizard of the Kansas City Monarchs, today was on his way back East after being credited with the 2-1 victory of the West over the East yesterday in the annual Negro all-star baseball classic staged before 51,723 spectators in Comiskey Park.

"The folks who turned out yesterday, especially those that were lucky enough to get in the park (some 10,000 were turned away at the gate because of lack of seating room) will long remember Paige. The tall, slender, easy-moving right-hander, who started on the mound for the West squad, blanked

(L to R) Dorothy Harris (wife of Vic Harris), Chet Brewer, Dorothy Thurman (wife of Bob Thurman), Unknown, Gladys Souell (wife of Herb Souell). In a 1934 exhibition game, Brewer defeated Earle Mack's All-Stars in Jamestown, North Dakota, striking out Heinie Manush of the Washington Senators three times. That was no small achievement, considering Manush had struck out only twenty-three times while batting .349 in 556 at-bats during the regular season.

J.B. Martin and President Dwight D. Eisenhower. Martin, a doctor, was a successful real estate investor in Memphis. Also politically active, he backed Alf Landon for president in 1936 and invited him to a rally, which drew the ire of Boss Crump, the most powerful man in Memphis. A series of death threats followed and Martin was forced to relocate to Chicago, where he became equally successful.

(L to R) Satchel Paige, Unknown, Lionel Hampton, Lorenzo (Piper) Davis. William Lowe, the manager of the Chattanooga Black Lookouts who signed Paige to his first contract in 1926, stated, "Paige was destined to become a great pitcher; he had great control and speed from the very beginning to the monumental end of his career."

Jack Marshall. He was a sure-handed second baseman who enjoyed a nineteen-year career in Negro baseball. After retiring he opened several bowling alleys in Chicago.

Bill Byrd (left) and Seeward Posey (Cumberland's brother), 1945. Posey was the business manager of the Homestead Grays. In 1940-41, Byrd, then a member of the Caguas, led the Puerto Rican Winter League with fifteen wins.

the foe without a hit or run for the first three innings he was permitted to pitch. During this brief span, Paige looked like the Paige of old. He had to face only ten batters, giving up no hits, whiffing four and walking only one."

After a few more paragraphs on Paige's exploits, the story finally began describing the nail-biting ninth inning, when Buck Leonard's home run narrowed the West's margin to 2-1. After two successive singles further imperiled the West's lead, righty reliever Porter Moss of the Memphis Red Sox entered and preserved the victory.

The following year, 46,247 saw left-hander Verdel Mathis of the Memphis Red Sox and the Radcliffe brothers, Ted (Birmingham Black Barons) and Alex (Cincinnati Clowns), lead the West to a 7-4 triumph. Between them, the Radcliffes had a combined 35 years of experience in professional baseball. On this day, they collected two RBIs apiece, while Mathis, the league's top southpaw,

Negro League All-Stars, 1936 *Denver Post* Tournament. Kneeling (L to R): Paul Hardy, Robert Griffith, LeRoy (Satchel) Paige, Ray Brown, Sam Streeter, Josh Gibson, Horne (bat boy), Middle row: Hood Witter (trainer), Walter (Buck) Leonard, Chester Williams, James (Cool Papa) Bell, Felton Snow, Jack Marshall, Jim Taylor. Back row: Seeward Posey, Sammy T. Hughes, Victor Harris, Bill Wright, Hart (bus driver). In seven Tournament games, this team batted .356 and collected 138 total bases. Bell stole eight bases, Gibson hit four home runs and paced the series with fifteen RBIs. The three-man pitching staff of Brown, Paige and Griffith struck out 49% of the batters they faced and had an ERA of 0.88%. The All-Stars out-scored their opponents 75 runs to 8 en route to becoming the 1936 Tournament champions.

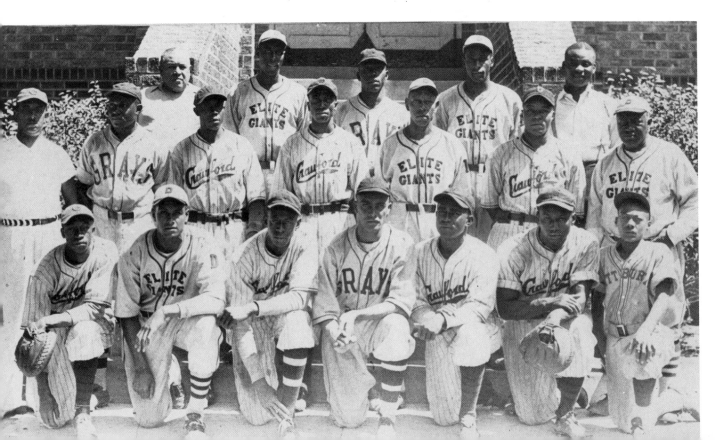

A vendor at Tandy Park in St. Louis does his best to help the fans quench their thirst.

Alex Radcliffe (left) and Walter (Bancy) Thomas. Radcliffe was an outstanding third baseman who appeared in eleven East-West Games, including seven straight (1933-39). In 1937 older brother Ted played in the annual event, giving the Radcliffes the distinction of being the first brother act to play in the summer classic.

Roy Partlow. According to William Cash, a catcher for the Philadelphia Stars, Partlow had four good pitches, but his greatest asset was his control. In 1945 the Grays traded him to the Stars for pitcher Roy Welmaker.

Theodore (Ted) Strong. He came from a baseball family. His father, Theodore Strong, Sr., was a pitcher for the St. Louis Stars, while a brother, Othello, played for the Chicago American Giants. As a member of the Monarchs, Ted appeared in the 1942 and 1946 World Series. He also played guard for the Harlem Globetrotters basketball team from 1940-47.

limited the East to three hits and one run in his three innings of work. And even though he didn't play, Satchel Paige received much of the attention, both before and after the game.

Paige, depending on which version of the story you believe, either was embroiled in a money dispute with the owners or was trying to use his considerable influence to help the war effort. As game day drew near his uncertain status became a hot story.

"The famous East vs. West baseball classic may be played here at Comiskey Park minus the colorful talents of one LeRoy 'Satchel' Paige on Sunday, August 13," an Associated Negro Press story said. "The reasons stated for Paige's probable absence from the lineup are that he first made demands for extra pay for his appearance in the game, then when they were rejected he proposed that the money from the baseball classic be donated to either a navy or army relief agency. On the other hand, Paige is said to have made such a proposal during the winter season, and has denied asking for extra pay for his services."

Whatever his motives were, Paige did not play, and afterward the press was preoccupied with the effect his absence had on the game. "The dream

The Kansas City Monarchs pitching staff, 1942. (L to R) Hilton Smith, Jack Matchett, Booker T. McDaniel, James (Lefty) LaMarque, Connie Johnson and Satchel Paige. LaMarque said of his fellow moundsmen: "We had the hardest-throwing pitching staff in the business. We learned that in order to win a majority of your games, you got to win a few when you don't have anything on the ball. That was something we didn't have to worry about too often."

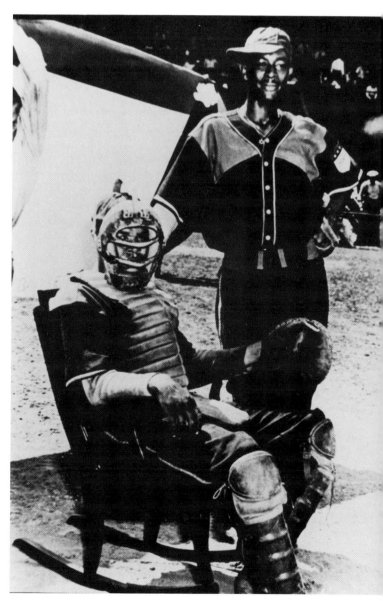

Left: Josh Gibson. A day after the Pittsburgh Crawfords captured the 1935 Negro National League Championship, they played in a four team doubleheader at Yankee Stadium that drew 27,000 fans. Across the Harlem River at the Polo Grounds, a twin-bill between the New York Giants and Brooklyn Dodgers drew only 12,000. The "Craws" blasted four home runs during their game, including a 475-foot shot by Gibson over the left-field fence.

Below: Lloyd (Pepper) Bassett (left) and Peanuts Nyasses. Nyasses' real name was Edward Davis. Bassett was a weak hitter when he started his career but eventually learned the craft and became a switch hitter.

Below: Larry Brown. In 1931, a New York daily newspaper said of Brown, "Speaking of great catchers, what of the Negro catcher of the Lincoln Giants? Look at his machine-like work behind the plate. He wears the earmarks of a perfect master, knows his game and plays it bang-up. Class, finish and polish are written in his every move. He is on a par, if not a little above, with the greatest catchers of modern times."

Satchel Page. In a 1934 game in Cleveland, Paige defeated the St. Louis Cardinal great, Dizzy Dean, who had won thirty games, by the score of 4-1. Paige struck out thirteen of the eighteen batters who faced him in six innings and didn't allow a hit. Dean remarked to a *Cleveland Plains Dealer* reporter, "Yeah, he's got a hell of a fast ball. Yes sir, he's got a fast ball."

Allen (Lefty) Bryant. A pitcher, he joined the Monarchs in 1939 after a successful stint with the All Nations team. Pitching for the Texas Sheepherders in the 1936 Wichita Baseball Tournament, he won the two games in which he appeared.

Left: The Memphis Red Sox parade into Kansas City's Blues Stadium on Opening Day in 1942. The Monarchs annually opened the season with a parade that went from Eighteenth and Vine to Twenty-second and Brooklyn, the site of the park.

Right: Joe Greene. He broke into the Negro American League in 1938 as a member of the Atlanta Black Crackers, playing catcher and second base. Before joining the Black Crackers, he played for the Macon Georgia Peaches, where he caught for Roy Welmaker, who later pitched for the Homestead Grays.

classic, the East-West All-Star Game of 1944, is a part of history now," wrote *Kansas City Call* sports editor Willie Bea Harmon, "but the fans are still wondering if Satchel Paige was missed . . . . That was the question on every lip. Many would say he was not missed . . . . but we say he was. Not a single player on either team has the color or should we say glamour which envelops Paige. He is, as they would say in Hollywood, a 'star.' "

The "star" stayed away again in '45, choosing instead to remain in Kansas City where he registered thirteen strikeouts in a victory over the American Giants. And while the Monarchs were

rolling at Ruppert Stadium, Jesse Williams, an unlikely hero, was doing his best to make the crowd at Comiskey Park forget Paige. The Monarch second baseman wasn't voted to the team but was pressed into service because Lorenzo (Piper) Davis of the Black Barons had been fined and

The Kansas City Monarchs, 1936. Standing (L to R): Andy Cooper, Pat Patterson, Woodrow (Lefty) Wilson, Curtis Harris, Floyd Kransen, Bob Madison, Willard Brown, Leroy Taylor. Seated: Newt Allen, Harry Else, Wilber (Bullet) Rogan, Henry Milton, Eddie Dwight, Owner J.L. Wilkinson had obtained Brown, Else, Wilson and Madison from the Monroe (Louisiana) Monarchs after the 1934 season. Leroy Taylor, despite a chronic knee injury, was a highly regarded outfielder. "Taylor would be chasing a fly ball or running a base when that trick knee would jump out of place." Chet Brewer recalled. "He would have to stop and pop it back into the socket, then proceed with the play."

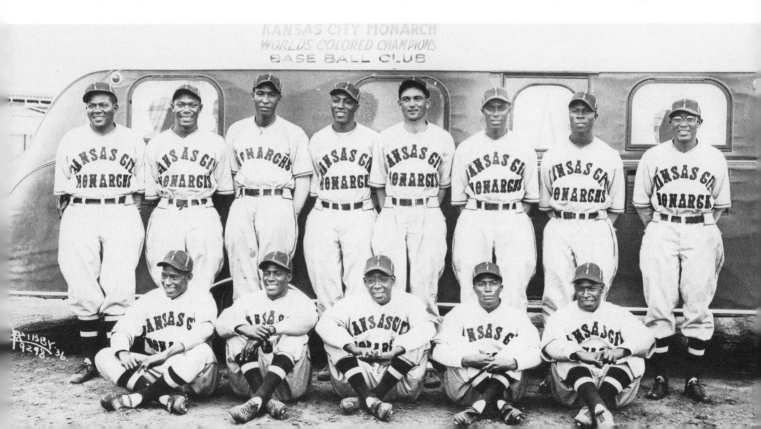

Above: (L to R) William Dismukes, Frank Duncan, Newt Allen, James Floyd (trainer). Duncan and Allen attended Lincoln High School in Kansas City together and became members of the same team at age 16. Duncan once said of his longtime friend: "I have watched Newt play for over twenty years and I still get a thrill when I know he's going to put on that uniform."

suspended for slugging an umpire in a game against the Buckeyes.

[The action taken against Davis was a rarity in the leagues, but a recent incident in a game between the Memphis Red Sox and the American Giants at Wrigley Field had triggered an outcry against violence on the field. In that game, Red Sox third baseman Jimmy Ford, with bat in hand, had chased after an umpire during a dispute over a call. No penalty was imposed. Thus, Davis' suspension was roundly applauded in the press. "It almost took an

Left: Pat Patterson. Kansas City sports promoter J. Cordell White called him the greatest third baseman in Monarchs' history. White explained, "[Newt] Joseph was good on bunts and a good fielder, but he didn't bat for average. [Bartolo] Portuando, the Cuban, was also a good third sacker, but Patterson could hit, run and field, plus he had good brains. He was always a .300 plus in the old apple orchard." Patterson was a graduate of Wiley College in Marshall, Texas.

Right: Willard Brown. In 1937 he played three games at Ward Field in Kansas City, Kansas, against the strong Schneiders' Jewelry team. He hit seven home runs in those games as the Monarchs outscored their opponents 26-7. While Brown was rounding the bases after blasting his seventh home run, he remarked to the Schneiders' pitcher: "Thanks, cousin."

Below: (L to R) Willard Brown, Ted Strong, Newt Allen. All were shortstops at various times in their careers. Brown was from Shreveport, Louisiana, where the Monarchs used to go for spring training. As the team's bat boy in 1929, Brown saw Newt Allen and Newt Joseph fielding ground balls during infield practice and dreamed of someday playing for the Monarchs. In 1935, his dream came true when he signed with Kansas City and played shortstop between his idols, second baseman Allen and third baseman Joseph.

Left: Josh Gibson. During the 1938-39 Cuban Winter League season, he batted .356 and belted three triples and eleven home runs in 163 plate appearances. He was joined in Negro baseball by his brother, Jerry, and son, Josh Gibson, Jr. An infielder, Josh Gibson, Jr. played for the Homestead Grays in the late '40s and then became the first non-white player to appear in the Middle Atlantic League, a minor league.

Josh Gibson. Here he accepts one of his many batting awards. Former Monarch John (Buck) O'Neil said of the great slugger: "Gibson hit the ball high and far and demonstrated no weakness. The only instruction our pitchers had was to throw him some of everything you had and hope."

(L to R) Ted (Double Duty) Radcliffe, Larry Brown, Olan (Jelly) Taylor, Richard (Subby) Byas, William (Nat) Rogers, Neil Robinson. Though not built like a power-hitter, Rogers could hit the long ball. He played professionally for twenty-three straight years, beginning in 1923 with the Illinois Giants of Spring Valley, Illinois.

Escobar Field. Puerto Rico's Santurce and San Juan teams shared this field during the late '30s and early '40s. According to Roy Partlow's wife, Dorothy, "The umpires in Puerto Rico hated to call a game off if it was raining, because the fans would get very violent if they felt the game could have been played."

(L to R) Fred Bankhead, Neil Robinson, Willie Hutchinson, Robert Keyes, 1942. Nicknamed "Shotgun," Keyes got beaned in 1942 and the ball ricocheted over the backstop. The players gave Keyes such a ribbing that he left and never returned to the team again.

Right: Allen (Lefty) Bryant. He joined the Kansas City Monarchs in 1939 and later had this to say about his years in baseball: "I was out of baseball before I really understood what it meant to be a Kansas City Monarch. The ball players had two things in mind back then: one was to be the best that you could be and the second was to outplay racism."

Below: George Walker. He was one of two great pitchers from Waco, Texas, the other being Andy Cooper of the Detroit Stars and Kansas City Monarchs. Walker played for both the Monarchs and Homestead Grays.

Right: Mary Jo Weaver. In 1940, the Monarch Booster Club held its second annual Miss Monarch contest, which was won by Mary Jo. Each of the contestants represented a local business. Mary Jo's affiliation was with the Crown Drug Store on Vine Street.

Herb Souell. Because he was a left-handed hitter, most lefty pitchers threw him curveballs. However, Souell was one of the best breaking-ball hitters in the game.

Ted Page. Longtime Negro leaguer Clint Thomas called Page, "the best right-fielder I have ever seen. He made playing the outfield one of the fine arts."

earthquake to do it," wrote Willie Bea Harmon of the *Kansas City Call*, "but President J.B. Martin of the Negro American League came to life and fined Lorenzo (Piper) Davis $50 and suspended him indefinitely for hitting 135-pound umpire Jimmy Thompson. This is the kind of action needed long ago."]

Williams was making his second East-West appearance, having collected two of the West's six hits in the '43 Game. A native of Henderson, Texas, he had joined the Monarchs in 1939 and had been their starting shortstop since 1940. In '45, he had fought off a tough spring training challenge from a rookie named Jackie Robinson. The much-heralded Robinson had been coaching baseball at Sam Houston State College in Huntsville, Texas, when

he was invited to the Monarchs' Houston training camp on the recommendation of pitcher Hilton Smith, who'd seen him play in California.

Robinson, then twenty-six, had a good spring but was unable to unseat Williams until the thirty-two year old veteran injured his arm. Jackie stepped in at shortstop and went on to have an outstanding year, leading the team in hitting with a .341 average, including ten doubles, four triples

Veracruz, 1941. Josh Gibson (fourth from left), Ray Dandridge (fifth from left), Bill Wright (second from right) and Johnny Taylor (third from right) were lured by the higher salaries of the Mexican League. In ninety-seven Mexican League games, Gibson batted .374, with thirty-three home runs and thirty-one doubles.

and five home runs. Robinson was playing so well that manager Frank Duncan left him at short and shifted Williams to second when the veteran's arm healed.

The Trujillo All-Stars 1937. Back row (L to R): Josh Gibson, Chester Williams, Antonio Caselnos, Rodolpho Fernandez, Robert Griffith, Perucho Cepeda, William Perkins. Middle row: Lazaro Salazar, Don Jose Enrique Ayubar, Satchel Paige. Front row: Enrique Lantiqua, LeRoy Matlock, Julio Vasquez, James (Cool Papa) Bell, Sam Bankhead, Silvio Garcia, Cho-Cho Correa. The team was sponsored by the president of the Dominican Republic, Rafael Trujillo, who took the game very seriously. According to Paige, the Americans were watched closely. "If we went swimming, [Trujillo's] soldiers chaperoned us. We had soldiers on our hotel floors, too. Trujillo gave orders [that] anyone in town selling us whiskey would be shot." Perucho Cepeda was the father of former major leaguer Orlando Cepeda.

Robinson, who'd made quite a reputation for himself as an all-around athlete at UCLA in the early '40s, was one of the prime attractions that day at Comiskey Park, but it was Williams who provided the thrills. While Jackie was taking an 0-for-5 collar, Jesse was driving in four runs with a single and triple as the West jumped to an 8-0 lead after two innings and coasted to a 9-6 victory, its third straight. "It's a good thing that Jesse Williams was permitted to go to the East-West Game by the owners of the Kansas City Monarchs," wrote the *Call's* Harmon. "Not only was Williams superb in his performance on the field, but he engaged a triple and a single and got credit for batting in four runs at the Dream Classic."

There were 37,714 on hand at Comiskey Park for the '45 East-West Game, which was actually a disappointing turnout in comparison to the previous four years (50,256, 48,400, 51,723 and 46,247). In each of those years, the East-West Game outdrew the major league "Midsummer Classic."

Above: Harry Kincannon (left) and Josh Gibson. When Gibson started to struggle at the plate in the mid '40s, manager Vic Harris benched him. Sonnyman Jackson, part-owner of the Homestead Grays, questioned the decision to sit the team's star attraction. Harris replied, "Josh is in no condition to play and these people came out to see a good game. If you want him to play, I'm through, you can have my uniform."

Below: (L to R) Ted Trent, Richard (Subby) Byas, Walter Thomas and Willie (Sug) Cornelius, 1936. Trent defeated the New York Black Yankees, 4-3, in 1934 at Yankee Stadium, but was tagged for two home runs by Clint Thomas, the second of which traveled 450 feet.

Above: The Birmingham Black Barons, 1940. Standing (L to R): Paul Hardy, Parnell Woods, Unknown, Unknown, Thomas Sampson, Unknown, Dan Bankhead, Lyman Bostock. Seated: Jim (Candy) Taylor, Gentry Jessup, Unknown, Robert (Black Diamond) Pipkin, Unknown, Ulysses Redd. Pipkin, a native of New Orleans, had a sharp breaking curve and lively fastball and was considered one of the league's top pitchers. Bostock's son, also named Lyman, batted .311 during four seasons in the major leagues. He died at age 27, the victim of a shooting in Gary, Indiana.

Below left: Unknown entrant in swimsuit contest draws a crowd before a Memphis Red Sox game.

Below right: James Ford. A hard-hitting infielder, he reputedly started a fight during a game in Chicago to get some additional press. The next morning he purchased several hundred newspapers, sat outside his hotel and shouted, "Extra! Extra! Read all about it. Jim Ford, the great St. Louis shortstop, starts near-riot in Comiskey Park."

Newark Eagles, 1939. Front row (L to R): Leon Day, Dick Seay, Dick Lundy, Willie Wells, Leon Ruffin, Jimmy Hill, Vernon Riddick. Back row: Monte Irvin, Fred Wilson, Lennie Pearson, George (Mule) Suttles, Max Manning, Harry Cozart, Ed Stone, James Brown, Johnnie Hayes.

(In 1945 the major league game was canceled because of the war.) But then again, business was up throughout the Negro leagues. When the '45 World Series concluded in late September, there was good reason to be optimistic about the coming year.

The war in Europe had ended in May; Japan had surrendered in August. As the nation rejoiced, players who'd been serving their country abroad straggled home to resume serving their teams. In their absence, a new wave of talent had burst onto the scene. Some, like Hank Thompson of the Monarchs and Larry Doby of the Newark Eagles, made brief appearances before they themselves were drafted. Others, like Robinson, Joe Black and Jim Gilliam of the Baltimore Elite Giants, Don

The Rev. D.A. Holmes chats with his catcher before throwing out the first ball at the Kansas City Monarchs' 1942 opener.

CHESTER WILLIAMS

(L to R) Clarence Palm, Nenene Rivera, Rafael Polanco, Geraldo Rodriquez and Roy Partlow, 1939. Palm, a catcher, was heckled frequently by his colleagues because of his very dark color. According to Partlow's wife, Dorothy, the pitchers told Palm to put white tape on his fingers because they couldn't see the signals he was giving during night games.

Chester Williams. After a Pittsburgh Crawfords-Philadelphia Stars game in 1934, sportswriter Nat Trammell offered this description of Williams' play at second base: "Williams turned in several beautiful fielding plays. He dived on his eyebrows to stop [Raleigh] Mackey's hit going across second base. Williams then somersaulted and threw perfect to [Leroy] Morney to force [Jud] Wilson at second and rob Mackey of a sure single. Williams again electrified the fans when he went back of [Oscar] Charleston to spear Chaney White's drive and tossed him out at first as well."

The Memphis Red Sox, 1941. Standing (L to R): Casey, Porter Moss, Verdell Mathis, "Winky" James, Neil Robinson, Fred Bankhead, Olan (Jelly) Taylor, William (Nat) Rogers, Richard Byas. Kneeling: Unknown, T. Brown, Cowan (Bubber) Hyde, Willie Hutchinson, Robert Keys, Wyman Longly, Marlin Carter, Larry Brown, Ted (Double Duty) Radcliffe. None were more respected in Memphis baseball circles than Robinson, Moss Mathis, Carter, Hyde and Larry Brown. Hyde was an outstanding student-athlete at Rust College in Holly Springs, Mississippi and Morris Brown College in Atlanta, Georgia.

Newcombe of the Newark Eagles, Piper Davis and Artie Wilson of the Birmingham Black Barons and Sam Hairston of the Indianpolis Clowns, had established themselves as shining stars. They'd all be back in 1946. Yes, the future of the Negro leagues looked promising in the fall of '45.

And then, without warning, there came a postwar bombshell that would forever change the course of baseball history. On October 23, at a press conference in Montreal, the Brooklyn Dodgers informed the world that they had signed Jackie Robinson to a minor league contract. He would be assigned to the team's Triple A farm team, the Montreal Royals.

At long last, there was a crack in white baseball's great wall.

Effa and Abe Manley, owners of the Newark Eagles. Effa (top photo with Raleigh Mackey (left) and Leon Day) and Abe (bottom photo) started the Eagles in Brooklyn in 1935, naming the team after a local newspaper. They moved to Newark in 1936. While Abe, one of many eastern team owners who found his fortune in the numbers racket, tended to business, Effa ran the ball club. In 1946 they won the Negro World Series.

Chapter 8

The final act of the epic struggle was played by two men, Branch Rickey and Jackie Robinson. It has been well-documented how Rickey, the president of the Brooklyn Dodgers, handpicked Robinson from the Negro leagues, as much for his character as his ability, to carry the torch for integration. Forever, they will be historically linked in a two-man chain that pulled down baseball's color barrier. Too often, though, in recounting the story of integration, the enormous and virtually anonymous contributions of others are ignored. On April 18, 1946, when Jackie Robinson hustled onto the Roosevelt Stadium field in Jersey City, there were a great many who could say they helped him put on his Montreal Royals uniform.

The most important contributors were the players, managers and owners who perpetuated Negro baseball for more than fifty years. Without their relentless efforts to prove they belonged in the National Pastime, where would Branch Rickey have found Jackie Robinson? Also lost in the luster of Rickey and Robinson were the black sportswriters, men such as Sam Lacy, Wendell Smith, Fay Young, Mabray Kountze and David Wyatt, to name just a few, who tirelessly promoted the game and waged a long and determined battle "to get our boys" into the major leagues. Those of their lineage who saw it finally happen were among the most elated at the triumph. Their joy could also be shared by a few white sportswriters who joined the crusade in the '30s and '40s. They are the unsung heroes of integration; all helped make it possible for Branch Rickey and Jackie Robinson to take their prominent place in history.

In the 1880s, before the dugout door was fully closed, several players provided proof positive that the barrier was being built for all the wrong reasons. George Stovey of Newark was the best pitcher in the International League. Frank Grant, the great second baseman for Buffalo, led the IL in several offensive categories. Bud Fowler had a long and productive minor league career. And Fleet Walker, the first black player in the major leagues, was a top-rated catcher for Toledo and Syracuse. And there were others, legitimate stars driven out of the game, not because they couldn't play, but for their skin color.

One early organization that established a color line was the Ohio State League. Welday Walker, Fleet's brother, who had played for Akron in 1886, was outraged when he read of the league's decision in February of 1887. In a letter to the league's president, dated March 5, 1887, he made a heartfelt plea to the league, asking that it rescind the rule.

"It is not because I was reserved and have been denied making my bread and butter with some clubs that I speak," Walker wrote, "but it is in hopes that the action taken at your last meeting will be called up for reconsideration at your next.

"The law is a disgrace to the present age, and reflects very much upon the intelligence of your last meeting, and casts derision at the laws of Ohio — the voice of the people — that say all men are equal. I would suggest that your honorable body, in case that black law is not repealed, pass one making it criminal for a colored man or woman to be found in a ball ground.

Satchel Paige. Pitching against major leaguer Bobo Newsom in a California Winter League game in November of 1933, Paige struck out thirteen and allowed five hits in an 11-3 victory. Teammates Cool Papa Bell, Sam Bankhead and Willie Wells stole a total of six bases as Newsom was ripped for fifteen hits.

Roy Campanella. He was discovered by Tom Wilson, owner of the Baltimore Elite Giants. In Negro baseball circles, Campanella was known as "Poochie," a name he was rarely called when he went to the major leagues.

"There is now the same accommodation made for the colored patron of the game as the white, and the same provision and dispensation is made for the money of them both that finds its way into the coffers of the various clubs.

"There should be some broader cause — such as lack of ability, behavior and intelligence — for barring a player, rather than his color. It is for these reasons and because I think ability and intelligence should be recognized first and last — at all times and by everyone — I ask the question again, 'Why was the law permitting colored men to sign repealed?' "

Welday Walker's impassioned letter was reprinted in *Sol White's Official Base Ball Guide,* White's 1907 historical account of blacks in baseball. White, too, addressed the issue of the color line, devoting a short chapter to its burdens.

"The colored players are not only barred from playing on white clubs," White wrote, "but at times games are canceled for no other reason than objections being raised by a Southern ball player, who refuses to play against a colored ball club. These men from the South who object to playing are, as a rule, fine ball players, and rather than lose their services, the managers will not book a colored team."

Regarding travel problems encountered by black teams, White said:

"The colored ball player suffers great inconvenience at times, while traveling. All hotels are

(L to R) Long Island Rail Road president Tom Goodfellow, Roy Campanella, Dodger executive Buzzy Bavasi. In mid-October 1955, the week that the Brooklyn Dodgers won the World Series, the Long Island Rail Road replaced its last four steam locomotives with brand-new diesels. One of the quartet of old steamers was No. 39 — the same number that Dodgers catcher Roy Campanella wore on his uniform. The LIRR management gave the big number plate from engine 39 to Campanella.

generally filled from the cellar to the garret when they strike a town. It is a common occurrence for them to arrive in a city late at night and walk around for several hours before getting a place to lodge.

"The situation is far different today in this respect than it was years ago. At one time the colored teams were accommodated in some of the best hotels in the country.

"The cause of this change is no doubt due to the condition of things from a racial standpoint. With the color question uppermost in the minds of the people at the present time, such proceedings on the part of hotel-keepers may be expected and will be difficult to remedy."

In another chapter, entitled "Colored Base Ball

as a Profession," White cautioned players about being excessively demanding at the negotiating table. "The colored ball player should . . . remember," he said, "that, although possessing the ability in every particular of the white ball player, he is not in a position to demand the same salary as his white brother, as the difference in the receipts of their respective games are decidedly in favor of the latter: thousands attending games of the whites to hundreds of the blacks."

According to White's figures, the average major league salary in 1906 was $2,000 per year, compared to $466 in "colored base ball." Still, he counseled the Negro player to approach the game "seriously . . . . as honest efforts with his great ability will open an avenue in the near future wherein he may walk

Newark Eagles bus accident in the late 1930s. None of the players was hurt in this crash, which was caused by brake failure.

hand-in-hand with the opposite race in the greatest of all American games — base ball."

It wouldn't be the near future, but White's call for professionalism was beginning to be echoed by others, including Rube Foster. The great pitcher, manager and executive was one of the first to take his team south for spring training and also insisted that his Chicago American Giants adhere to a strict training regimen. "Training trips for colored clubs a few years back would have been looked upon as a joke," Foster wrote in a 1910 issue of the *Indianapolis Freeman*, "but at present such trips are considered a necessity, considering the class of teams that are demanded by the public."

It was a continual theme in Foster's writing — being prepared, physically and mentally. He, along with many others, was convinced that if the major leagues ever abolished the color line, it would not be for a lone individual, but, rather, for a whole team. (That was how the California Winter League was integrated in the early 1920s.) That team would have to be the product of a "major league" organization. In establishing the Negro National League in 1920, Foster hoped to show the barons of major league baseball that blacks could play the game, both athletically and economically. And until the league collapsed under the weight of the Great Depression, it did just that.

Foster's successor as Negro National League president, Judge William C. Hueston, also recognized the importance of blacks having their own

major league. "The league is the greatest leveler of prejudice today," Hueston said at the league's annual meeting in 1928. "It is also the best propaganda possible to advance the theory that Negroes could do anything as well as whites."

"The colored man has been forced to provide his own baseball opportunities," wrote Olympic long jumper DeHart Hubbard in the *Kansas City Call* in 1924, "and he is making rapid progress in so doing."

Nonetheless, it was an arduous fight that Foster and friends had on their hands. Aside from the overwhelming prejudice that had to be overcome, there was a very frustrating aspect to their struggle: nowhere in the bylaws of major league baseball was there a regulation prohibiting owners from hiring blacks. That it was a collusive agreement only served to strengthen the barrier, providing the conspirators with a pat response to questions about the color line: "What color line?"

As late as 1942, Commissioner Kenesaw Mountain Landis, who'd been hired to restore baseball's good name in the wake of the 1919 Black Sox scandal, was still insisting that the major leagues were an equal opportunity employer.

"There is no rule against major league clubs hiring Negro baseball players," Landis said. "Negroes are not barred from organized baseball by the commissioner and never have been during the twenty-one years I have served. There is no rule in organized baseball prohibiting their participation and never has been to my knowledge."

Interesting comments from a man who in the early 1920s ordered teams to discontinue wearing their major league uniforms during postseason barnstorming games against Negro league teams, an action that had come after a series of losses by the major leaguers. If there wasn't a rule, and the black teams were proving to be the equal of their white counterparts, then why weren't any jobs being offered to black players?

That's precisely what a reporter from the *Chicago Defender* wanted to know when he interviewed White Sox owner J. Louis Comiskey in 1933.

"Oh, yes, the Sox want color," Comiskey said. "That's why we brought Al Simmons in."

"But we are talking about colored players on your ball team," the reporter responded.

"Well, now," Comiskey replied, "I have never had reason to think of that."

"But that's why we are here today, Mr. Comiskey," said the reporter. "We wish to know how you stand."

"You can bet your last dime that I'll never refuse to hire a great athlete simply because he isn't the same color of some other players on my team if the bar you tell me is against them is lifted," Comiskey declared. "Had some good players come along and my manager refused to sign him because he was a Negro, I am sure I would have taken action or

attempted to. Although it isn't up to me to change what must be a rule."

The reporter then mentioned that Willie Foster of the Chicago American Giants was "one of the finest pitchers in baseball" and would be a great drawing card for the White Sox. Said Comiskey: "Yes, I expect so."

That same year National League president John Heydler offered his thoughts on the subject: "Beyond the fundamental requirement that a major league player must have unique ability and good character and habits, I do not recall one instance where baseball has allowed either race, creed or color to enter into its selection of players."

Whether dealing with the empty denials of Landis and Heydler or the inane double-talk of Comiskey, advocates of integration knew full well that the ban existed, and they knew why. Until racial attitudes softened, major league baseball would remain the "Irrational Pastime."

Through the years, the game's Southern influence provided the strongest fortification for the barrier. The prevailing notion was that if blacks were allowed to play, then the major leagues' large bloc of Southerners would quit. Also, teams held spring training in the South, where the law forbade blacks and whites from participating together. Sportswriter Lloyd Lewis of the *Chicago Daily News* explained baseball's fear of a Southern backlash in a 1938 story:

Booker McDaniel (right) and unknown Veracruz teammate. In 1946 he jumped to San Luis of the Mexican League with former Monarchs Jesse Williams and Bonnie Serrell. Other American blacks who went south of the border in the mid '40s were James Fillmore, James Clarkson, Ray Dandridge, Edward Hunter, Johnny Taylor, Terris McDuffie, Ray Brown, Tom Glover, Bill Wright, Jesse Douglas, Theolic Smith, Martin Dihigo, Lloyd Davenport, Pete Pages, Art Pennington, Ed Stone and Leon Gerard. Both the Monterrey and Tampico Clubs of the Mexican League were all-black teams. Many of these players upstaged the major leaguers who jumped south. The Mexican press proclaimed, "The colored ballplayers are the very backbone of the Mexican Baseball League."

(L to R) Celois Street, Unknown, Emma Jean, Othello Renfroe, Rabbit (a local comedian), Willa Street, Ruth and Felix Street. This photograph was taken at the Scotts Theater restaurant. Ball players were renowned for their propensity to socialize, some becoming better known for their activities off the field than on the field.

"There were 212 Southerners among the 512 players on the rosters of the big league clubs in February. Few of these 212 would continue playing if the gates were opened to Negro athletes.

"Several owners of major league clubs are known to wish they could employ Negro stars like LeRoy (Satchel) Paige, but they hesitate for fear the Southerners in the league would secede and form an all-Dixie major league. This league could prosper by selecting eight cities from a list comprised of Washington, Atlanta, Richmond, New Orleans, Houston, Dallas, Tulsa, Little Rock, Oklahoma City, Kansas City, Birmingham or Memphis."

It may have been reasonable to fear the Southerners' reaction, but it also may have been a legitimate assumption that they wouldn't have surrendered the lofty status and salary that a major league career afforded. As for the Southern ban on whites and blacks playing together, spring training might have been a problem, though not an insurmountable one. In 1946, when Jackie Robinson went to Daytona Beach with the Montreal Royals, the mayor was quick to lift the restriction rather than lose the revenue generated by the team.

Another stated reason for not allowing blacks into the big leagues was the concern about violence, both on the field and in the stands. Bill

(L to R) Max Manning, Carl Erskine, Frank Meagher. Manning signed with the Newark Eagles in 1939 after an illustrious high school career. During his senior year he received a letter from the Detroit Tigers asking him to try out. The scout obviously had only read of Manning's exploits and didn't realize that he was black.

Rufus Lewis. He pitched for the Pittsburgh Crawfords, Newark Eagles and Houston Eagles. Lewis also enjoyed two successful seasons in Cuba in 1947 and 1948, where he appeared in a total of fifty-five games, winning nineteen and helping Havana win the winter league championship in 1947.

Dave Barnhill. In 1943 he pitched two games against Satchel Paige in Yankee Stadium. Paige won the first contest, 6-3, before a crowd of 20,000. Later in the season, Barnhill avenged the defeat by shutting out the Monarchs before a crowd of 18,000.

Cunningham of the *Tyler* [Texas] *Morning Telegraph* viewed this as the biggest obstacle. "Fear of physical trouble on the field and race riots in the stands is frankly the most of it," he wrote in 1942. "The majority of the ball players are Southerners and many of them cracker confederates. Maybe they're not right, but you try telling 'em and see how far you get.

"A collision, a case of high spikes, a Negro batter hit with a beanball flung by a Southern pitcher, a player roughed at the plate, trouble in the locker rooms, on into the stands and even the streets is the real background of the unwritten rule."

It was a theory that had already been disproved. For years blacks and whites had been competing against one another, if not amiably, then without rancor. In the Cuban and California Winter Leagues, in postseason barnstorming games, black teams and major leaguers (including Southerners) had proved they could coexist on a baseball diamond.

(L to R) Tom Baird, C.A. Franklin, J.L. Wilkinson, 1943. Wilkinson and Baird, the Monarch owners, had asked Franklin, the editor of the *Kansas City Call*, for help in overturning an order from the Office of Defense Transportation that required Negro league teams to travel by trains rather than buses. If allowed to stand, the order would have been financially disastrous to league teams. Here, they are looking over petitions that helped to overturn the ruling.

Standing (L to R): Maurice Wiggins, Unknown, Bill Veeck, Unknown. Front row: Unknown, Al Smith and Mrs. Sarah Foster (Rube's wife). Veeck, owner of the Cleveland Indians, signed Larry Doby in 1947 to break the color barrier in the American League. "When we signed Larry Doby, the first Negro player in the American League, we received 20,000 letters, most of them in violent and sometimes obscene protest," Veeck wrote. "Over a period of time, I answered all. In each answer, I included a paragraph congratulating them on being wise enough to have chosen parents so obviously to their liking."

And there were no riots. There was good, tough, hard-nosed baseball, but there were no riots.

Another excuse offered for not admitting blacks centered on the difficulties they would encounter while traveling — the Jim Crow hotels and restaurants. It was hollow reasoning at best. If there was one facet of baseball life that Negro leaguers were prepared for, it was the road. They would have been willing to cope with that hardship in the majors just as they did in their own leagues.

The last, and perhaps the most ridiculous, doubt, was the one that some people expressed about the Negro players' ability. Were they good enough to play in the major leagues? Ty Cobb knew they were. He was caught stealing twice by Bruce Petway during a game in Cuba and eventually refused to compete against minority players.

Carl Hubbell, the great New York Giants pitcher in the '30s, knew there were several Negro league players who were qualified to cross the line. "I've seen a lot of colored boys who should have been playing in the majors," he once said. "First of all I'd name this big guy, Josh Gibson, for a place. He is one of the greatest backstops in history, I think. Any team in the big leagues could use him right now. Bullet Rogan of Kansas City, and Satchel Paige could make any big league team. Paige has the

fastest ball I've ever seen."

Others were equally complimentary. Dizzy Dean, who spoke of Paige only in superlatives, also had kind words for Monarchs' catcher Frank Duncan. "That fellow Duncan which [sic] catches for Kansas City," Dean said, "is almost as good a catcher as Gabby Hartnett, and I can't say no more than that about a catcher."

Eddie Herr, a Cleveland Indians' scout who signed Carl Hubbell to his first contract, was overwhelmed by the performance of the Trujillo All-Stars pitching staff at the 1937 *Denver Post* tournament. "Judging by what the big leagues are paying for pitching talent now," Herr said of the group that included Chet Brewer, Ernest Carter, Leroy Matlock, Robert Griffith and Satchel Paige, "I would place a collective price tag of one-quarter of a million dollars on the Negro pitching staff."

Ray L. Doan, a scout for the St. Louis Cardinals who also promoted games for the House of David team, witnessed the '37 *Denver Post* tournament and came away raving about the All-Stars. "The Negro club is as good as any team in the big leagues and I don't bar the New York Yankees," Doan said after watching the black players defeat Roger Hornsby's Denver Bay Refiners team, 12-0.

Jesse Williams. In the 1945 East-West game, Williams, representing the Kansas City Monarchs, collected two hits and drove in four runs to lead the West to a 9-6 victory.

"They've got a pitching staff that any big league manager would like to have. They've got marvelous fielding and every man in the lineup is a good hitter. And nowhere will you see a fielding first baseman like David (Showboat) Thomas."

Gabby Hartnett, the Cubs' great catcher of the '20s and '30s, also was impressed by what he'd seen of the Negro leaguers. "There are any number of good Negro players around the country," he said. "And I'm sure that if we were given permission to use them, there'd be a mad scramble between managers to pick them up."

Permission was a long time coming, but as the years passed there grew a loudening cry from the black press, which began to pound away relentlessly at the barrier.

The *Chicago Defender,* citing the success of J.L. Wilkinson's All Nations team in 1916, said that "colorphobia" had cost the White Sox and Cubs the pennant, noting that the Chicago American Giants and All Nations had many players who could have helped either team. The story said, "Yet . . . the fans go back to sit another winter to figure out why no World Series came to Chicago. The truth is in a few words. Color of a man's skin did it."

In the November 3, 1922, edition of the *St. Louis Argus,* Charles Starks of the Associated Negro Press applauded the great strides being made in Negro baseball. "Now comes the Negro National Baseball League finishing its third year in which they

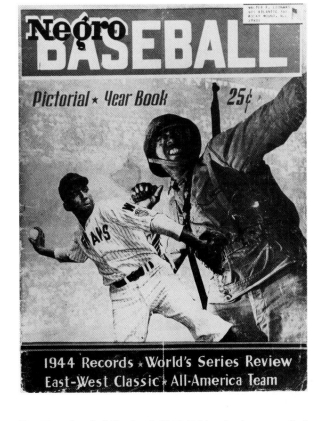

The *Negro Baseball Yearbook,* 1945. Making the throws are Buck Leonard (in baseball uniform) and a G.I. During World War II, more than fifty Negro league players served in the armed forces. Ralph Johnson was the only player killed in combat. Among the injured was Rusty Payne, an outfielder with the Toledo Crawfords who was stabbed in the side with a bayonet.

(L to R) Larry Doby, Don Newcombe, Roy Campanella and Art Pennington. In 1946, while with Nashua of the New England League, Campanella and Newcombe became the minor leagues' first black battery since the nineteenth century. Newcombe posted a record of 14-4, while Campanella batted .290 with ninety-six RBIs.

without question raised the quality of their brand of baseball," Starks wrote. "In New York we read of the colored Bacharach Giants taking the first two games from the World Series champions [New York Giants]. In St. Louis we find the representatives of the Negro League fairly running away with Detroit [Tigers] with all players intact except Ty Cobb and the same Negro team playing rings around 'Stars' from the Browns and Cardinals. The Kansas City Monarchs, possibly the best Negro team in the country, outplayed the K.C. Blues American Association team in every phase of the game. The Monarchs won five out of six games played, taking the first four."

In the same article, Starks asked why "should the public accept the results of a 'World Series' between two white teams as conclusive when perhaps there are one or several colored teams in the country better than the contenders?"

DeHart Hubbard sounded a pessimistic chord in 1924, when he wrote: "A Cuban can play in organized baseball, a Mexican is good enough to play, but never a man of African descent. We have some ball players who could qualify in any company. Dick (Cannonball) Redding, Oscar Charleston, Elwood (Bingo) DeMoss, John Henry Lloyd, Bruce Petway, Oliver Riggins, and many others could make the grade, but will never get the chance."

That's really all they wanted — the chance. It didn't have to be in the majors; any of the above mentioned would have been willing to play their

Sarah Foster, Rube's widow, was the featured guest at the dedication of the Rube Foster Memorial Baseball Field at Ft. Huachuca, Arizona. At the dedication, she stated, "I learned that for a woman married to a public figure, there are a lot of things to consider. The most important thing to consider is that your husband just doesn't belong to you. I tried to remember that, and I didn't try to get into everything he was in." Above, she is flanked by Colonel Hardy and Brigadier General Benjamin O. Davis.

On rare occasions, Negro teams were forced to abandon their buses for an alternative form of travel. Here, the Memphis Red Sox arrive home after a game in Chicago.

way up from the minor leagues. As one Associated Negro Press story put it: "The American Negro wants no special class, no special place, no special street, no special trains, no special nothing. He wants to be regarded as an American citizen, with all the rights belonging to such. He asks no special favors and will be satisfied with none."

Along the way, the black sportswriters were joined by a few of their white colleagues, who also were disturbed by the injustice. Roger Pipen of the

Baltimore Evening News saw the local Black Sox play in 1925 and was "astonished" by their ability. "If colored players were permitted in the National, American and International Leagues," Pipen declared, "three or four of the Sox would have their names in big type in every sports page around the country."

Shirley Povich of the *Washington Post* returned from a spring training swing through Florida in the '30s and wrote about "a couple million dollars'

Roy Campanella. As the Baltimore Elite Giants catcher in 1944, he was named over Josh Gibson to the All-American Baseball Team, selected by the *Negro Baseball Yearbook*. According to the *Yearbook* writer, "Campanella out-hit the great Josh Gibson .350 to .338 and played in six more league games, had more doubles than any other player in either league, eighteen, and was a top run-getter."

Sarah Bell Wood. She married Larry Brown on October 10, 1948. When the 1949 baseball season began, she decided to travel with her husband's Memphis Red Sox to see how baseball players lived. Over the next thirty days, she made visits to thirteen cities and slept in a hotel only one night. The rest of the nights, the team slept on the bus while traveling to the next game.

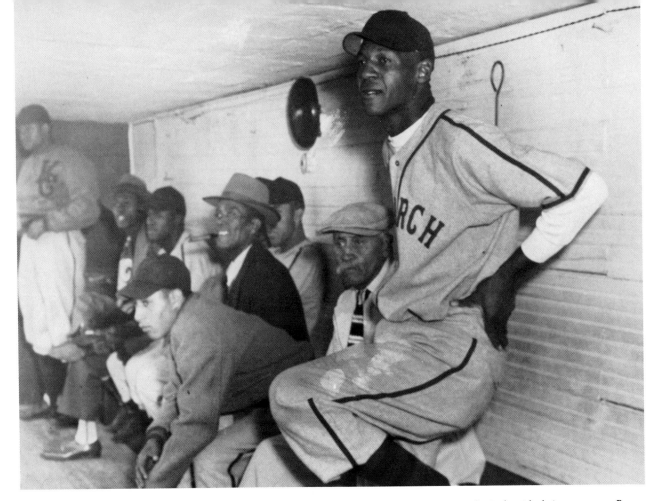

Inside the Kansas City Monarchs dugout. Many of the old-timers came back to watch the games and mingle with their successors. Percy Staples, with cigar and hat, had been a member of the Tennessee Rats for eleven seasons. Seated next to Buck O'Neil (standing, far right) is Frank Duncan, whose son, also named Frank, was a Monarch catcher and manager for many years.

In 1942, 48,400 people paid to see the East All-Stars defeat the West, 5-2. Satchel Paige took the loss, allowing five hits in his three-inning stint.

worth of baseball talent on the loose, ready for the big leagues, yet unsigned by any major league."

He complained of the "tight little boycott" that major league baseball had established against the black players. "Only one thing is keeping them out of the big leagues," Povich wrote, "the pigmentation of their skin. That's their crime in the eyes of the big-league club owners."

Others, like Jimmy Powers of the *New York Daily News* and Dan Parker of the *New York Daily Mirror,* were equally critical. "Negroes belong in big league baseball competition," Powers wrote in 1938. "They have ability and it is only fair to them as Americans that they be given an equal chance. I believe big league ball would gain added sparkle if the great Negro stars were admitted."

In the same year Parker added: "I see no reason why Negroes should not be admitted to major league baseball. If it weren't for them, where would America [have been] in Hitler's Olympics? There is no place for racial discrimination in the American National game."

Parker touched on an important point in his

Above: (L to R) Jim Taylor, J.B. Martin (Negro American League president), William Little, Frank Young (sportswriter), and Arthur Tony (Monarch Booster Club president). Taylor became manager of the Chicago American Giants in 1941 after a successful season with the Birmingham Black Barons. The Giants played that year in Comiskey Park because the bleachers in their park at Thirty-ninth and Wentworth had burned down.

reference to Jesse Owens' remarkable feat at the '36 Olympics in Berlin. Under the disdainful eye of Adolph Hitler, Owens had sprinted and jumped his way to an unprecedented four gold medals (100 meters, 200 meters, long jump and 400-meter relay). He returned home on the *Queen Mary* and received a hero's welcome upon disembarking in New York. Other track stars, such as John Woodruff, Ben Johnson, Mack Robinson, Dave Albritton, Ralph Metcalfe and Eddie Tolan were making their marks as well, regularly competing against and regularly beating white athletes.

In boxing, few championship opportunities had existed since 1915, when Jess Willard took the heavyweight title from Jack Johnson. But in the '30s, black fighters again were beginning to flex their muscles. John Henry Lewis, a member of Gus Greenlee's stable of fighters, staked a four-year claim to the light heavyweight championship starting in 1935. Henry Armstrong held the featherweight, lightweight and welterweight crowns between 1937 and 1940. And Joe Louis, the "Brown

Bob Thurman. He holds the record for the most career home runs by an American in the Puerto Rican Winter League with 120. In various years, he led that league in walks (69 in 1949), hits (112 in 1950), doubles (22 in 1950), triples (8 in 1951), and home runs (18 in 1948).

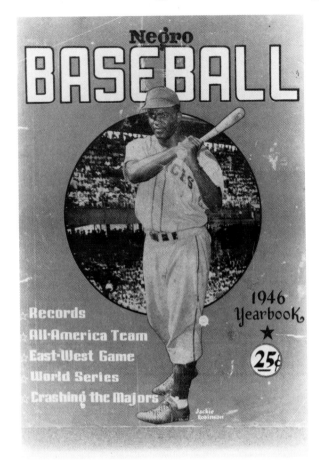

The *1946 Negro Baseball Yearbook*, with Jackie Robinson pictured on the cover. On October 23, 1945, at a press conference in Montreal, it was announced that Robinson had signed a contract to play for the Montreal Royals, the Brooklyn Dodgers' Triple A farm team. The historic signing made him the first black player in the twentieth century to be under contract to a major league team. "I can't begin to tell you how happy I am that I am the first member of my race in organized ball," Robinson said that day. "I realize how much it means to me, to my race, and to baseball. I can only say that I'll do my very best to come through in every manner."

Bomber," began a twelve-year hold on the heavy-weight title in June of 1937 when he knocked out James Braddock. Louis ultimately became one of America's most beloved athletes.

In track, in boxing, on many of the country's collegiate athletic fields, blacks were proving they belonged in the mainstream of America's sporting life. Why, then, were the major leagues clinging to their rigid views on the race issue?

An answer of sorts came in 1938 when Jake Powell, a journeyman outfielder with the New York Yankees, casually remarked during a radio inter-view in Chicago that he stayed in shape during the off-season by working as a policeman and "cracking niggers over the head." Naturally, the black com-munity of Chicago was outraged, and the firestorm quickly spread to other cities. Landis's office was

Local fans at the El Capitan Bar in Kansas City following a Monarchs game. Felix Street (standing, far right) was a longtime fan who began going to Monarch games as a child in 1923. "All the players on the Monarchs were real nice men," Street said. "In those days we called them professional fellows."

New Orleans Pelicans of the Negro Southern League, 1946. Kneeling (L to R): Unknown, Joe Buggage, "General" Jackson, Joe Willis, Robert (Black Diamond) Pipkin, Ike Wheeler. Standing: Clarence Fernandez, Edward Ducey, Billy Rivers, Joe Warmington, Clarence Adams, Robert Bissant. Many players continued to wear the hats of their former teams.

deluged with letters demanding that Powell, a native of Silver Spring, Maryland, be banned from the game. The commissioner slapped a ten-day suspension on Powell, but the protesters were unappeased, and they let Powell know it at every stop in the American League. In Washington he was pelted with bottles, while in New York a petition bearing 6,000 signatures demanded he receive a lifetime ban.

League officials and team owners all decried Powell's insensitive remark, making them vulnerable to a spate of caustic commentary from the press. The *New York Post* pointed out the hypocrisy in an editorial. "[The owners] express outward horror at Powell's hasty and uncouth comment," the *Post* said. "Then they calmly proceed with their own economic boycott against this minority people."

Left: Herbert Barnhill. Originally from Jacksonville, Florida, he was a solid catcher for the Chicago American Giants in the late '30s and '40s.

Below: (L to R) Jim Brown, Oscar Moore, Felix Street, Irvin, Sylvester Trailer, Unknown. Going to a game was a social event, and the fans dressed the part.

Left: Booker T. (Cannonball) McDaniel. A pitcher, he was the first Negro leaguer to sign a Chicago Cub contract. Wayne Terwilliger, who was a teammate of McDaniel's with the minor league Los Angeles Angels in 1949, said, "Booker T. was a very enthusiastic player, very aggressive. He was popular with his teammates. He had some success with us, but I think he was a little short of stuff." Terwilliger was unaware that McDaniel was thirty-eight years old at the time, not twenty-seven as announced by the Cubs. McDaniel never made it to the majors.

Troubling as it was, the Powell incident did shine a spotlight on the major leagues' hiring practices. However, *Kansas City Call* sportswriter Ernest Brown, Jr. and others wondered how many more "Powells" were in the employ of major league baseball. "With Negro sportswriters the country over attempting to bring pressure so that Negro ballplayers will be admitted to the big leagues, this was indeed a drastic setback," Brown wrote. "If this expression by any means typifies the type of baseball players that are now present in the big leagues, it will be some time before Negroes will have the doors of major league baseball opened to them."

Certainly there were others who shared Powell's outlook. Bucky Harris, manager of the Washington Senators, uttered some truly offensive remarks about his white Cuban players in 1940. In a preseason story that appeared in the *Washington Daily News*, Harris was quoted as saying, "I'm

Below: Satchel Paige's All-Stars used this airplane to travel about the country in 1948, when they played a series of games against Bob Feller's All-Stars. Pictured here (L to R): Hilton Smith, Howard Easterling, Barney Brown, Sam Jethroe, Gentry Jessup, Hank Thompson, Max Manning, Othello Renfroe, William (Dizzy) Dismukes, Rufus Lewis, Gene Benson, Buck O'Neil, Frank Duncan, Artie Wilson and Quincy Trouppe. In the doorway are a valet and Paige. Said Hank Thompson of the barnstorming tour: "This was a gravy train. My share was $7,500 for seventeen days' work. Actually, we played more than seventeen games. We'd play a game in New York in the afternoon, and one at night in Baltimore. Each team had a private plane. Segregated luxury."

Above left: Bob Boyd. He invited himself to a Memphis Red Sox tryout camp in the mid '40s. The Red Sox liked what they saw in the left-handed first baseman, and he was immediately signed and farmed out to the Knoxville (Tennessee) Giants of the Negro Southern League. His pay for that season was $175 per month.

Above right: Jackie Robinson. He played only one season (1945) as a member of the Kansas City Monarchs. On a recommendation from manager Frank Duncan, Robinson appeared in the annual East-West Game at shortstop. When league president J.B. Martin received the news of Robinson's signing with the Brooklyn organization, he remarked, "I feel that I speak the sentiments of fifteen million Negroes in America who are with you one hundred per cent and will always remember the day and the date of this great event. I wish Robinson, the Montreal baseball club and all concerned the greatest success."

Right: Willard (Sonny) Brown. As a boy in Shreveport, Louisiana, he used to play baseball until sunset, then find a lighted street and play some more. He joined the Monroe (Louisiana) Monarchs in 1934 and signed with the Kansas City Monarchs as a shortstop in 1935. He was once asked by a minor leaguer, "How do you swing that big forty-ounce bat?" Replied Brown: "I don't swing it, I just lay it on the ball."

Above: (L to R) Wilber Rogan, Robert Boone and Hurley McNair. In a 1946 game between the host Kansas City Monarchs and the Birmingham Black Barons, a dispute broke out between Birmingham manager Tommy Sampson and umpire McNair over a close call at first base. Sampson began pushing McNair, who responded by pulling a knife out of his pocket. Sampson wheeled and made a beeline for his dugout, with McNair close behind waving his blade. Sampson snatched a bat from one of the players and regained the offensive, chasing McNair back across the diamond and whacking him once on the back of his leg. When the brawl was finally broken up, McNair was removed from the field.

Porter Moss. In the 1943 East-West Game, Moss, with two outs in the ninth inning and the West nursing a 2-1 lead, relieved Theolic Smith, who had given up back-to-back singles to Josh Gibson and Howard Easterling. Vic Harris, the next batter, swung at Moss's second pitch, but connected only for a harmless fly ball. The West players and fans mobbed Moss as he headed for the locker room.

going to rid my clubhouse of everything that speaks with an accent. They're trash, they are doing no good and they aren't in place here. They don't fit. They've all got to show me something, and show it quick, or I'm cleaning out the joint. If I have to put up with incompetents, they must at least speak English." (If Harris didn't want assistance from the Cubans, there were several English-speaking Negro league players who would have been glad to help the Senators in their yearly quest to escape the American League basement.)

There were others, though, who recognized that there was a large pool of untapped talent in the Negro leagues. The Senators' owner, Clark Griffith, told *Washington Tribune* reporter Sam Lacy in 1938 that he could envision the day when blacks would be playing in the majors. "There are few big-league magnates," Griffith said, "who are not aware of the fact that the time is not far off when colored players will take their places beside those of other races in the major leagues."

A few years later, Griffith invited Josh Gibson and Buck Leonard of the Washington Homestead Grays to his office for a conversation. Griffith, like other regulars at the Grays' games, had marveled at the hitting exploits of this prodigious pair. After quizzing them about the possibility of playing in the majors, to which both expressed interest, Griffith merely went on to predict that a rough road awaited the first to cross the color line.

Philadelphia Phillies owner Gerry Nugent once told Rollo Wilson of the *Pittsburgh Courier* that blacks had to gain entrance to the minor leagues before the big leagues would consider using them. "Comparisons on ability are made in the minors and the best come to the majors," Nugent said. "Negro players are better, on an average, than most of the white semipro players, and I have no doubts that many of them could stick if they entered the big loops. I, for one, will be glad to see Negro players in organized baseball if and when that time comes."

That time was coming, but for all the supportive words, the Jake Powell incidents, the players' proven ability, nothing came close to illustrating the absurdity of the color line like World War II. It was during the war, in which blacks joined whites

Above: (L to R) Buck O'Neil, Frank Duncan, James (Jew Baby) Floyd, Wilber (Bullet) Rogan. All four enjoyed long careers in the Monarch organization. Duncan came to the Monarchs in 1922 and retired in 1947. O'Neil joined the team in 1938 and remained until it was sold in 1955. Rogan, an original Monarch, signed with the club in 1920 and retired at age forty-nine in 1938. Floyd was the team's trainer from 1920 to 1949.

Below: Larry Doby, with the Newark Eagles in mid-'40s. He was a four-sport star at Eastside High in Paterson, New Jersey. In 1943, Doby, nineteen, was batting .342 for the Newark Eagles and had been selected to play in the East-West Game when he was drafted. He was stationed at the Great Lakes Naval Training Center in Illinois. Doby batted .334 in 1942 while playing second base for the Eagles.

Left: Alex Radcliffe. In 1932 he was with the Chicago American Giants, while his brother, Ted, was playing for the Pittsburgh Crawfords. During a game between the two teams, Ted fired a two-hitter but lost, 1-0, because one of the two hits he allowed was a home run by Alex.

(in separate regiments) in the fight for democracy, that big league baseball became an easy and frequent target. The unarguable point was simply this: if blacks were good enough to die for their country, then they were good enough for the major leagues.

Associated Negro Press reporter Mabray (Doc) Kountze was one of many journalists who continually used the theme in his wartime writing.

"The very fact that colored boys have to organize their own league and their own clubs in order to

Left: Othello Renfroe. He was born in Newark, New Jersey, in 1923. An infielder/catcher, Renfroe was nicknamed "Chappy" after Chappy Gray, a great semipro player. In 1946 Renfroe, while playing for the Kansas City Monarchs, hit three home runs in a game against the Memphis Red Sox.

Below: The Birmingham Black Barons, 1944. Front row (L to R): Johnny Scott, Ed Steele, Ted (Double Duty) Radcliffe, Winfield Welch, Bubber Gipson, Leandy Young. Middle row: Lester Lockett, Lafayette Washington, Alfred Saylor, Tommy Sampson, Lloyd (Pepper) Bassett, Lorenzo (Piper) Davis. Back row: Felix McLaurin, John Britton, Leroy Morney, Artie Wilson, Jimmy Newberry, Butch Huber. Britton joined the Barons in 1943 when the Clowns traded him for Jesse (Hoss) Walker. In 1950, Britton batted .328 for Winnipeg of the Canadian Man-Dak League. He returned to the league in 1951 and batted .310 as a member of the Elwood Giants. In 1952 Britton became the first black to play in the Japanese league when he signed with the Hankyu Braves. In 194 games, he collected 222 hits in 758 at-bats.

Above: During World War II, many army units organized baseball teams. This team featured the home-run hitting of Joe Greene (standing, fourth from left). Before the war, he played for three Negro league clubs, the Atlanta Black Crackers, the Kansas City Monarchs and the Homestead Grays. After the war, he also played with the Cleveland Buckeyes.

Below: Josh Gibson. Photo was taken at East-West Game in 1946, his last appearance in the annual classic. According to photographer Ernest Withers, "There were fifty-one photographers on the field, but Gibson would only pose for a few of us."

gain major league recognition is one of the unpleasant situations of our democracy," Kountze wrote in 1942. "I must remind the most skeptical persons that there were no German-American leagues, no Italian-American leagues, no Polish-American leagues, no French-American leagues. No, ladies and gentleman, we are the only Americans who have to parade our boys around like a circus establishing them somewhat in the class of foreigners who just came over on the boat.

"I'm just puzzled," Kountze added. "They seem to want our boys for the wearing worries of war, but they don't want them sharing the more peaceful pursuits of major league baseball. I just thought I'd write about it to sort of inform some of those folks who keep hammering about the sins of the Axis."

They could man the battlefields, but not the baseball fields of the major leagues. The paradox was becoming increasingly offensive to anyone, white or black, with a social conscience. Ric Roberts of the *Pittsburgh Courier* noted in a 1945 story about the success of the Negro leagues that "the continued rebuff of Negro baseball players by the major white leagues is winning many race-conscious citizens over to our brand of ball — many of them refusing to patronize the lily-white big league games."

(L to R) Unknown, Larry Brown, Verdel Mathis. In addition to having a great arm, Brown, a catcher, was superb at running down and catching foul pops. As one player said, "If Larry took off his mask, you were out. He wasn't in the habit of chasing balls that landed several rows up in the bleachers."

Sympathetic voices also were being heard from on Capitol Hill. As mentioned in the previous chapter, President Roosevelt had established the Fair Employment Practices Commission, which was designed to curtail discrimination in hiring. In the spring of 1945, Representative Vito Marcantonio of New York introduced a resolution in Congress calling for the Secretary of Commerce to investigate baseball's hiring practices. "The purpose of the bill," Marcantonio said, "is to take the whole discussion from within the four walls of the baseball clubs and bring it before the greatest American forum." The resolution read:

"Resolved by the Senate and House of Representatives of the United States of America in Congress assembled that the Secretary of Commerce be and is hereby directed to investigate employment policy and practices of baseball clubs affiliated with the National and American Leagues. The purpose of this investigation shall be to determine the extent of discrimination in employment of baseball players because of race, color or

The Baltimore Elite Giants, 1944. Standing (L to R): Roy Campanella, Lester Lockett, Unknown, Thomas Glover, Lamon Yokeley, Wesley (Doc) Dennis, William Hoskins, Andy Porter. Kneeling: Unknown, Felton Snow, Bill Harvey, Henry Kimbro, Norman Robinson, Thomas (Peewee) Butts, Frank Russell, George Scales. As manager for Ponce of the Puerto Rican Winter League, Scales, a native of Montgomery, Alabama, led his teams to four consecutive pennants in the early '40s. He won his last flag in 1946-47, giving him a total of five pennants, a league record.

The East All-Star team, 1946. Kneeling (L to R): Henry Kimbro, Jonas Gaines, Murray Watkins, Bill Ricks, Gene Benson, Leon Day, Sam Bankhead, Howard Easterling. Standing: Felton Snow, Josh Gibson, Monte Irvin, Buck Leonard, Raleigh (Biz) Mackey, Pat Scantlebury, Lennie Pearson, Larry Doby, Fernando Pedroso, Silvio Garcia, Vic Harris. The East lost to the West, 4-1, before 45,474 at Comiskey Park. For Gibson, who went 0-for-3, it was his final appearance in the East-West Game.

creed."

In August of 1945, New York Mayor Fiorello La Guardia assembled a ten-man committee to study the color line. The group's purpose was to "give this one subject thorough study and make specific recommendations to the major leagues." Among the members were sportswriter Arthur Daley, entertainer and longtime Negro League backer Bill

Robinson, New York Yankee general manager Larry MacPhail and Branch Rickey.

As the committee discovered, Larry MacPhail, along with many other baseball men, took a dim view of integration, mainly because they figured it would translate into a loss of revenue. The Yankees were making $100,000 a year in the mid-'40s by

Bill Cash. An outstanding catcher for the Philadelphia Stars, he was earning $500 a month when signed by the Chicago White Sox. During several years in the Chicago farm system, his monthly salary never topped $325.

John Richard Wright. A former member of the Homestead Grays, he joined the Montreal Royals with Jackie Robinson in 1946, but his career in the International League was short-lived. He pitched in only two games before being sent down to Three Rivers of the Canadian-American League. There he had a record of 12-8 and finished sixth in the league with 105 strikeouts.

renting Yankee Stadium and their minor league parks to Negro league teams. If the best and the brightest of the black stars were to join the major leagues, he reasoned, teams like the New York Black Yankees and the New York Cubans might not need to rent a big house like the one Ruth built. Said MacPhail: "There aren't too many players of major league caliber in the Negro National and American Leagues, so if they should lose their best players to the majors, their own clubs would be hurt at the gate." And MacPhail would have to share the pain.

Organizations outside of government also began getting involved in the cause during the '40s. The Young Communist League circulated petitions and collected more than 100,000 signatures calling for

blacks to be allowed into the major leagues, while the National Maritime Union unanimously adopted a resolution "demanding a square deal for Negro ballplayers in the major leagues."

Another plea came from the chairman of the National Athletic Commission (the International Workers Order) who sent a letter to Chicago Cubs owner Phil Wrigley in which he wrote: "I speak authoritatively for my organization of over 155,000 members, of whom several thousand are Negroes. Mr. Wrigley, many of our boys, Negro and white, are giving their lives on the sands of North Africa and around the world so that democracy may live. They are carrying on our fight against Hitlerism and its vile ideology of race superiority. You and other club owners have the opportunity of serving your

(Clockwise from left) Gread (Lefty) McKinnis, Lonnie Summers, Jesse Douglas, Art (Superman) Pennington of the Chicago American Giants. They were the heart and soul of manager Winfield Welch's 1949 Western division championship club which met the Baltimore Elite Giants in the World Series that season. Without the services of Pennington, who had signed with the Dodgers, the American Giants lost the fall classic in four straight games.

country in a very important manner at this critical time. I urge you to hire Negro ball players in the major leagues now."

The chances of Phil Wrigley or any other owner signing a black player increased in 1944 with the death of Judge Landis, who'd helped perpetuate the major leagues history of discrimination for more than twenty years. It didn't take long for his successor, Kentucky Senator Albert (Happy) Chandler, to raise hopes for change. Shortly after he was appointed by the owners, Chandler was

questioned about the issue of allowing blacks into the majors. He responded, "If they can fight and die on Okinawa, Guadalcanal, in the South Pacific, they can play baseball in America."

In early April of 1945, sports editor Joe Bostic of the *People's Voice* newspaper in New York decided the time was right to gauge the cumulative effect of the forces that had been working toward integration. Barging into the Dodgers' wartime spring training facility at Bear Mountain, New York, he demanded that veteran Negro leaguers Dave (Showboat) Thomas and Terris McDuffie receive tryouts. Dodger President Branch Rickey, whose secret search for a candidate to cross the color line was already under way, reluctantly allowed the players to work out. For forty-five minutes, Rickey watched as Thomas, a thirty-nine year old first baseman for the New York Cubans, and McDuffie,

Chicago American Giant players, 1948.

Harry Rhodes

Sunday games if it didn't begin fair hiring practices. Its arm sufficiently twisted, the team agreed to offer a tryout to three Negro leaguers. *Pittsburgh Courier* sportswriter Wendell Smith, an outspoken critic of the color line, readily agreed to supply the players.

On April 16, Smith escorted outfielder Sam Jethroe of the Cleveland Buckeyes, second baseman Marvin Williams of the Philadelphia Stars and shortstop Jackie Robinson of the Kansas City Monarchs to Fenway Park for their "opportunity." With manager Joe Cronin and coach Hugh Duffy observing, the talented trio went through batting and fielding practice. "There is no doubt about it that they are ballplayers," Duffy said. "They looked good to me." Despite the encouraging comment, the players were dismissed with a "don't call us, we'll call you." The call, of course, never came.

Nevertheless, the press was not entirely disheartened. After all, not since Charlie Grant had worked out with John McGraw's Baltimore Orioles in 1902 had there been a black player in a major league camp. The two ventures also generated a great deal of publicity. "Newspapers throughout the nation have reported on the two incidents," wrote Willie Bea Harmon, sports editor of the

Riley Stewart

a thirty-six year-old pitcher for the Newark Eagles, went through their paces. The Dodger executive was unimpressed.

"I would not be interested in Thomas if he were twenty-four instead of thirty-four [the age he gave]," Rickey said. Of McDuffie, he said, "He has good control, but does not follow through on any delivery. It might take considerable time before he broke that habit." Rickey, of course, had his own blueprint for breaking the color line and wasn't about to have a newspaper reporter alter it.

Not long after the Bear Mountain episode, another tryout was arranged in Boston, where pressure was being brought on the Red Sox to begin signing black players. A city councilman named Isadore Muchnick had threatened to block issuance of a permit the team needed to play

McErvin

Clyde McNeal

Rhodes was a first baseman and pitcher. McNeal was an accomplished hitter whom Ted Radcliffe called one of the best ball players that he'd ever managed. John Williams (page 266) was a policeman from Hot Springs, Arkansas, before entering baseball.

Jake Tolbert

Kansas City Call. "Every time a colored player dons a suit in one of the major league camps he breaks down one of the bars that keeps him from playing on major league teams. Muchnick is a white man who has interested himself in the unwarranted discrimination against colored players . . . . There are others like him. Let us continue to fight."

The fight continued, but it also grew more frustrating. With so many major leaguers in the armed services, there was hope throughout the war that Negro league players might be used to replenish the labor supply. That hope was virtually dashed in 1945 when the St. Louis Browns signed Pete Gray, a one-armed outfielder.

"How do you think I felt when I saw a one-armed outfielder?" veteran pitcher Chet Brewer asked.

As hopeless as the situation seemed to Brewer and his colleagues, there was a discreet movement under way to bring down the barrier. Principally, it involved two men, although by no means was it a two-man job.

It was on August 28, 1945, exactly two weeks after Japan's surrender had closed the curtain on World War II, that Branch Rickey first met Jackie Robinson. Dodger scout Clyde Sukeforth had been directed to bring Robinson to the team's offices at 215 Montague Street in Brooklyn. Neither Robinson nor Sukeforth knew precisely why they had been summoned, though Sukeforth had his suspicions. Jackie was under the impression that he was being courted to play for the Brooklyn Brown Dodgers, Rickey's entry in the new United States Baseball League. Branch Rickey, "The Mahatma," as he was respectfully known, had his own agenda.

Wesley Branch Rickey was born December 9, 1881, on a farm in Lucasville, Ohio. He was raised in a fundamentalist family, and he maintained his devout beliefs throughout his life, even refusing to play Sunday games during his brief major league

Jesse Williams

Chicago American Giant players, 1948.

John Williams

career. As a part-time catcher/outfielder for the St. Louis Browns and the New York Highlanders, Rickey compiled a .240 average from 1905 to 1907. Given his batting average, his managers, Jimmy McAleer of the Browns and Clark Griffith of the Highlanders (later Yankees), probably weren't overly upset about his weekly sabbatical. After retiring in 1907, the serious-minded Rickey, who previously had coached baseball at Ohio Wesleyan University, attained his law degree from the University of Michigan, where he also coached the baseball team. He was named manager of the Browns in 1913, a post he held through the 1915 season. He became manager of the St. Louis Cardinals in 1919 and remained in that position until 1925, when he was named the team's general manager.

During his ten years as field general, Rickey's teams never finished higher than third place, but he quickly found his niche in his new role, building the "Cards" into a National League powerhouse that won five pennants and three World

Hank Thompson. In 1943, at age seventeen, he joined the Kansas City Monarchs. The following year he was drafted into the army and later was a machine gunner with the 1695th Combat Engineers, fighting at the Battle of the Bulge. In 1949 he hit .303 in fifty-five games for Jersey City of the International League.

The Monarchs saw this sign in 1946 while making a tour through Oklahoma. The proprietor of the cafe evidently wanted to cash in on the fine culinary reputation of black people.

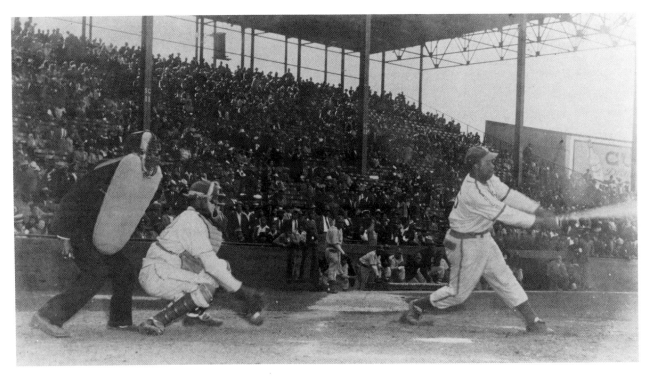

Action during a Kansas City Monarchs-Memphis Red Sox game in 1942.

Hank Baylis (third from left). Like many players, he was a versatile athlete who played baseball in the summer and basketball in the winter. A native of Topeka, Kansas, he played baseball with the Baltimore Elite Giants, Birmingham Black Barons, Chicago American Giants and Kansas City Monarchs.

(L to R) Luis Diaz, Luis A. Marquez, Hiram Arroyo and Mario Perez, 1941. They played for the Aguadilla Stars of the Puerto Rican League. Marquez later played for the Homestead Grays.

Series' over the next ten years. Their success was due in no small part to Rickey's development of baseball's first farm system — a business arrangement whereby specific minor league teams were used to groom players for a major league team. It was an innovation that soon was adopted throughout the majors.

By 1945, Rickey, who'd left the Cardinals three years earlier to become the Dodgers' president and general manager, was ready to begin implementing another "innovation." He set his plan in motion by entering a Brooklyn team in the United States Baseball League, a Negro circuit that was formed in early 1945 and also included franchises in Pittsburgh, Philadelphia, Detroit, Chicago and Toledo. Rickey stated that he was becoming involved because "I am interested in renting our park," and "as an individual I am interested in the successful operation of a sound Negro baseball league." In announcing his commitment, he also took a swipe at the Negro leagues, declaring that they were "in the zone of a racket," a thinly veiled reference to the preponderance of numbers

Clyde Nelson. While playing for the Indianapolis Clowns in a 1949 game in Philadelphia, he went back to catch a pop-up behind first base and suddenly fell to the ground. The players rushed to his side, but were unable to revive him; Nelson was dead of an apparent heart attack.

Above: The Memphis Red Sox with Lionel Hampton, 1949. Standing to the right of Hampton is Willie Wells. "Wells was one of the greatest shortstops to ever spike a baseball diamond," said Cool Papa Bell. "He could hit with power, run, throw and tag." In 1950, at age forty-five, Wells batted .304 for Winnipeg of the Man-Dak League. He batted .310 in 1951.

Below: James (Lefty) LaMarque. He started in Potosi, Missouri, pitching for a mixed team. Kansas City Monarchs secretary William Dismukes read about LaMarque in a St. Louis newspaper and invited him to try out for the Monarchs in 1941. LaMarque played with K.C. from 1941 to 1950. Between 1946 and 1948 he pitched in fifty-three Cuban Winter League games, posting a record of 18-13.

bankers in the leagues.

Longtime Negro league watchers were convinced that Rickey's motivation was simply to cash in on the Negro baseball boom; that, like promoters/booking agents Abe Saperstein and Eddie Gottlieb, he was more interested in exploitation than in the "operation of a sound Negro baseball league." His sanctimonious remarks regarding the established leagues' unsavory elements were easily dismissed, since the owner of the new league's Pittsburgh franchise was none other than Gus Greenlee, whose numbers' money had resuscitated the Negro National League in the early '30s. Nevertheless, Rickey had developed a perfect cover for his plan.

Throughout 1945, Dodger scouts combed the Negro leagues, supposedly in search of players for the Brooklyn Brown Dodgers. Rickey sifted through glowing reports on Buck Leonard, Josh Gibson, Satchel Paige, Roy Campanella, Lorenzo (Piper) Davis, Minnie Minoso, Sam Jethroe, Silvio Garcia and Jackie Robinson. He was impressed by many, but he was captivated by the Monarchs' rookie shortstop.

Right: Gentry Jessup runs the bases during a Cuban Winter League game. Jessup was an outstanding pitcher for the Chicago American Giants. He played in Cuba only one season (1946-47), finishing with a 5-3 record in sixteen appearances.

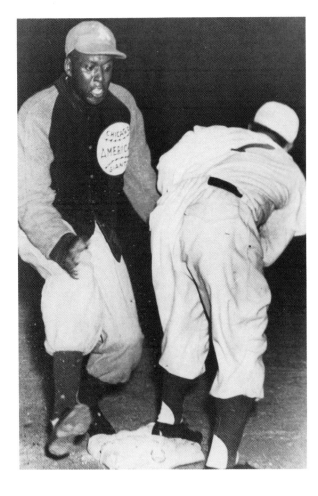

Below left: John O'Neil (left) and William Dismukes. In 1911, Dismukes pitched three games in two days for the Indianapolis ABCs, winning them all, including one that lasted twelve innings. He pitched a no-hitter against the Chicago American Giants in 1912 and duplicated the feat versus the Chicago Giants in May of 1915. In 1916, in what was billed as the "World Series," he defeated the Chicago American Giants three times to lead the ABCs to the title.

Below right: Thomas (Peewee) Butts. He entered professional baseball in 1938 as a member of the Atlanta Black Crackers of the Negro Southern League. He was such an outstanding shortstop that he, along with Willie Wells, became the measuring stick against which prospects were compared. To be referred to as "another Peewee Butts or Willie Wells" was considered high praise.

Above: Herb Souell. He went to the Kansas City Monarchs' second team in 1939 after playing with the Monroe (Louisiana) Drillers, where he went by the name of Herb Cyrus. Toward the end of his career, after losing much of his hair, he was known as "Baldy."

Left: John Hundley. The St. Louis native began his career as a catcher with the Claybrook (Arkansas) Tigers in 1935. In 1943 he joined the Cleveland Buckeyes, signing for a salary of $250 per month. Three weeks after signing that contract Hundley received a letter informing him that he had been drafted into the armed services — at a salary of $52 per month.

Allen Bryant (front row, shirtless). He was a former Kansas City Monarch who fought in the South Pacific during World World II. According to a book entitled *The Negro Soldier in World War,* "Propagandists emphasized racial discrimination of one kind or another and unfortunately were able to refer to the facts that the black American, supposedly a citizen, was in many states denied the ballot; that he was 'Jim Crowed' on many of the railroads and public carriers, although charged first-class fare for transportation; that he was denied admission to most public places of amusement, hotels and the like."

Gene Baker. "The most interesting thing I remember about my first game in the National League," Baker recalled, "was that it was the first time in my career that I had ever played second base."

Herb Souell gets a few words of encouragement from his wife, Gladys, before the start of a California Winter League game in 1947. He played the following winter in Puerto Rico as a member of Ponce. With the Kansas City Monarchs, he was named the top defensive player of the 1942 World Series in which K.C. defeated the powerful Homestead Grays.

Like so many other blacks, the story of Jackie Robinson begins on a plantation. He was born in Cairo, Georgia, on January 31, 1919, the youngest of Jerry and Mallie Robinson's five children. His father left the family when Jackie was only six months old, and it wasn't long after that that his mother, children in tow, moved to Pasadena, California. He grew up poor in a mixed neighborhood, but, like his brother, Mack, an outstanding track star who won the silver medal in the 200-meter dash at the '36 Olympics, Jackie used his versatile athletic ability to escape the anonymity of his impoverished surroundings.

At Pasadena Junior College and then UCLA, Robinson, 5′11½″, 190 pounds, was a standout in football, basketball, track and baseball. It was on the gridiron, though, where he achieved his

greatest collegiate acclaim, teaming at UCLA with All-America Kenny Washington, whose father, Edgar, had played for the 1920 Kansas City Monarchs, to give the Bruins one of the best backfields in the country. After leaving school in 1941 because of financial difficulties, Robinson found employment as a coach for the National Youth Administration and as a member of the Los Angeles Bulldogs, a semipro football team. In the spring of '42 he was drafted into the army and went on to spend two and a half sometimes stormy years on limited duty because of bone chips in his ankle. He was stationed at Fort Hood, Texas, in June of 1944, when he refused a bus driver's order to "get to the back of the bus." Even though the army

recently had ordered that military buses be desegregated, Robinson, a lieutenant, was charged with insubordination and court-martialed. He won his case, however, and received an honorable discharge in November. He landed a job with the Kansas City Monarchs the following spring and was in the process of compiling some impressive statistics when Clyde Sukeforth approached him before a game at Comiskey Park.

Branch Rickey wasn't looking for just a purebred baseball player as he plowed through his scouts'

Left: Buck Leonard applies tag to a New York Cubans player during a game in 1946. "Leonard was the first baseman that I admired the most," said the Monarchs' Buck O'Neil, himself a first baseman. In 1953, at age forty-six, Leonard batted .333 in the Piedmont League, his only year in minor league baseball. On August 7, 1972, he was inducted into the Baseball Hall of Fame. "The greatest thrill of my life," Leonard said.

Above: (L to R) Joseph Taylor, Clyde McNeil, Jesse Douglas and Arthur (Superman) Pennington of the Chicago American Giants. Manager Jim (Candy) Taylor first saw McNeil play when he was a junior in high school. The next year Taylor sent him a contract to play for the American Giants for $360 a month. Although he had twenty-four scholarship offers to play basketball, including one from Notre Dame, McNeil signed with the American Giants.

Frank Barnes (left) and Connie Johnson. Both were from the South, played for the Monarchs, and made it to the major leagues. Barnes played with the Cardinals, while Johnson became the first black to pitch a season opener for the Baltimore Orioles.

Left: Jackie Robinson. He used to tell his black teammates and other black players: "The kids are playing baseball as never before, because now there is a future in the game. The gates have opened, and, given time, this is one game we will rule." Jackie played his first major league game on April 15, 1947, against the Boston Braves in front of 25,623 at Ebbets Field in Brooklyn.

Below: Dan Bankhead. A pitcher, he was the highest-paid player on the Memphis Red Sox in the late '40s, earning more money than catcher Larry Brown and outfielder Neil Robinson, who were both superior players. Unlike Brown and Robinson, however, Bankhead was not hesitant about asking for a raise. When Bankhead made it to the Dodgers in 1947, he hired an agent to negotiate his contract. Appearing in a mere fifty-two major league games, he nonetheless obtained contracts to endorse both the Stacy Adams and Stadler shoe companies.

reports. He knew, as did anyone familiar with Negro baseball, that there was a bountiful reservoir of talent from which to draw. In Rickey's mind, though, the task at hand required more than the ability to hit, run and field. Rickey was searching for a man who could do all that while withstanding perhaps the greatest pressure any athlete would ever face. He knew full well the burden that awaited this man — the torrents of racial abuse from opponents and fans, the frequent knockdown pitches, the Jim Crow accommodations in certain cities, and the encumbrance of living day-to-day under the press's microscope.

For many reasons, Robinson was Rickey's man. In his extensive background check on Robinson, Rickey saw a young man who was accustomed to interacting with whites, having grown up in a mixed neighborhood and competed with and against them all his life. He saw a religious man

Jose Fernandez. A native of Cuba, he served as manager for Syd Pollock's Cuban Giants before becoming the skipper for Alex Pompez's New York Cubans. He was joined on the New York Cubans by his brother, Rudolfo, a pitcher.

who lived clean and played hard, a fierce and fearless man who was quick to stand up when challenged. He saw an intense competitor who couldn't tolerate losing. He saw anger and pride, toughness and intelligence. He saw the will and the determination to succeed.

Jackie Robinson and Clyde Sukeforth walked through the doors at 215 Montague Street, stepped into the elevator and rode to the fourth floor. It was August 28, 1945, and Brooklyn was in the middle of a suffocating heat wave. For Jackie, the anticipation of the unknown made it seem even hotter. To be called to a meeting by Branch Rickey, one of the most revered men in baseball, was downright unnerving.

Jackie sat down across a desk from the Dodger president, and for the first several minutes, the two of them said little. It was Rickey who began to

expand upon their introduction, asking, "Are you a good player?" Sukeforth, a former catcher, fielded the question: "He is the Dodgers' kind of player."

Rickey eventually revealed the true purpose of the meeting, telling Robinson that he was being considered as a prospect for the Dodger organization. In a scene often since recounted, Rickey then proceeded to give Robinson a crash course in what lay ahead for the twentieth-century's first man to cross the color line. Jackie sat and listened as Rickey acted out a series of hostile roles: the racist player and fan, insulting him with the most vile remarks; the hotel clerk at a Jim Crow hotel, telling him "his kind" wasn't welcome; the antagonistic umpire, never giving him a fair call, baiting him into a confrontation. After several hours, Robinson finally had heard enough.

"Mr. Rickey, do you want a ballplayer who's afraid to fight back?" he asked.

"I want a ballplayer with guts enough NOT to fight back," Rickey responded. "Other people are going to say worse things to you. And we can't fight prejudice by force. We must recognize what we're

Jim Pendleton. He started out as a shortstop with the Asheville (North Carolina) Blues of the Negro Southern League in 1947. The following year he joined the Chicago American Giants of the Negro American League. Pendleton played 120 games in 1953 with the Milwaukee Braves, mostly as an outfielder. Often shifting between the majors and minors, he ended his career with the Houston Colt 45's in 1962.

up against, and fight the problem with good will and moral courage. You must be the one man in baseball who can't lose his temper. You're not going to like all the umpires' decisions. And all the insults. Swallow them and grin. Because if you get in a brawl, Jackie, people will stigmatize your people because of you. Out on the field you've got to be almost a saint."

That was very important to Rickey: Jackie's willingness to "turn the other cheek" in the face of manifest hatred. Before he left the Dodger offices that day, Robinson agreed to Rickey's demands, and in return for his compliance he received a contract for $600 a month and a $3,500 signing bonus to play for the Dodgers Triple A affiliate, the Montreal Royals. Rickey had one other demand: Robinson was to tell no one, except for his mother and fiancee, Rachel, what had transpired at the meeting.

The Dodger president had hoped to delay the announcement until after the end of the football season, when the story would receive the most media attention. Furthermore, he was interested in signing several other Negro league players, among them catcher Roy Campanella of the Baltimore Elite Giants, pitcher Don Newcombe of the Newark Eagles and John Wright of the Washington Homestead Grays, and felt that one general announcement would be best. Fiorello La Guardia, however, forced his hand.

In late October, New York's mayor wanted to

Sam Hairston. "Sam was the kind of ball player that you could play anywhere you wanted," said Don Gutteridge, who managed Hairston when he played for the Colorado Springs Sky Sox. The MVP of the Western League in 1953, Hairston also won that league's batting title in 1955 with a .350 average. He had two sons, John and Jerry, who played in the major leagues.

release his committee's report, which called for the major leagues to begin providing "equality of opportunity for all." Rickey, who did not want it to appear that he was signing Robinson because of political pressure, requested that the mayor delay his announcement. La Guardia consented, and Rickey told Robinson, who was in New York, to fly to Montreal the following day.

AIEA Naval Barracks team, 1944. Shortly before baseball was integrated, blacks and whites were playing together on service teams. This club had Barney McCosky (front) of the Detroit Tigers, Johnny Lucadello (sitting, fourth from left) of the St. Louis Browns, and Hugh Casey (standing, fourth from right) of the Brooklyn Dodgers. Jim Zapp (standing, second from right) played for the Birmingham Black Barons from 1948 to 1950. He batted .330, slugged twenty-one home runs and collected 136 RBI's for Paris (Texas) of the Mississippi-Ohio Valley League in 1951.

Ball players stand on dock after arriving in a Latin American country. That's Josh Gibson shaking hands with a local promoter. In 1943, Gibson hit 10 home runs in Griffith Stadium, a single-season stadium record.

Left: Roy Partlow. He was among several Homestead Grays who served in World War II. Joining him in the service were Howard Easterling, Matthew Carlisle, Johnny Wright, Garnet Blair, Frank Williams, Wilmer Fields and Jerry Gibson.

Larry Doby. He was the first black player in the American League, making his debut with the Cleveland Indians on July 5, 1947. "[Cleveland manager] Lou Boudreau lined up all the players and one by one introduced me to each one," Doby recalled. "All the guys but three shook my hand. Bill Veeck, owner of the Cleveland club, as quickly as possible got rid of these fellows."

Ernie Banks. A Dallas native, Banks was playing semipro baseball with the Amarillo Colts when the Kansas City Monarchs signed him in 1950. He was hitting .380 with the Monarchs in 1953, when the Chicago Cubs bought his contract. The opportunity thrilled Banks. "I think I can make it in the majors," he said. "I'm sure going to try. They told me last week that the Cubs were going to buy my contract from K.C. I've been too excited to sleep much since." Edgar Munzel, a Cub official, stated, "I believe Banks is a cinch .300 hitter in that he's the best batter against breaking stuff of any rookie I've ever seen come to the big leagues, and I'm not barring anybody."

The story was front-page news all across the country, and the media continued to buzz about Rickey and Robinson throughout the off-season. Most supported the move, recognizing that it was long overdue. Naturally, the black press was most laudatory, hailing Rickey for his "democratic action" and offering encouragement to Robinson. "Wherever he goes and whatever he faces," wrote *Kansas City Call* sportswriter John Johnson, "millions of American Negroes will be pulling for him,

There were more than two dozen newspaper and radio men in the offices of the Montreal Royals on Tuesday, October 23. Representing Royal management were team president Hector Racine, vice-president Romeo Gavreau and Branch Rickey, Jr., who headed the Dodger farm system. Racine delivered the proclamation: Jackie Robinson had signed a contract to play for the Montreal Royals in 1946.

After a mad scramble to inform their employers of this startling news, the press reassembled to hear Racine's comments. "We made this step for two reasons," he explained. "First, we are signing this boy because we think of him primarily as a ballplayer. Secondly, we think it a point of fairness."

Satchel Paige. In 1942 he became the highest paid player in baseball with an annual salary of more than $40,000. Alberta Gilmore, secretary for the Monarchs, stated, "We used to stop his income earnings at the $12,000 level, and then give him the balance of his pay under the table to keep him out of tax problems."

Above: The Memphis Red Sox get together at a football game between two Memphis Negro high schools, Manassas and Booker T. Washington. Back row (L to R): Marlin Carter, Ted Radcliffe. Middle row: Willie Hutchinson (wearing glasses), Frank Pearson (second from left), Larry Brown (second from right), Homer (Goose) Curry (far right). Front: James Ford. Ford, who played second base in the 1941 East-West game, saw his career threatened when he became infected with rabbit fever while hunting in the mid '40s. His illness might have been fatal were it not for the development in 1939 of penicillin.

Below: Homestead Grays, 1946. (L to R) Dan Wilson, Luis Marquez, Matthew Carlisle, Sam Bankhead and Buck Leonard. Wilson, a native of St. Louis, was not a big man but he could hit with power. Leonard went from making two and three dollars a game when he started out to being the third highest-paid player in Negro baseball, right behind Satchel Paige and Josh Gibson.

Above left: Larry Brown and Lionel Hampton. During the off-season, Brown worked at the Gayaso Hotel in Memphis, which was located on Main and McCall Streets. He loved to socialize and enjoyed meeting celebrities who stayed at the hotel.

Above right: Josh Johnson. He was a right-handed hitter who pulled everything to the left side early in his career. While serving in World War II, he learned how to hit to all fields, which came in handy when he rejoined the Homestead Grays after the War. When the Grays met the Chicago American Giants, manager Jim Taylor put the shift on for Johnson, moving his second baseman to the shortstop side of the base. To Taylor's surprise, Johnson rapped a sharp single to right. He was a graduate of Cheyney State College in Cheyney, Pennsylvania, and received a Master's degree in education from Penn State in 1941.

Below: The Vargas Team (Caracas, Venezuela), 1947-48. Standing: Verdel Mathis (second from left), Don Newcombe (fifth from left), John Wright (sixth from left). Front row: Harry (Suitcase) Simpson (far left). Simpson said the hardest part of being a major leaguer was that "all your friends thought you were rich and were constantly hitting you up for a loan."

Monarch players and friends enjoy a night out, 1946. Johnny Scott (far right) was born in Magnolia, Arkansas. The 5'10″ left-handed hitter joined the Shreveport (Louisiana) Sports in 1938 and then played with the Muskegon (Michigan) Reds from 1939 to 1943. After a year with the Birmingham Black Barons, he signed with the Kansas City Monarchs in 1945.

for they know he is their pathfinder, pioneering in organized baseball, making way for future Negro ballplayers not yet toddlers."

Somewhat dimming the glorious moment was the immediate reaction of Kansas City Monarchs co-owner Tom Baird, who received no compensation for Robinson. "We won't take it lying down," he said. "Robinson signed a contract with us last year and I feel that he is our property. If [Commissioner] Chandler lets Montreal and

Brooklyn get away with this he's really starting a mess."

Baird's comments were described as "the most interesting" by the *New York Post*. "It had been generally felt that the revolutionary move would be universally hailed by Negro baseball as the long-sought opening wedge into the big leagues," the story said.

Baird, under pressure, quickly retracted his remarks. One day later he said, "I am happy to

Harry (Suitcase) Simpson (left) and Jesse Williams in Puerto Rico. When Williams, from Henderson, Texas, became the Monarchs' starting shortstop in 1939, he had been playing the game for only two years — one professionally. Simpson, who played for the Philadelphia Stars, first joined the Negro National League in 1945 as a pitcher with the Cincinnati-Indianapolis Clowns.

Andy Porter. The Little Rock, Arkansas, native joined the Nashville Elite Giants in 1932 and remained with them until 1939. He then spent several seasons in Tampico, Mexico, before returning to the Elite Giants in 1943. Standing 6'3", he was a hard thrower who also played for the Indianapolis Clowns in 1948-49.

Quincy Trouppe. In 1943 Jorge Pasquel, president of the Mexican League, struck a deal with the United States government in order to bring Trouppe and Theolic Smith, who were eligible for the draft, to Mexico. According to Trouppe, the agreement called for Mexico to lend the United States 80,000 workers to fill the manpower shortage caused by the war in return for allowing the two players to play ball in Mexico.

Left: (L to R) William (Sonny) Randall, LeRoy Coates, Isaiah White. Randall and Coates had been members of the Homestead Grays before being drafted and joining the Great Lakes Naval Varsity in 1944.

know that Jackie Robinson has been selected to play in the big leagues. It is a well-deserved advancement for the Negro race. He has my best wishes for his success. [The Monarchs] have no wish to hold any player down." In truth, Robinson had no written agreement with the Monarchs, only a verbal one for the '45 season. And even if they did have his signature on a contract for '46, Rickey likely would have ignored it, given his contempt for the Negro leagues. When Senators owner Clark Griffith told Rickey the Dodgers should have

Above: Herb (Doc) Bracken. A native of St. Louis, Missouri, he'd had experience with the St. Louis Giants before joining the Great Lakes Club. Bracken played for the Cleveland Buckeyes after getting his discharge from the navy.

Left: (L to R) Leon Triado, Antonio Aponte, Robert Clark. In 1938, when Puerto Rico formed its winter league, the only Americans invited to participate were members of the Negro leagues. During the 1945-46 season, Clark, a catcher who'd debuted in the early 1920s with the Richmond Giants, managed San Juan to the league championship.

Below: Jim Brown. A member of the Birmingham Black Barons, he is shown here during World War II as a member of the Great Lakes Naval Varsity.

Above: Booker McDaniel. When his mother died, McDaniel and his three brothers (the oldest being 16) were forced to raise themselves. Each brother took a job in the community and around the house. Booker's job was to do the wash. He became so adept at it that it was said he could give any housewife in Morrilton, Arkansas, a run for her money in the laundry department.

Below: (L to R) William Harridge, president of the American League; Judge Kenesaw Mountain Landis, commissioner of baseball; and John Heydler, president of the National League. The powers of baseball are pictured at a meeting in Chicago in December of 1931. Both Landis and Heydler maintained that there was no such thing as a color line in major league baseball.

compensated the Monarchs for Robinson, Rickey responded, "I have not signed a player from what I regard as an organized league."

Publicly, other Negro league owners applauded the signing of Robinson. To do otherwise would have created the impression that they were putting their bankbooks ahead of social progress. As Newark Eagles owner Effa Manley said, "We were in no position to protest and [Rickey] knew it. The fans would never have forgiven us." Privately, though, they shared the same fear that triggered Baird's initial reaction. What would become of their business, which had taken so many years to build into a profitable venture, if the major leagues seized their most important assets? They were about to find out.

(L to R) Herb Souell, Connie Johnson, Ted Strong, Willard Brown, Hilton Smith, (all women unknown). Johnson stated, "We would take the entire team, go into a night spot and someone would announce that the Kansas City Monarchs were in the place, and we would have a table full of ladies."

Chapter 9

Before the 1946 season began, Branch Rickey reached into the Negro leagues three more times, signing Roy Campanella of the Baltimore Elite Giants, Don Newcombe of the Newark Eagles and John Wright, who'd played for the Washington Homestead Grays before completing a tour of duty in the Navy. Shortly after the season started, he struck again, taking Roy Partlow from the Philadelphia Stars. All were signed to minor league contracts, all without compensation to their teams. Clearly, if the leagues were going to survive, even for a little while, they were going to have to stop the wholesale piracy.

"Was Mr. Rickey truthful when he said there was no organized Negro baseball league?" asked *Kansas City Call* sports editor John Johnson soon after Jackie Robinson signed with the Royals. "If this is true . . . then Negro baseball should organize to protect itself. A club can spend a lot of money in developing and training a ball player. If a baseball magnate wants a player, let him pay the price. This is the American way."

The owners took Johnson's point to heart and soon had each player's name on a standardized contract. With that measure of protection in place, the leagues sailed through the '46 season in the wake of wartime prosperity, the immediate effect of integration proving negligible. As Robinson and his compatriots tested their skills in the minors, the Negro leagues continued to reap the profits from booming attendance. The East-West Game drew

45,474, an increase of almost 14,000 over the '45 game. A second all-star game, staged at Griffith Stadium in Washington, D.C., wasn't nearly as successful as the Comiskey Park extravaganza, but it did draw 16,000. The Newark Eagles, led by Leon Day, Larry Doby and Monte Irvin, capped the season with a seven-game victory over the Kansas City Monarchs in the World Series.

Despite the continued good fortune, there wasn't a player in either league who wasn't casting a wary eye on Jackie Robinson's performance in 1946. Many among them were of the opinion that Branch Rickey could have selected a better player. Robinson had played only one year in the Negro leagues. To the players he had left behind he was only a rookie, a talented one surely, but nevertheless thought by some to be too inexperienced for the challenge ahead. Make no mistake, they were thrilled that *somebody* was getting the opportunity, but they didn't want their big chance possibly undermined by someone who wasn't the best they had to offer.

"How would you feel seeing a rookie selected?" asked outfielder Jimmie Crutchfield, who'd broken into the leagues in 1930. Veteran infielder Pat Patterson said he could name "five or six players that were better" than Robinson. And Jesse Williams, Jackie's Monarch teammate, said, "He was a good ballplayer, but he wasn't the best ballplayer we had." Still, Williams conceded that Robinson "was the best for that particular role he

The Baltimore Elite Giants, 1949. Standing (L to R): Joe Black, Luther Ferrell, Robert Davis, Lennie Pearson, William Byrd, Alfred Wilmore, Robert Romby, Johnny Hayes, James (Junior) Gilliam, Jesse (Hoss) Walker. Seated: L. Davis, Lester Lockett, S. Rodgers, Henry Kimbro, Vic Harris, Hank Baylis, Frazier Robinson, Frank Russell, Thomas (Peewee) Butts, Leon Day. They beat the Chicago American Giants to win the Negro American League championship.

played." Within the league, it was felt that a better choice could have been made. Names often mentioned were Monte Irvin of the Newark Eagles, Willard Brown and Bonnie Serrell of the Monarchs, Sam Jethroe of the Cleveland Buckeyes, Artie Wilson of the Birmingham Black Barons and even Satchel Paige, who at age forty was still one of the top pitchers in the league.

Bob Feller, who had faced Robinson during a barnstorming tour, also expressed skepticism about

his ability. "He will be in a tough spot," said the ace of the Cleveland Indians pitching staff. "I'm not prejudiced against him, either, and I hope he makes good. But, frankly, I don't think he will."

It didn't take long for Jackie to begin earning the respect of those who doubted him. In his first game with Montreal, before a crowd of more than 25,000 at Jersey City's Roosevelt Stadium, Robinson cracked four hits, including a home run, drove in four runs, scored four runs and stole two bases to

Birmingham Black Barons, 1948. (L to R) Herman Bell, Lloyd (Pepper) Bassett, William Greason, Joe Scott, Roosevelt (bat boy), Jehosa Heard, Wiley Griggs, Lorenzo (Piper) Davis, Alonzo Perry, Jim Newberry, Jim Zapp, Ed Steel, Johnny Britton, Art Wilson, Nathaniel Pollard, Unknown, William Powell, Willie Mays. After defeating the Kansas City Monarchs for the Negro American League pennant, the Barons lost the World Series to the Homestead Grays, four games to one. Their only victory came in Game 3, which they won, 4-3, on Willie Mays' RBI single in the ninth inning.

lead the Royals to a 14-1 triumph. "This would have been a big day for any man," wrote Joseph M. Sheehan in the *New York Times*. "Under the circumstances that prevailed, it was a tremendous feat. Robinson fully justified [Branch Rickey's] break with tradition. He looked, as well as acted, the part of a real ballplayer."

Jackie went on to have a superb year with the Royals, leading the International League in batting (.349) and runs scored (113) and finishing second in stolen bases (forty). And though Robinson, who was named the league's Rookie of the Year, received most of the press, the other newcomers performed well, too. Twenty-five year old Roy Campanella, a squat 5'9½", 190-pound catcher, had already had nine years of professional experience, having learned his craft under the great Raleigh (Biz) Mackey with the Baltimore Elite Giants. With Nashua (New Hampshire) of the Class B New England League, "Campy" batted over .300 and led the team in home runs with fourteen. Don Newcombe, who turned twenty during the season, had pitched two years for the Newark Eagles. A 6'4" hard-throwing right-hander, he posted a 14-4 record for Nashua. Pitcher John Wright, who was with Robinson on Opening Day in Jersey City, played briefly with Montreal and then was sent down to Three Rivers (Quebec) of the Class C Canadian-American League, finishing the season with a 12-8 record. Roy Partlow, also a pitcher, followed the same course as Wright, going from Montreal to Quebec and posting a 10-1 mark.

Financially, the Negro leagues were largely unaffected by the first year of integration. The minor league newcomers had been dispatched to baseball's outposts, with Robinson, Wright and

Buck O'Neil. In 1950 former player Hallie Harding, then the sports editor of the *Los Angeles Sentinel*, wrote a story in which he maligned Negro baseball. O'Neil responded: "There are approximately two hundred men in the Negro league now. They earn from $200 to $800 monthly for five months. Some eighty-odd of these will draw this amount from winter league baseball. These salaries, of course, will not compare to those of [Ted] Williams or [Joe] DiMaggio with their multi-thousand dollar draws. But it beats the hell out of loafing on Beale Street [Memphis] or Eighteenth and Vine [Kansas City]."

January 22, 1951

Mr. T. Y. Baird, Pres.
Kansas City Monarchs
1418 No. 27th Street
Kansas City 2, Kansas

Dear Tom:

I have just returned to this country and found your correspondence awaiting me regarding the contract of player Elston Howard. In view of the probability of boys of this age entering the military service, we could not, at this time, be interested in purchasing him for $7500.00. I appreciate your offering the man to us.

Very truly yours,

Harry C. Jenkins,
Farm Director

HCJ:cjh
cc: Hugh Wise.

Above: Elston Howard. A native of St Louis, Missouri, and a graduate of Vashon High School, he was scouted by Dizzy Dismukes before joining the Kansas City Monarchs on June 28, 1948. Shortly thereafter, he replaced Johnnie Scott as the team's regular left-fielder, batting .306 with forty-nine hits, eleven home runs, four triples and eleven doubles in his rookie year.

Top right: Elston Howard was offered to other clubs before the Yankees signed him to a minor league contract in 1951. In 1954 he went to spring training with the Yankees but was sent down to the minors by manager Casey Stengel. With Kansas City of the American Association, he was the team's MVP, batting .331 with twenty-two home runs and fifteen triples.

Right: Jose Santiago. He broke the color line in the Central League when he signed with Dayton in 1948.

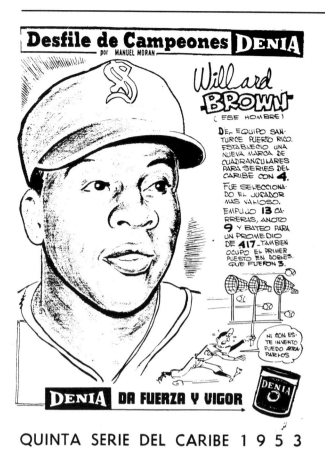

Desfile de Campeones DENIA
por MANUEL MORAN

Willard BROWN
(ESE HOMBRE)

DEL EQUIPO SAN-
TURCE PUERTO RICO.
ESTABLECIO UNA
NUEVA MARCA DE
CUADRANGULARES
PARA SERIES DEL
CARIBE CON **4.**

FUE SELECCIONA-
DO EL JUGADOR
MAS VALIOSO.
EMPUJO **13** CA-
RRERAS, ANOTO
9 Y BATEO PARA
UN PROMEDIO
DE **417**—TAMBIEN
OCUPO EL PRIMER
PUESTO EN DOBLES.
QUE FUERON **3.**

NI CON ES-
TE INVENTO
PUEDO ATRA-
PARLOS

DENIA DA FUERZA Y VIGOR

QUINTA SERIE DEL CARIBE 1 9 5 3

Left: Willard Brown. He was among the most respected hitters in the Puerto Rican Winter League, having hit a league record twenty-seven home runs during the 1947-48 season, when he also won the Triple Crown.

Below: Albert (Buster) Haywood. He began his career in 1935 with the Portsmouth (Virginia) Firefighters. He had a brief tryout with the Brooklyn Eagles in 1935 but didn't make the Negro major leagues until 1940 when Jim Taylor gave him a shot with the Birmingham Black Barons. While playing under the alias of "Khora", as a member of the Ethiopian Clowns, Haywood was named MVP of the 1941 *Denver Post* tournament after batting .423.

Partlow based in Canada, and Campanella and Newcombe in New Hampshire. Since Negro league teams all were located in the country's urban centers, there was little in the way of competition for the black baseball fan's dollar. As the owners tallied their receipts at season's end in 1946, there was no indication that the good times were about to end.

Just before the '47 season started, Branch Rickey announced that the Dodgers were purchasing Robinson's contract from Montreal; Jackie was about to break the major league color barrier. In July the Cleveland Indians purchased the contract of twenty-two year old Larry Doby from the Newark Eagles, making him the first black in the American League. Shortly thereafter, Willard Brown and Hank Thompson, both of the Monarchs, signed with the St. Louis Browns. For the Negro leagues, especially the Negro National League, the impact was devastating. The integration of major league baseball was embraced as an important step forward, one that spawned hope for a segment of society that lived under the constant constraints of segregation. Fans of black baseball, who'd supported the leagues for so many years, suddenly turned their

Gene Baker (standing) and Ernie Banks. When these two former Kansas City Monarchs infielders joined the Cubs as rookies in 1953, they became the first Negro double play combination in the major leagues. They were nicknamed "Bingo and Bango."

James (Junior) Gilliam. Before signing with the Brooklyn Dodgers, he played for the Baltimore Elite Giants from 1945 to 1950. In 1953 he was named the Dodgers' first-string second baseman, forcing Jackie Robinson, who'd been the regular second sacker, to divide time between third base and the outfield.

The Memphis Red Sox, 1949. (L to R). Sam Raif (bus driver), Larry Brown, Willie Wells, Sr., Joe Scott, Orlando Verona, Mora, Unknown, Cowan (Bubber) Hyde, Willie Wells, Jr., Bob Boyd, Willie Hutchinson, Unknown, Unknown, Neil Robinson, Ernest (Spoon) Carter, Unknown, Unknown, Casey Jones, Unknown, Leslie (Chin) Evans. Willie Wells and his son were the second father-son duo to play on the same team. Frank Duncan, Sr., and Frank Duncan, Jr., of the Monarchs were the first.

Saturnino Orestes Armas Arrieta Minoso. Known as Minnie, he started in black baseball with the New York Cubans in 1946. After retiring from the major leagues in 1964, he continued his career with Gomez Palacio of the Mexican League until 1973, when he collected 108 hits at age fifty-one. He returned to the Chicago White Sox in 1976 and again in 1980, making brief appearances that gave him the distinction of being the only major leaguer to play in five decades.

Joe Scott. In 1942, while playing military baseball in Dayton, Ohio, the New York Black Yankees gave Scott $500 to sign a notarized document stating that upon his release from the service, he would join their club. Scott finally joined the Black Yankees in 1946 and was paid $300 per month. However, by midsummer he jumped to the Pittsburgh Crawfords of the United States League where he earned $750 a month playing for owner Gus Greenlee.

Below: Nathaniel Peeples. In 1951 Peeples became the first Negro to sign a Southern League contract when he joined the Atlanta Crackers. Other Southern League teams boycotted the signing and Peeples was released. The owner's only comment was: "We tried, but no one else in the league would go along with us." Peeples batted .325 for Evansville of the Three I League in 1955.

Left: Bob Gibson (left) and Buck O'Neil. The Monarchs had a talent for signing the best ballplayers in the country. However, future Hall of Famer Gibson, who was just a schoolboy when this photo was taken in 1954, eluded the Kansas City club. The St. Louis Cardinals signed him in 1957, and he went on to win 276 games in his seventeen years in the major leagues.

Right: Elston Howard. In 1955 he became the first black to play for the New York Yankees. Manager Casey Stengel once remarked to longtime Yankee Hank Bauer, "It took the Yankees all these years to get a Negro ball player, and we had to get a slow one." Howard, who played for the Kansas City Monarchs in the early '50s, stole only nine bases during his fourteen-year major league career. His lack of speed didn't prevent him from being named the American League's Most Valuable Player in 1963.

Below: Manager Robert Clark (left) gives Roy Campanella, then a young catcher for the Baltimore Elite Giants, a few tips on how to play his position. Campanella became the starting catcher for the Elite Giants in 1937 at the age of sixteen. By the time he joined the Brooklyn Dodgers in 1948, he was already a seasoned veteran, having honed his skills not only in the Negro leagues but in the Puerto Rican Winter League, too. He was named the National League's Most Valuable Player in 1951, 1953 and 1955.

attention and curiosity almost exclusively toward the major leagues.

Teams with the misfortune of being based in or near a big league city, which included the entire NNL and several NAL clubs, soon were crippled by a sudden drop in attendance. The Newark Eagles, the New York Black Yankees and the New York Cubans suffered dismally as fans flocked to Ebbets Field to see Robinson. The Cleveland Buckeyes experienced a similar decline once Doby was signed. Even in Kansas City, 250 miles west of the nearest major league city, owners J.L. Wilkinson and Tom Baird were dismayed when their fans trekked to St. Louis whenever Robinson and the Dodgers visited. And with each passing year, the situation worsened.

Left: Willard Brown with Dallas of the Texas League. He won the 1951 Negro American League batting title with a .417 average. Parnell Woods of the Chicago American Giants was second (.375) and Henry Kimbro of the Baltimore Elite Giants was third (.374). Leonard Pigg of the Indianapolis Clowns, the 1949 batting champion, finished with a .362 average.

Below: A happy ending to a Cuban Winter League game in 1947. Jesse Williams of the Kansas City Monarchs is about to shake the runner's hand. Also in the picture (far right) is Lloyd (Ducky) Davenport, a member of the Chicago American Giants.

(L to R) Buck O'Neil, Vaughn, Robert Motley, Frank Duncan and Oscar Charleston before a game in 1949. In 1933, Henry L. Farrell of the *Chicago Daily News* wrote of Charleston: "The boy, Oscar Charleston, who played first base for the eastern team, could handle the same job on at least ten clubs in the big leagues. He is rated as the greatest of all Negro baseball players, and he handles the base with the grace and agility of Hal Chase."

(L to R) Jackie Robinson, Larry Brown, Luke Easter. Easter, who had played in the Negro leagues with the Homestead Grays, joined the Cleveland Indians in 1949 at age 35. His best years were 1950, 1951 and 1952, when he hit twenty-eight, twenty-seven and thirty-one home runs, respectively. His thirty-one homers in 1952 were second only to teammate Larry Doby's thirty-two in the American League.

Jackie Robinson listens as legendary Cardinal infielder Frankie Frisch offers some helpful hints.

The plight of the Newark Eagles was typical. In 1946 they drew 120,000 to Ruppert Stadium, which they leased from the Newark Bears, a New York Yankee farm club. By 1948, their attendance had plunged to 35,000. Effa Manley, who with her husband, Abe, had owned the team for thirteen years, had listened long enough to the sound of a silent stadium. After the '48 season she was forced to sell the team, blaming Branch Rickey for her predicament. "Our troubles started after Jackie Robinson joined the Dodgers," she complained. "[Negro fans] are stupid and gullible in believing that Rickey has any interest in Negro players other than the clicking of his turnstiles. Baseball has become a rich man's hobby and we're not rich."

The Memphis Red Sox, 1949. (L to R) Canidido Mara, Orlando Verona, Jose Colas, Unknown, manager Larry Brown. The Memphis Red Sox bolstered their lineup with Cubans during the twilight years of the Negro leagues. The Latin players presented no language problem for Brown, who was fluent in Spanish.

Above: (L to R) Comedian King Tut, Oscar Charleston, female star Connie Morgan, 1954. Charleston, the Negro leagues' greatest outfielder, was named manager of the Indianapolis Clowns for the '54 season, his last. He died on October 5 of that year.

Female stars Toni Stone (below) and Connie Morgan (right). At age fifteen, Toni Stone, from St. Paul, Minnesota, quit her girls' softball team and joined a men's team. Connie Morgan was a native of Philadelphia, where she played with the North Philadelphia Honey Drippers, an all-girls baseball team. When the popularity of Negro baseball started to decline after integration, the Indianapolis Clowns signed Morgan and Stone to contracts in hopes of bolstering attendance. Stone, who also played for the Monarchs, proved to be the best of the female baseball players. Mamie (Peanut) Johnson of Long Branch, New Jersey, also played for the Clowns.

Above: Sam Hairston (right) and Chicago White Sox manager Paul Richards. After injuries to both of their catchers in July of 1951, Hairston joined Chicago for four games, becoming the first black player to wear a White Sox uniform. He was a contact-hitter who batted .310 for the Colorado Springs Sky Sox in 1953, striking out only nineteen times in 535 at-bats. With the same team in 1955, he hit .350 with only thirty strikeouts in 546 at-bats.

Though disparaged for her remarks by the black press, Manley wasn't alone in suggesting that Rickey's motives weren't solely humanitarian. "When did [integration] happen?" asked former Chicago American Giants player/manager Dave Malarcher. "When the major leagues saw those 50,000 Negroes in the ball park [at the East-West game]. Branch Rickey had something else on his mind other than a little black boy. He had those crowds." In 1949 Tom Baird, still bitter about not being compensated for Robinson, wrote: "I have

Gene Richardson. A 5'10" left-hander, he was named Southern California High School Player of the Year in 1946. He won fourteen of fifteen starts, and during the three-game state championship series, Richardson allowed no earned runs while striking out fifty-four men in twenty-seven innings. The following year he joined the Kansas City Monarchs.

NEW YORK **Giants** OPERATED BY **NATIONAL EXHIBITION COMPANY**

E C. STONEHAM, *President*
ES S. FEENEY, *Vice-President*
P. FEELEY, *Treasurer*
RD T. BRANNICK, *Secretary*

OFFICES · 100 WEST 42ND STREET, NEW YORK 18, N. Y.
POLO GROUNDS · 157TH ST. & 8TH AVE, NEW YORK 30 N.Y.

January 31, 1949

Mr. T. Y. Baird,
Kansas City Monarchs Base Ball Club,
1418 No. 27th St.,
Kansas City, 2, Kansas.

Dear Mr. Baird:

Enclosed please find three copies of an agreement to cover the assignment of the contract of Player Henry Thompson by the Kansas City Monarchs to the Jersey City Giants. We have already received a terms acceptance from Thompson and have sent him a 1949 contract to sign. As soon as we have received two copies of the enclosed agreement signed by you and Thompson's signed contract, we will send you our check for $5,000.

I want to thank you for your courteous cooperation in this matter.

Sincerely yours,

Charles S. Feeney

Charles S. Feeney

Sale of Hank Thompson. When he joined the New York Giants in 1950, he became the first black to play in both the American and National leagues, having played with the St. Louis Browns in 1947.

been informed that Mr. Rickey is a very religious man. If such is true, it appears that his religion runs toward the almighty dollar.''

Maybe Rickey was simply looking for an edge. After all, he was hired to bring Brooklyn its first World Championship, and what better way to accomplish that than by signing the best of the black players? The Dodgers, in fact, almost reached their goal in 1947, when they lost the World Series to the New York Yankees in seven games. Whatever Rickey's motives may have been, the deed, heroic and welcomed as it was, effectively doomed the leagues.

The Cleveland Buckeyes, 1947. (L to R) Sam Jethroe, Tommy Harris, Bill Reynolds, Willie Grace, Joe Greene, Al Smith, Othello Renfroe, Archie Ware. Although Jethroe didn't report to the Montreal Royals until July 8, 1948, he still led the league in stolen bases. Clay Hopper, the manager of the Royals, said of Jethroe: ''He is fast in the outfield and an excellent hitter. I don't see how he can miss filling a berth in major league baseball.''

Birmingham Black Barons celebrate a 5-4 victory over the Kansas City Monarchs in the opener of the 1948 Negro American League playoffs. Seventeen-year-old Willie Mays (arrow) drove in the game-winner when he beat out an infield hit with two outs and the bases loaded in the eleventh inning.

Dan Bankhead slides home during an exhibition game. Bankhead won a combined twenty-four games with Nashua of the New England League and St. Paul of the American Association in 1948. Included in his twenty-four victories was a no-hitter against Springfield on July 25. The next year he won twenty games for Montreal of the International League. In 1948 Branch Rickey of the Dodgers said of Bankhead: "He's plenty strong and he has courage. He has improved; he's a little more at ease with white boys than he was when we had him over at Brooklyn in 1947."

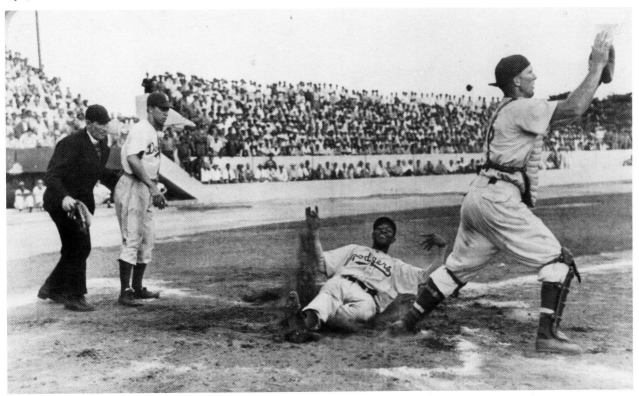

With Negro baseball's popularity fading, promoters hoped to revive interest with novelty teams. The Zulu Cannibal Giants was one team that reorganized after a twenty-year absence. Female baseball players were signed by the Indianapolis Clowns, who continued to tour until the early 1970s. Unfortunately, many people who saw the clown teams tended to regard all of Negro baseball as a comedy act. In reality, the vast majority of teams were very serious about their sport.

Desperate for ways to cut their losses, teams began slashing salaries, invoking a $6,000 salary cap for the '48 season. Sideline managers were released and replaced by player/managers. Long-time skippers such as Frank Duncan of the Monarchs and Candy Jim Taylor of the Chicago American Giants were among those victimized by the austerity program. Mostly, though, team owners sought to balance their books by selling players to major league clubs. It became a vital source of revenue.

With their players now under legally binding contracts, the leagues became a breeding ground for the majors. Building a championship team became secondary to finding players who had major league potential. Veteran players who'd been in the league for several years were replaced by youngsters who, it was hoped, someday soon would bring a bounty. Owners could command anywhere from $5,000 to $15,000 for a player, depending on his perceived potential.

Several teams sought to form working relationships with major league clubs as unofficial farm teams. The New York Cubans, who were owned by Alex Pompez, developed such an arrangement with the New York Giants, as did the Chicago American Giants with the St. Louis Browns. The Monarchs, who sold more players than any other

Lorenzo (Piper) Davis. As a member of the Birmingham Black Barons in 1946, he led the Negro American League with sixty-nine RBIs and batted .354, fifth in the league. In a game against the Baltimore Elite Giants, Joe Black struck him out with the bases loaded to preserve a victory. Davis got his revenge a day later, cracking a home run off Black to win the game.

(L to R) Olan (Jelly) Taylor, Neil Robinson, Bob Boyd, Verdel Mathis, Ernest (Spoon) Carter, bat boy. Nat Rogers has his foot in the dugout. In 1948 Boyd finished second in the Negro American League batting race with a .376 average and led the league with eight triples. His 114 hits, sixty-two runs and fifty-one RBIs also placed him among the league leaders.

team, targeted the New York Yankees, who had a farm team in Kansas City. "I want to give the Yankees first shot at any player on the Monarchs I think they are interested in," owner Tom Baird wrote in a letter to Lee MacPhail, the Yankees' farm director in the late '40s. When the Giants expressed interest in Hank Thompson, who had returned to the Monarchs after his brief stint with the St. Louis Browns in 1947, Baird wrote to MacPhail, "I told [the Giants] that I wanted $10,000 for Thompson. Do you want me to contact you before I make any deal with the New York Giants? I feel as though I am a part of the Yankee organization and I want to give you first chance at any players that your organization might want."

One of the first owners to cash in on selling players was Effa Manley, who in 1947 was reported to have received $15,000 from the Cleveland Indians for Larry Doby. A slugging second baseman, Doby was one of six players who went from the

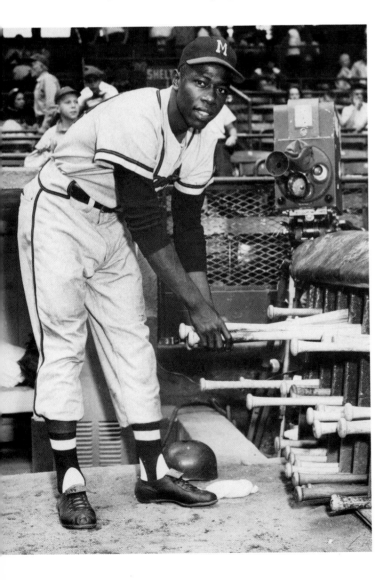

Above: Theolic Smith. A native of St. Louis, he began his professional career with the Claybrook (Arkansas) Tigers in 1935. Oscar Charleston, then the manager of the Pittsburgh Crawfords, saw him pitch and was so impressed that he signed him for the 1936 season. In 1951, he was the top pitcher in the Negro American League with a 15-2 record and 1.81 ERA for the Chicago American Giants. He ended his career in the Pacific Coast League.

Left: Hank Aaron. In 1952 he signed with the Indianapolis Clowns and played under manager "Buster" Haywood. Haywood told former New York Cubans owner Alex Pompez, then scouting for the New York Giants, about his great young outfielder. Shortly thereafter, another Giant scout went to see Aaron play, but was unimpressed after seeing Aaron get only one hit. Following the East-West Game, Aaron's contract was sold to the Boston Braves for $15,000. He finished the 1952 season at Eau Claire (Wisconsin) of the Northern League where he batted .336.

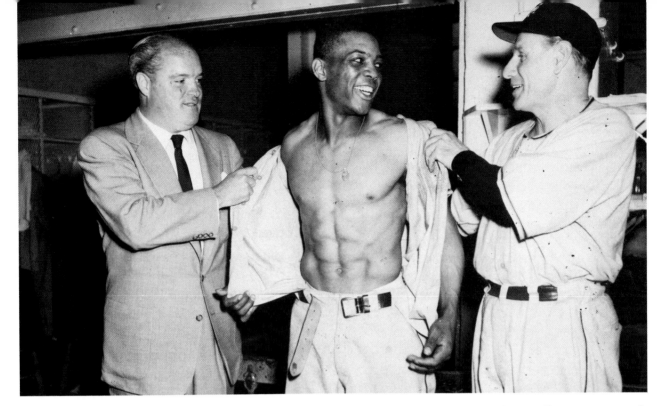

New York Giant owner Horace Stoneham (left) and manager Leo Durocher (right) with their great young outfielder, Willie Mays. Mays started his professional career as a fifteen-year-old with the Chattanooga Black Lookouts of the Negro Southern League. While with Chattanooga, he played against future major leaguers Bob Boyd of Knoxville, and William Greason and Jim Pendleton, both of Asheville, North Carolina.

black leagues to the majors without detouring through the minors. (The others were Hank Thompson, Willard Brown, Satchel Paige, Ernie Banks and Dan Bankhead.) For Effa, the transaction likely was the difference between selling the team and returning for her swan song in '48.

Even though all players were under contract, Branch Rickey still believed as late as 1948 that he could operate with impunity in pursuing Negro league players. His prey after the '48 season was Monte Irvin, the star outfielder of the Newark Eagles. Effa Manley, who was in a fight for survival,

The Cleveland Indians, 1954. The Indians won the American League pennant with a 111-43 record. There were four black players on the team, including Larry Doby (top row, far left), Al Smith (bottom row, far left), Dave Hoskins (bottom row, second from left) and Dave Pope (bottom row, third from right). Hoskins, a pitcher who lost his only decision in 1954, was 9-3 the previous season. Doby led the league in home runs (thirty-two) and RBIs (126). Pope led the Venezuelan Winter League in batting with a .345 average in 1953.

threatened to sue Rickey for compensation, citing a valid contract and the Negro league reserve clause. The Dodger president retaliated by releasing the story to the black press, which in turn vilified Effa for holding back her players and showing an unwillingness to sacrifice for the cause. Undaunted, the Eagle owner held her ground and Rickey eventually capitulated, announcing, "The Brooklyn baseball club is not interested in Irvin if Mrs. Manley's statement about the reserve clause or contract is true." It was an important victory for the leagues — if Branch Rickey couldn't get away with heisting players, then neither could anyone else. In

one of her last moves before selling the team, Manley sold Irvin to the New York Giants for a mere $5,000.

Years later, Monte Irvin told Jerry Izenberg of the *New York Post* that Effa used half of the money from his sale to buy a fur coat. "The last time I saw her," Irvin said, "which must have been thirty years later, she was wearing it.

"You made a good buy," Irvin told her.

"So did the Giants," Effa replied.

The following is a complete list of the players who made it to the majors after having played in the Negro leagues:

ATLANTA BLACK CRACKERS: Charlie Neal.

BALTIMORE ELITE GIANTS: Joe Black, Roy Campanella, Jim (Junior) Gilliam, Dave Hoskins.

BIRMINGHAM BLACK BARONS: Bill Greason, Jehosie Heard, Willie Mays, Artie Wilson.

CHICAGO AMERICAN GIANTS: Jim Pendleton, Joe Taylor.

CLEVELAND BUCKEYES: Sam Jones, Sam Jethroe, Al Smith, Quincy Trouppe.

HOMESTEAD GRAYS: Luke Easter, Luis Marquez, Bob Trice.

INDIANAPOLIS CLOWNS: Henry Aaron, Paul Casanova, Sam Hairston, Larry Raines, George Smith, John Wyatt.

KANSAS CITY MONARCHS: George Altman, Gene Baker, Ernie Banks, Frank Barnes, Ike Brown, Willard Brown, J.C. Hartman, Pancho Herrera, Elston Howard, Connie Johnson, Lou Johnson, Hank Mason, Satchel Paige, Curt Roberts, Jackie Robinson, Hank Thompson, Bob Thurman.

MEMPHIS RED SOX: Dan Bankhead, Bob Boyd, Vibert Clark.

NEWARK EAGLES: Larry Doby, Monte Irvin, Don Newcombe.

NEW YORK BLACK YANKEES: George Crowe.

NEW YORK CUBANS: Edmundo (Sandy) Amoros, Orestes (Minnie) Minoso, Ray Noble, Hector Rodriguez, Jose Santiago, Pat Scantlebury.

PHILADELPHIA STARS: James Clarkson, Charles Peete, Harry (Suitcase) Simpson.

Tom Alston. A native of North Carolina, he became the first nonwhite member of the St. Louis Cardinals in 1954. The rangy 6'5" first baseman played parts of four seasons in the major leagues, all with the Cardinals.

Many more players were sold, of course, but never made it beyond the minor leagues. Some, like Al Pinkston of the Chicago American Giants and Nate Peeples of the Kansas City Monarchs, spent more than ten years kicking around the

NATIONAL LEAGUE BASEBALL CLUB

OF *Boston, Inc.*

The Boston Braves

WILLIAM H. SOUTHWORTH
MANAGER
GEORGE E. (DUFFY) LEWIS
TRAVELING SECRETARY

BRAVES FIELD
COMMONWEALTH AVENUE
BOSTON, 15

March 9, 1951

Mr. T. Y. Baird, President
The Kansas City Monarchs
1418 North 27th Street
Kansas City 2, Kansas

Dear Tom:

I regret that there has been a delay in answering your letter
of February 19, offering the contract of pitcher Jim LaMarque
for $3500. The truth is we now have three colored boys at
Milwaukee, and if we take another, I am fearful that the club
would get top-heavy.

I am certain you can recognize this is a factor to be
considered. I firmly believe the pitcher would perform
creditably in AAA baseball, but we simply are in no position
to add him to our roster at this time.

Yours truly,

Harry C. Jenkins
Farm Director

jkp

Above: As this letter proves, once the color line was broken in 1946, black players still had to overcome a quota system. As the Negro leagues began to fade in the 1950s, so, too, did opportunities for minority players.

Monte Irvin. After selling Irvin to the New York Giants in 1948, Newark Eagles owner Effa Manley sold the team to a couple of businessmen who moved it to Houston. With the Negro National League having folded, the Houston Eagles joined the Negro American League for the 1949 season.

Ernie Banks (seated, center) pays a visit to Grambling State University. Standing to Banks' left is Dr. Waldo Emerson Jones, the school's president, and Eddie Robinson (standing front, right), holder of the record for the most victories by a college football coach. At far left is former Monarch Buck O'Neil. Dr. Jones was such a baseball enthusiast that he named himself coach of the team.

minors. Others, greats like Ray Dandridge, Thomas (Peewee) Butts and James (Buster) Clarkson, who would have been surefire major league stars ten years earlier, were in the late autumn of their careers when they reached the minors. And legends such as Cool Papa Bell, Wilber Rogan, Willie Wells and Martin Dihigo never even made it that far, their stellar careers already behind them.

For the leagues, selling players was strictly a stopgap remedy. No matter how many they sold, their fate was sealed. In 1948, the same year President Harry S. Truman desegregated the armed forces, there were only four black players in the majors — Robinson and Campanella with the

Left: Ray Noble (left) and manager Leo Durocher.
Below: (L to R) Jim Hearn, Hank Thompson, Bill Connelly.
Right: Monte Irvin.

In 1950 Thompson set a record for double plays started by a third baseman (43). Noble, whose real name was Rafael Miguel Noble, was a native of Cuba who played several years with the New York Cubans of the Negro National League. When Monte Irvin joined the New York Giants in 1949, there were only five blacks in the National League.

Dodgers, and Doby and Satchel Paige, who'd signed in midseason, with the Indians. As far as the Negro National League was concerned there might as well have been four on every team. While Doby, Paige and the Cleveland Indians were working their way toward a World Series championship, the NNL, plagued by another year of plummeting attendance, was forced to close operations at season's end. Fittingly, the Washington Homestead Grays, the circuit's power for so many years, won the pennant, their ninth in fourteen years, and then beat the Birmingham Black Barons in the World

Al Pinkston. He was 6'5½", weighed 227 pounds and played for the Cleveland Buckeyes, the Chicago American Giants and the New Orleans Creoles in the Negro leagues. He went on to have an outstanding minor league career, batting .352 with 2,368 hits in fifteen years.

William (Bonnie) Serrell. A native of Dallas, Texas, he was a sure-handed infielder who jumped from the Kansas City Monarchs to the Mexican League in 1945. Like others who left for Mexico, he was barred from the Negro American League, though he was allowed to return to the Monarchs in 1949. He was later sold to the San Francisco Seals of the Pacific Coast League, but by 1955 he was back in the Mexican League, batting .338 for Nuevo Laredo.

Series. (The Black Barons, who defeated the Monarchs in a playoff for the Negro American League pennant, featured, among others, a seventeen year-old outfielder named Willie Mays.)

By the time the NNL folded, the Grays had already been crippled by the loss of their two most prominent figures — Cum Posey and Josh Gibson. Posey, whose steady hand had guided the Grays since the early 1900s, died in March of 1946, while Gibson, thirty-seven, their great slugger and top drawing card for so many years, suffered a stroke and died in January of '47. After the league collapsed, the Grays, who'd lost $45,000 in 1947-48 according to one report, joined the new Negro American Association, whose teams were located mainly in North Carolina and Virginia. In the spring

Above: (L to R) Gene Hermanski, Pee Wee Reese, Marvin Rackley and Jackie Robinson. Robinson led the league in stolen bases in two of his first three years in the majors with a personal high of thirty-seven in 1949. Reese, with thirty thefts in 1952, was the last white player to lead the league in stolen bases.

Below: Orestes (Minnie) Minoso poses with bat and ball after extending his hitting streak to thirteen games in 1955. After playing three years for the New York Cubans of the Negro National League, he was signed by the Cleveland Indians and assigned to Dayton of the Central League in 1948. It was apparent that he didn't belong in the low minors when he batted .525 in the eleven games he played.

Left: John Ritchey. A former member of the Chicago American Giants, he became the first black player in the Pacific Coast League in 1948 when he signed with San Diego. The lefty-hitting catcher batted .323 for the season.

Larry Doby. He was one of six players to jump directly from the Negro leagues to the majors. Willard Brown, Hank Thompson, Dan Bankhead, Satchel Paige and Ernie Banks were the others. Brown appeared in only twenty-one games in 1947, for the St. Louis Browns, but his inside-the-park home run on August 13 was the first home run by a black player in major league history.

Above: Jackie Robinson played himself in "The Jackie Robinson Story," which was made in 1950. Actress Ruby Dee, who played the part of Jackie's wife, Rachel, said, "I recall that Jackie was a lovely and gentle man. I found him very easy to work with, most cooperative, as was Rachel, in helping me prepare for the role."

Below: (L to R) Unknown, Eddie Dwight, Wilber Rogan, John Donaldson, 1949. Donaldson was in Kansas City scouting for the Chicago White Sox and found time to rehash old times with Rogan and Dwight.

of '49, however, the Grays' suffered another crucial loss when financial backer Rufus (Sonnyman) Jackson died. Posey's brother, Seeward, managed to keep the team afloat for a couple of years but was forced to fold it after the 1950 season.

The Grays sold several players to big league organizations, including Josh Gibson, Jr., the son of their great slugger; Luis Marquez, the NNL batting champ in '48; and Sam Bankhead, who became the first black manager in "white" baseball when he was named skipper of Farnham of the Provincial League (Canada). None, though, attracted more attention than Luke Easter, a 6'-4", 240-pound slugging first baseman. He was thirty-four years old when he debuted with San Diego of the Pacific Coast League in 1949, batting .363 with twenty-five home runs and ninety-two RBIs. In 1950 Big Luke

was called up to the Cleveland Indians and went on to slug eighty-six home runs over the next three years. He played sparingly in 1953 and returned to the minors in 1954, finally retiring in 1964.

The New York Black Yankees also joined the Negro American Association in 1949, moving from New York and changing their name to the Black Yankee Travelers. In subsequent years they became mostly a traveling team, taking their last junket in 1955.

The rest of the Negro National League was absorbed by the Negro American League, which was divided into two divisions in 1949. The Eastern Division was comprised of the Louisville Buckeyes, who had moved from Cleveland, along with the Baltimore Elite Giants, the New York Cubans, the Philadelphia Stars and the Indianapolis Clowns, all

Above: (L to R) Roy Campanella, Emory James, Wesley Jackson and Junius (Rainey) Bibbs. Photo was taken at Crispus Attucks High School in Indianapolis, where Campanella addressed the students. Bibbs, a former Negro league infielder, taught for twenty-five years at the school.

Left: Buck O'Neil. In 1962 he became the first black coach in the major leagues when the Cubs signed him to work with their infielders. Upon hearing the news, former Monarch owner Tom Baird said, "O'Neil was a real leader. All the players respected him. He gave sound advice and seldom raised his voice when a player made a mistake. He's a credit to baseball and deserves the honor of becoming the first Negro coach in major league baseball."

(L to R) Taylor Hayes, Larry Brown, Hugh Cherry (owner of the Houston Eagles), Goose Tatum, Tom Hayes, Al Thompson. Tom Hayes was the owner of the Birmingham Black Barons when they won the Negro American League Championship in 1948. In 1950, he sold Willie Mays to the New York Giants for $15,000. He was also the only owner in Negro baseball who owned and flew his own airplane. Tatum, in addition to playing for the Harlem Globetrotters, was an outfielder/first baseman for the Indianapolis Clowns in the early '40s.

Memphis Red Sox owner W.S. Martin shakes hands with future major leaguer Bob Boyd. In the middle is Homer (Goose) Curry, manager of the Red Sox. Boyd played nine seasons in the majors, retiring with a .293 career batting average.

formerly of the NNL. The Western Division took in the Houston (formerly Newark) Eagles from the NNL, while maintaining its franchises in Birmingham, Chicago, Kansas City and Memphis.

Under the new structure, only two teams, the Monarchs and the Black Barons, showed a profit for 1949. In the South, where there were no blacks playing in any of the minor leagues, the Barons were still the only game in town for black fans. Kansas City, the league's sturdiest franchise through the years, continued to prosper, even though it had lost the services of its patriarch, J.L. Wilkinson. Wilkinson, whose affiliation with the Negro leagues had begun in 1920 with Rube Foster's original Negro National League, was seventy-four years old and suffering from failing eyesight when he sold his half interest in the team to co-owner Tom Baird in 1948.

The rest of the teams plodded through the '49 season, with the championship going to the Baltimore Elite Giants, who swept the Chicago American Giants in the playoff. The Elite Giants were led by the infield duo of Peewee Butts and Jim Gilliam and pitcher Joe Black, a graduate of Morgan State University. The first NAL team to bow out was the Cleveland Buckeyes. After moving to Louisville in '49, they returned the following year to Cleveland and disbanded in midseason.

Above: Roy Campanella, winner of the National League MVP Award in 1953, enjoys some music with Al Rosen of the Cleveland Indians, that year's American League MVP winner. In 144 games, Campanella rapped out 162 hits, including forty-one home runs and 142 RBIs. His RBI total was a major league record for catchers, breaking the mark of 133 set by Bill Dickey of the 1937 Yankees.

Below: Roy Campanella's wife, Ruthe, with a sportswriter and sons (L to R) David, Tony and Roy.

Elston Howard hits the deck. Following integration, black players became frequent targets when they stepped up to the plate. Former major leaguer Dixie Howell, who was with Jackie Robinson at Montreal in 1946, was amazed by Robinson's experience, calling it "the worst you ever saw. Man, you never saw nothing like that. Every time he came up, he'd go down. Man, did they ever throw at him."

It was during 1950 that an old problem — uneven scheduling — surfaced again. The Indianapolis Clowns, who won the first half of the split season, played thirty-nine games in the second half, while the New York Cubans played just eight and the Philadelphia Stars only twelve. The Clowns, who finished in third place, were awarded the title on the basis of having played more than thirty games. The league's credibility was diminishing rapidly.

Chuck Connors. The famous actor, who played briefly for the Brooklyn Dodgers and Chicago Cubs, poses with some of his fans. Connors also played in the Cuban Winter League for Almendares, teaming up with Negro leaguers Sam Jethroe and Monte Irvin.

Equally harmful was the dwindling newspaper coverage. As more and more players reached the majors, the black press, which had played such an important role in promoting the game before integration, began devoting less and less attention to the league. The new class of major leaguers was written of extensively, their triumphs extolled, their failures bemoaned. Newspapers rejoiced as each team dropped its barrier and acquired its first black player. Until 1955 the New York Yankees hadn't had a nonwhite player. On April 14 of that year, Elston Howard, who'd been purchased from the Monarchs for $7,500 in 1953, was inserted into the lineup by manager Casey Stengel. In its report the Associated Negro Press gave the exact time of Howard's debut (4:32 pm), proclaiming, "Howard's appearance at-bat signalled the fall of a dynasty that had been assailed on all sides as being anti-Negro. The fans gave Howard a well-deserved round of applause, marking his debut on the heretofore lily-white Bronx Bombers."

Above: Willie Kirkland. After a noteworthy minor league career, Kirkland enjoyed nine years in the major leagues before retiring in 1966. From 1968 to 1973, he played in Japan, where he hit 126 home runs and collected 559 hits in 703 games.

Below: The Memphis Red Sox and Kansas City Monarchs get together with Lionel Hampton after a game. Back row (L to R): Bullet Rogan, Eugene Collins, Frank Duncan, Hampton, Eugene Richardson, Larry Brown, Curt Roberts. Front: Earl Taborn (above), Willard Brown.

Edmundo (Sandy) Amoros and Joe Black. Amoros, a 5'7", Cuban born outfielder, played in 1950 for the New York Cubans. He led the International League in batting (.353) and four other offensive categories in 1952. Black, who had played for the Baltimore Elite Giants from 1943 to 1950, enjoyed his best major league season in 1952, when he posted a 15-4 record with fifteen saves and a 2.15 ERA for the Brooklyn Dodgers.

In 1945 President J. Alvin Gardner of the Texas League stated, "I imagine that Branch Rickey has been put under terrific pressure. I'm positive you'll never see any Negro players on any of the organized baseball teams in the South as long as the Jim Crow laws are in force." In 1953 James (Buzz) Clarkson (second from left) and Willard Brown (second from right) showed off their new Texas League (Dallas Eagles) uniforms as a sportswriter named Dixon and a team official looked on. Clarkson finished the season with 18 home runs and a .330 batting average, while Brown batted .310 and belted twenty-three home runs.

Still, despite mounting woes, the league trudged on. The New York Cubans, whose lone championship had come in 1947, dropped out of the circuit in 1951, leaving the league with eight teams and one division. For the second straight year, Indianapolis won both halves of the split season.

The Clowns opened the following season with an eighteen year old slugger named Henry Aaron in their outfield. It was rare at this point for a top prospect like Aaron to escape the tentacles of the big league scouts. From the early days of integration major league teams increasingly had been scouting black players in high school and college, hiring retired greats like John Donaldson and Bill Yancey to do their bird-dogging in an effort to avoid paying the middlemen — the Negro league owners. Some-

how, they missed Hammerin' Henry of Mobile, Alabama, though Indianapolis' traveling secretary Bunny Downs didn't. Downs signed Aaron in April of 1952 after seeing him play an exhibition game against his Clowns. Aaron didn't last long in Indianapolis, however. In midseason, after a New York Giant scout passed on the opportunity to pair Willie Mays and Hank Aaron in the same outfield, the Boston Braves bought Aaron's rights from the Clowns' owner, Syd Pollock.

Among the many players the scouts didn't miss was Bob Gibson, a seventeen year old phenom in Omaha, Nebraska, who was being wooed by the Monarchs in 1952. In his biography, *From Ghetto to Glory: The Story of Bob Gibson,* written by Phil

Kansas City Monarchs' games were popular with both white and black fans. For years blacks were not allowed to purchase box seats at the minor league Kansas City Blues games. There was no such ban, however, for Monarch games. Pictured in the front row here are (L to R) Betty Peeler, Christine Roberts (wife of Monarch second baseman Curtis Roberts), Charles Hinkle and Celia Peeler.

Al Andrews (left) and Elston Howard. They were the first two black players signed by the New York Yankees. Jackie Robinson's claim that the Yankees didn't want blacks on their team may have helped to get these players signed. Andrews never made the grade, but Howard became a fan favorite at Yankee Stadium.

Sam Jones (middle) savors historic game of May 12, 1955, when he fired a no-hitter against the Pittsburgh Pirates. It was the first time a black had accomplished that feat in the majors. In the ninth inning of that game, he walked the first three batters, then proceeded to strike out Dick Groat, Roberto Clemente and Frank Thomas.

Paul Smith of the Pittsburgh Pirates is forced at second base as Junior Gilliam throws to first to complete double play. Gilliam learned the finer points of infield play from Jesse (Hoss) Walker, a former infielder and his manager with the Baltimore Elite Giants in 1950.

Pepe, he explained why the Monarchs weren't an attractive alternative for a young player with major league ability and ambitions.

"Negroes were beginning to appear in major league uniforms more frequently, and thanks to Jackie Robinson and Branch Rickey and everybody who came after them, the Kansas City Monarchs were no longer the be-all and end-all for Negro ballplayers."

In the ensuing years, the Clowns fought to stave off the inevitable by fielding a team that was more reflective of their name. Resorting to clowning more and more, they also added two women, Toni Stone and Connie Morgan, to their roster. Both were accomplished semipro players and provided a boost at the gate. Stone later played for the Monarchs, who were in similar straits. In 1955 the Clowns, coming off another championship season, withdrew from the league. "Our relations with the league have always been pleasant," Pollock announced, "and we hope to cooperate fully in any way we can. But we desire to go independent to develop more younger players and give them a better chance to make the major leagues. We want to concentrate more on having the team and its comedians get in more of their stunts."

Indianapolis was out, and, by 1955, so were the Chicago American Giants, Philly Stars and New Orleans (formerly Newark and Houston) Eagles, all because of the waning interest in black baseball.

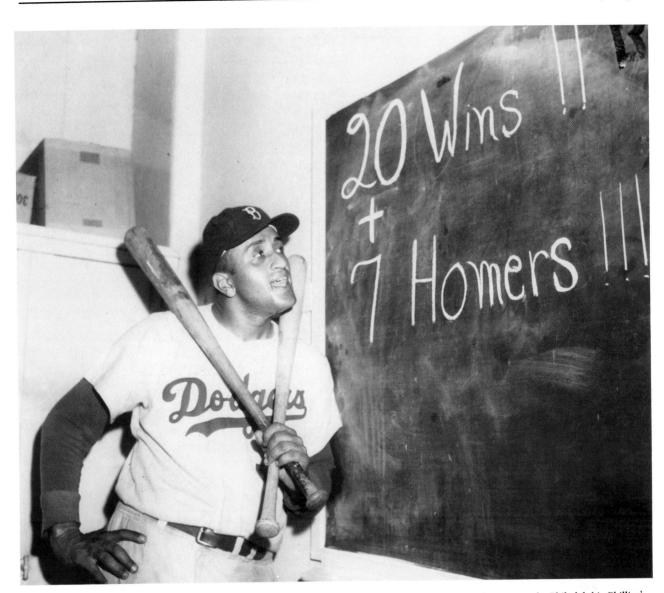

20 Wins !!!
+
7 Homers !!!

Don Newcombe. In 1955 he won twenty games for the Brooklyn Dodgers, second only in the National League to the Philadelphia Phillies' Robin Roberts (twenty-three). "Newk" was also renowned for his hitting ability, batting over .300 four times, belting fifteen home runs and driving in 108 runs in his ten-year major league career.

The American Giants knew the end was near in 1951, when only 500 fans showed up at Comiskey Park for their home opener against the Monarchs. In the years before integration, Opening Day was a cause for great celebration and could be counted on to attract anywhere from 15,000 to 20,000. Those days were gone forever. In 1955, a year after the U.S. Supreme Court, ruling in the case of Brown v. the Board of Education, had struck down the "separate-but-equal" doctrine, the Negro American League was comprised of just four teams — the Kansas City Monarchs, the Memphis Red Sox, the Birmingham Black Barons and the Detroit Stars.

For the Monarchs, 1955 marked their worst financial year. The major league Philadelphia A's moved to Kansas City that year and cut even deeper into the Monarchs' dwindling core of supporters. For owner Tom Baird, who'd started with the Monarchs as a promoter in the 1920s, the team was no longer a viable business venture. Though he'd sold more players than any other team owner had (seventeen of whom made it to the majors), there was no way he could compete once big league baseball moved into his backyard.

Baird found a buyer in Ted Rasberry, a former school teacher in Cedar Bluffs, Mississippi. Rasberry's affiliation with black baseball had begun in 1946, when he formed the Grand Rapids (Michigan) Black Sox and entered the team in a mixed league in the Midwest. In '53 he revived the Detroit Stars and joined the Negro American League. When he bought the Monarchs, giving him

The Kansas City Monarchs' bus burns on a Florida roadside after some clothing on board caught fire. As the bus burned, Buck O'Neil, the manager, overheard a voice on the police radio say, "Don't worry, it's just some niggers broke down."

Brooklyn Dodgers, 1953. (L to R): Gil Hodges, Roy Campanella, Jackie Robinson, Duke Snider, Carl Furillo. Robinson was viewed as the "ideal man for integration." Sam Lacy, the sports editor of the *Afro-American Newspapers*, wrote in the *1945 Negro Baseball Yearbook*: "[Robinson] would have neither the inferiority complex we must avoid nor the cocky bulldozing attitude we likewise should abandon."

two of the league's four teams, he moved them to Grand Rapids, though they returned to Kansas City for several games each year. Olan (Jelly) Taylor, the longtime first baseman for the Memphis Red Sox, was named manager, replacing Buck O'Neil.

The NAL, now virtually ignored by the press, stumbled through the late '50s and into the early '60s. During the final years, they were reduced to playing mostly small towns, the days of staging four-team doubleheaders before throngs in big league parks a distant memory. The East-West Game, a final link to the glory years, continued to be held annually, though the crowds were getting smaller and smaller. The 1957 Game featured two all-stars who were better known for their success in other realms. The starting pitcher for the West was Charlie Pride, a right-hander for the Memphis Red Sox. Pride became slightly more famous for his voice than his arm. For the East, Nat (Sweetwater) Clifton of the Detroit Stars started in left-field. A Harlem Globetrotter in the late '40s, Clifton, 6′6″, played from 1950 to 1958 with the New York Knicks and the Detroit Pistons of the National Basketball Association.

Above: Roy Campanella opened a liquor store in Harlem during the 1951 season. He used to park his custom made Cadillac El Dorado in front of the establishment. "When people see that car — and how can they miss it — they know I'm in the store," Campanella said. "That's when they come in and start buying. It's just good business. It ain't vanity."

Below: Campanella and Duke Snider. In 1955, after winning his third MVP Award in five seasons, Campanella stated, "I'm sorry that Snider couldn't have won it this year. But that doesn't mean I don't appreciate it. I couldn't tell you how much I appreciate the honor."

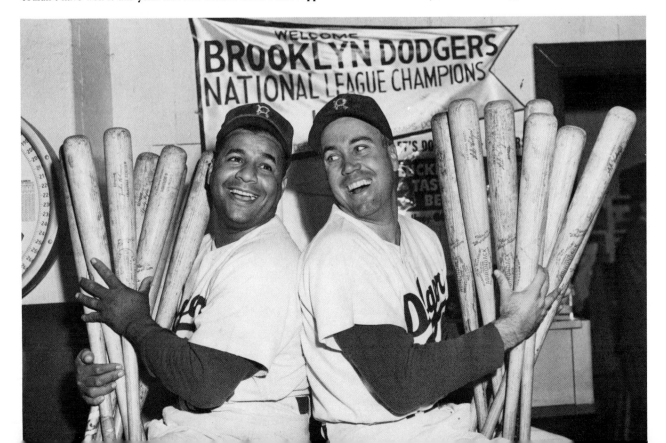

Jackie Robinson. At the persistent urging of a Boston city councilman, the Red Sox reluctantly gave tryouts to Jackie Robinson, Sam Jethroe and Marvin Williams in 1945. Though all performed well, none were invited back. It was because of this incident that Robinson was skeptical when the Brooklyn Dodgers first expressed interest in his services. "When Clyde Sukeforth, Dodger scout, approached me and said that he represented the Brooklyn Dodgers and had come to see me play, I almost laughed in his face," Robinson said.

Monarchs' Opening Day at Blues Stadium, 1953. In 1944 the *Negro Baseball Yearbook* reported that "at least one franchise in organized Negro baseball has grossed close to $300,000 in a single season, and paid higher salaries than are paid in the Class A Southern League."

(L to R) George Crowe, Billy Bruton, Jim Pendleton, Sam Jethroe of the Boston Braves. Photo was taken at spring training 1952 when they were known as the "Tan Quartet." During the winter of 1945-46, Crowe played professional basketball with the Renaissance team of New York.

In 1960, one year after the Boston Red Sox became the last major league team to employ a black player, the league was comprised of the Grand Rapids Monarchs, the Detroit-New Orleans Stars, the Birmingham Black Barons and the Raleigh (North Carolina) Tigers, who had replaced the Memphis Red Sox. Playing for the Monarchs that season was Ike Brown, an eighteen-year-old outfielder who often entertained the fans by playing all nine positions during games. Brown was signed by the Detroit Tigers in 1961 and became the last player from the Negro leagues to reach the majors when he made the Tigers' roster in 1969.

Larry Brown and Bob Boyd. After more than thirty years in the Negro leagues, Brown became a scout for the St. Louis Browns. Boyd was one of the top hitters to emerge from the Negro leagues.

SCORE CARD

Score by Innings	1	2	3	4	5	6	7	8	9	10	R	H
MONARCHS												
NEW YORK CUBANS												

KANSAS CITY MONARCHS		NEW YORK CUBANS	
Lineup and Probable Batting Order		**Lineup and Probable Batting Ord**	
25	Herb Souell, ...3b	8	Amando Yvanes ....
24	Curtis Roberts 2b	1	Edmundo Amoro ....
21	Gene Collins, ...cf	9	Pedroso Diaz ....
10	Elston Howard, ...lf	17	Rene Gonzalez ....
16	Bonnie Serrell, ...1b	12	Louis Loudon ....
29	Nat Peeples, ...c	20	Cleveland Clark ....
23	Tom Cooper, ...c	7	Walter Hardy ....
20	Bill Breda ....rf	5	Luis Caballoro ....
28	Ernest Banks, ...ss	11	John Johnson .... Ir
22	Buck O'Neil, ...1b-Mgr.	2	Renaldo Fernandoz ....
	PITCHERS	19	Willie Patterson ....
18	Bob Betts	15	Jose Fernandoz .... Mg
19	Frank Barnes		**PITCHERS**
26	Jim LaMarque	3	Pat Scantlebur
15	Cliff Johnson	18	Jose Gara
17	Mel Duncan	21	Riley Stew
12	George Walker	10	Raemundo Navarret
Wm. "Dizzy" Dismukes, Sec.		4	James "Pee Wee" Jenkin
		22	Robert Watso

The Kansas City Monarchs, who were strongly supported by the white business community, continued to scout and sign great players well into the mid-1950s. This 1951 scorecard features the names of Ernie Banks, Curtis Roberts, Elston Howard, Frank Barnes and Connie Johnson, all of whom made it to the major leagues. The Cubans' lineup also featured the names of a couple of players who made it to the majors — Pat Scantlebury and Edmundo "Amoro" [real name Edmundo Amoros], who was known as Sandy Amoros when he joined the Brooklyn Dodgers later in the year.

Sam Hill snags a fly ball. A native of Birmingham, Alabama, he was selected for the 1948 East-West Game. After a stint in the minors, he returned to the league and appeared in the 1957 East-West Game.

The Negro American League, practically unnoticed, dissolved after the 1963 season. The Monarchs, operating strictly as an independent, took their last gasp in 1964, with fifty-eight year old Satchel Paige making several appearances for them. After that, the only visible reminder of segregated baseball was the Indianapolis Clowns, who continued to take their act on the road into the early '70s. It is unfortunate that the freshest memories of black baseball were provided by the Clowns; they were a distant relative of the serious-minded teams that traversed the country during the glory years of the Negro leagues.

In their heyday, the Negro leagues rewarded their patrons with sights and memories every bit as wondrous and meaningful as those gleaned from the other side of the color line.

John Beckwith or Mule Suttles or Josh Gibson slugging a mammoth home run . . . . Bullet Rogan and Willie Foster locked in a scoreless, late-inning duel . . . . Bingo DeMoss, the game's greatest bunter, squeezing home a runner for Rube Foster's Chicago American Giants . . . . Jimmie Lyons or Oscar Charleston or Cool Papa Bell outrunning a long fly ball and depriving an unlucky batter of extra bases . . . . The Kansas City Monarchs and Homestead Grays, the class of the leagues, going head-to-head in the World Series . . . . The All-Stars displaying their enormous talents before a crowd of 40,000 or more in the East-West Game . . . . And, of course, Satchel Paige.

The essence of Negro baseball died in the fall of 1945, when Jackie Robinson signed his historic contract with the Montreal Royals. Until then, a player in the Negro American or Negro National League had climbed as high as he could; he was in the "majors." When the barrier came down, the leagues lost that "major league" status and instead became no more prestigious than a minor league. Their eventual passing prompted no elegies, no mourning. The Negro leagues were designed to provide opportunity where opportunity was denied and to offer vibrant proof that there was no legitimate basis for the major leagues' unwritten rule.

Their death was their ultimate victory.

Jackie Robinson and Branch Rickey. This photo was taken July 20, 1962 — three days before Jackie was inducted into the Hall of Fame and seventeen years after they shocked the baseball world with the announcement that Jackie had signed a contract to play for the Brooklyn Dodgers' farm team in Montreal.

Appendices

19th CENTURY BLACK PLAYERS
IN THE MINOR AND MAJOR LEAGUES

1878
INTERNATIONAL ASSOCIATION
John (Bud) Fowler, P, Lynn, MA

NEW ENGLAND LEAGUE
John (Bud) Fowler, P, Worcester, MA

1883
INTER STATE ASSOCIATION
Jack Frye, 1B, OF, Reading, MA

NORTHWESTERN LEAGUE
Moses (Fleet) Walker, C, Toledo, OH

1884
NORTHWESTERN LEAGUE
John (Bud) Fowler, P, Stillwater, MN

AMERICAN ASSOCIATION (Major league)
Moses (Fleet) Walker, C, Toledo, OH
Welday W. Walker, OF, 2B, Toledo, OH

1885
WESTERN LEAGUE
John (Bud) Fowler, 2B, Keokuk, IA
Moses (Fleet) Walker, C, Cleveland, OH
Welday W. Walker, OF, Cleveland, OH

EASTERN LEAGUE
Moses (Fleet) Walker, C, Waterbury, CT

COLORADO LEAGUE
John (Bud) Fowler, 2B, P, Pueblo, CO

1886
WESTERN LEAGUE
John (Bud) Fowler, 2B, Topeka, KS

EASTERN LEAGUE
George Stovey, P, OF, Jersey City, NJ
Moses (Fleet) Walker, C, Waterbury, CT
Frank Grant, 2B, Meriden, CT

INTERNATIONAL ASSOCIATION
Frank Grant, 2B, Buffalo, NY

PENN STATE ASSOCIATION
Jack Frye, 1B, OF, Lewiston, PA

1887
INTERNATIONAL ASSOCIATION
John (Bud) Fowler, 2B, Binghamton, NY
Frank Grant, 2B, Buffalo, NY
Robert Higgins, P, Syracuse, NY
Randolph Jackson, 2B, Oswego, NY
William Renfro, P, Binghamton, NY
George Stovey, P, OF, Newark, NJ
Moses (Fleet) Walker, C, Newark, NJ

OHIO STATE LEAGUE
Richard Johnson, C, OF, Zanesville, OH
N. Higgins, CF, Columbus, OH
Welday W. Walker, OF, Akron, OH
Sol White, 2B, 3B, Wheeling, WV

CENTRAL INTERSTATE LEAGUE
Richard Johnson, C, OF, Springfield/Peoria, IL

VERMONT LEAGUE
John (Bud) Fowler, 2B, P, Montpelier, VT

NORTHERN MICHIGAN LEAGUE
Alex Ross, 3B, Greenville, MI

1888
INTERNATIONAL ASSOCIATION
Frank Grant, 2B, OF, Buffalo, NY
Robert Higgins, P, Syracuse, NY
Moses (Fleet) Walker, C, Syracuse, NY

NEW ENGLAND LEAGUE
George Stovey, P, OF, Worcester, MA

TRI-STATE LEAGUE
Richard Johnson, OF, Zanesville/Lima, OH

CENTRAL INTERSTATE LEAGUE
John (Bud) Fowler, 2B,
Crawfordsvile/Terre Haute, IN

NEW MEXICO LEAGUE
John (Bud) Fowler, 2B, P, Santa Fe, NM

1889
INTERNATIONAL ASSOCIATION
Moses (Fleet) Walker, C, Syracuse, NY

MICHIGAN STATE LEAGUE
John (Bud) Fowler, 2B, Greenville, MI
Alex Ross, OF, 3B, Greenville, MI

ILLINOIS-INDIANA LEAGUE
Arthur Grace, P, 1B, Champaign, IL
R.A. Kelly, IF, Danville, IL

COLORADO STATE LEAGUE
William Castone, OF, Aspen, CO
George Taylor, C, IF, OF, Aspen, CO

MIDDLE STATES LEAGUE
Cuban Giants
All black team representing Trenton, NJ

Ben Boyd, OF	Jack Frye, 2B
Frank Grant, 2B	Abe Harrison, SS
Ben Holmes, 3B	John Nelson, P, OF
Harry Johnson, OF	William H. Seldon, P, OF
George Stovey, P, OF	Arthur Thomas, 1B, OF
Shep Trusty, P, OF	William T. Whyte, P, OF
Clarence Williams, C, 3B	George Williams, 1B, 3B
William H. Malone, P, 1B	

New York Gorhams
All black team representing Philadelphia, PA

Frank Bell, OF	Harry Cato, 2B, P, OF
Chamberlain, 1B	Emory, C
Nat Collins, P	Ross Garrison, SS
Andrew Jackson, 3B	Oscar Jackson, OF
Frank Miller, P	Barton, C, OF
Sol White, 2B, 3B	John Nelson, P, OF
George Stovey, P, OF	

1890
EASTERN INTER-STATE LEAGUE
Cuban Giants
All black team representing York, PA

Ben Boyd, OF	Jack Frye, 1B, P
Ross Garrison, SS	Good, OF
Abe Harrison, SS	Andrew Jackson, 3B
Oscar Jackson, OF	William H. Malone, P, 3B
William H. Selden, P, OF	William Terrill, SS
Arthur Thomas, C, 1B	Sol White, 2B, 3B
George Williams, 1B, 3B	William T. Whyte, P, OF
William Jackson, C, 2B, OF	

ATLANTIC ASSOCIATION
Frank Grant, 2B, OF, Harrisburg, PA
Clarence Williams, C, 3B, SS, Harrisburg, PA

CENTRAL INTERSTATE LEAGUE
John (Bud) Fowler, 2, Galesburg, IL
Richard Johnson, C, OF, Peoria, IL

ILLINOIS—IOWA LEAGUE
John (Bud) Fowler, 2B,
Sterling/Galesburg, IL, Burlington, IA

NEW YORK—PENN LEAGUE
R.A. Kelly, IF, Jamestown, NY

NEW YORK STATE LEAGUE
George Stovey, P, Troy, NY

1891
CONNECTICUT STATE LEAGUE
Cuban Giants
All black team representing Ansonia, CT

Frank Bell, OF	Ben Boyd, OF
Cam, OF	Jack Frye, 1B, P
Frank Grant, 2B	Bob Jackson, OF
William Jackson, 2B, OF	John Nelson, P, OF
George Stovey, P, OF	Sol White, 3B
Clarence Williams, C	

NEW YORK—PENN LEAGUE
R.A. Kelly, IF, Jamestown, NY

1892
NEBRASKA STATE LEAGUE
William Castone, P, OF, Lincoln/Kearney, NE

John (Bud) Fowler, 2B, Lincoln/Kearney, NE
Frank Maupin, C, 3B, Plattsmouth, NE
John Patterson, OF, Plattsmouth, NE
John Reeves, 3B, Plattsmouth, NE
George Taylor, 1B, Beatrice, NE

CALIFORNIA LEAGUE
Wilds, C, Stockton, CA

1894
NEW ENGLAND LEAGUE
Herbert, OF, Pawtucket, RI
James Robinson, P, OF, Pawtucket, RI

1895
MICHIGAN STATE LEAGUE
William Binga, C, Adrian, MI
Pete Burns, C, Adrian, MI
John (Bud) Fowler, 2B, 3B, Adrian/Lansing, MI
Vasco Graham, C, Adrian, MI
Joe Miller, P, Adrian, MI
George Wilson, P, OF, Adrian, MI

WESTERN INTERSTATE LEAGUE
Sol White, 2B, 3B, Fort Wayne, IN

KANSAS STATE LEAGUE
Bert Wakefield, 1B, 2B, Emporia, KS

1896
KANSAS STATE LEAGUE
Bert Wakefield, 1B, 2B, Emporia/Atchison, KS
Bert Jones, P, OF, Atchison, KS

COLORADO STATE LEAGUE
George Taylor, 1B, Denver, CO

1897
KANSAS STATE LEAGUE
Bert Jones, P, OF, Atchison, KS

1898
KANSAS STATE LEAGUE
Bert Jones, P, OF, Atchison, KS
Bert Wakefield, 2B, Salina, KS

IRON AND OIL LEAGUE
All black team representing Celoron, NY

Al Baxter, OF	Billy Booker, 2B
Eddie Day, SS	George Edsall, OF
William Kelly, 3B	John Mickey, P
William Payne, OF	John Southall, C
Walter Williams, P	Edward Wilson, P
Clarence Wright, 1B	

1899
CANADIAN LEAGUE
Bill Galloway, OF, Woodstock, Ontario

MAJOR AND MINOR LEAGUE TITLES
1946-1955

Titles won by black players from 1946-1955, the first ten years after integration of the minor leagues (The major leagues were integrated in 1947.).

Henry Aaron

1953	Jacksonville	South Atlantic League	Average .362
1953	Jacksonville	South Atlantic League	Runs 115
1953	Jacksonville	South Atlantic League	Hits 108
1953	Jacksonville	South Atlantic League	Doubles 36
1953	Jacksonville	South Atlantic League	RBI 125
1953	Jacksonville	South Atlantic League	Total bases 305
1955	Milwaukee	National League	Doubles 37

Tom Alston

| 1953 | San Diego | Pacific Coast League | Games played 180 |

Edmondo (Sandy) Amoros

1953	Montreal	International League	Runs 128
1953	Montreal	International League	Hits 190
1953	Montreal	International League	Doubles 40
1953	Montreal	International League	Average .353

Gittian Applegate

1952	Superior	Northern League	Strikeouts 188
1952	Superior	Northern League	Walks 143
1952	Superior	Northern League	Shutouts 4

Alfred Armour (played under the name of Buddy Wilson to protect his college football eligibility)

| 1949 | Farnham | Provincial League | Average .342 |

Dan Bankhead

1948	Nashua	New England League	Wins 20
1948	Nashua	New England League	Strikeouts 248
1948	Nashua	New England League	Walks 128
1949	Montreal	International League	Strikeouts 176
1949	Montreal	International League	Walks 170

Ernie Banks

| 1954 | Chicago | National League | Games played 154 |
| 1955 | Chicago | National League | Games played 154 |

Quincy Barbee
| 1949 | St. Jean | Provincial League | Home runs 23 |

Charles Beamon
| 1955 | California | California League | Winning percentage 1.000 |
| 1955 | California | California League | Earned run average .136 |

Julio Becquer
| 1952 | Drummondville | Provincial League | Triples 11 |
| 1953 | Havana | Florida International League | Triples 11 |

Carlos Rodriquez Bernier
1949	Bristol	Colonial League	Runs 136
1949	Bristol	Colonial League	Stolen bases 89
1950	Bristol	Colonial League	Stolen bases 53
1951	Tampa	Florida International League	Runs 124
1951	Tampa	Florida International League	Triples 21
1951	Tampa	Florida International League	Stolen bases 51
1952	Hollywood	Pacific Coast League	Runs 105
1952	Hollywood	Pacific Coast League	Stolen bases 65
1952	Hollywood	Pacific Coast League	Stolen bases 29

Bob Boyd
1951	Sacramento	Pacific Coast League	Stolen bases 41
1952	Seattle	Pacific Coast League	Triples 18
1952	Seattle	Pacific Coast League	Average .320
1955	Houston	Texas League	Games 163
1955	Houston	Texas League	At-bats 635
1955	Houston	Texas League	Hits 197

Alonso Brathwaite
| 1951 | Farnham | Provincial League | At-bats 507 |

Bill Bruton
1950	Eau Claire	Northern League	Games 128
1950	Eau Claire	Northern League	At-bats 545
1950	Eau Claire	Northern League	Runs 126
1950	Eau Claire	Northern League	Stolen bases 66
1951	Denver	Western League	Triples 27
1952	Milwaukee	American Association	Games 154
1952	Milwaukee	American Association	At-bats 650
1952	Milwaukee	American Association	Runs 130
1952	Milwaukee	American Association	Hits 211
1953	Milwaukee	National League	Stolen bases 26
1954	Milwaukee	National League	Stolen bases 34
1955	Milwaukee	National League	At-bats 636
1955	Milwaukee	National League	Stolen bases 25

Marshall Bridges
| 1955 | Amarillo | West Texas-New Mexico League | Winning percentage .933 |

Ellis Burton
| 1955 | Phoenix | Arizona-Mexico League | Runs 140 |

Joe Caffie
1952	Duluth	Northern League	Triples 18
1952	Duluth	Northern League	Total bases 271
1952	Duluth	Northern League	Average .342

1952	Duluth	Northern League	At-bats 500
1952	Duluth	Northern League	Runs 105
1952	Duluth	Northern League	Hits 171

Roy Campanella
| 1953 | Brooklyn | National League | RBIs 142 |

Orlando Cepeda
| 1955 | Kokomo | Mississippi Ohio Valley League | Average .393 |

Ed Charles
| 1952 | Quebec | Provincial League | Triples 11 |
| 1955 | Corpus Christi | Big State League | Runs 135 |

Virbert Clark
1955	Charlotte	South Atlantic League	Starts 32
1955	Charlotte	South Atlantic League	Innings pitches 262
1955	Charlotte	South Atlantic League	Hits 260
1955	Charlotte	South Atlantic League	Runs 116

James (Buster) Clarkson
| 1948 | St. Jean | Provincial League | Home runs 29 |
| 1954 | Beaumont/Dallas | Texas League | Home runs 42 |

Wes Covington
| 1955 | Jacksonville | South Atlantic League | Average .326 |
| 1955 | Jacksonville | South Atlantic League | Total bases 270 |

George Crowe
1949	Pawtucket	New England League	RBIs 106
1950	Hartford	Eastern League	Games 139
1950	Hartford	Eastern League	Runs 122
1950	Hartford	Eastern League	Hits 185
1950	Hartford	Eastern League	Doubles 43
1950	Hartford	Eastern League	Average .353
1950	Hartford	Eastern League	Total bases 314
1951	Milwaukee	American Association	Hits 189
1951	Milwaukee	American Association	Doubles 41
1951	Milwaukee	American Association	RBIs 119
1951	Milwaukee	American Association	Total bases 316
1954	Toledo	American Association	Games 154
1954	Toledo	American Association	Hits 197
1954	Toledo	American Association	Doubles 38
1954	Toledo	American Association	RBIs 128
1954	Toledo	American Association	Total bases 343

Ray Dandridge
| 1950 | Minneapolis | American Association | At-bats 627 |
| 1950 | Minneapolis | American Association | Hits 195 |

Johnny Davis
1953	Ft. Lauderdale	Florida International League	Games 140
1953	Ft. Lauderdale	Florida International League	Runs 117
1953	Ft. Lauderdale	Florida International League	Total bases 292
1953	Ft. Lauderdale	Florida International League	Home runs 35
1953	Ft. Lauderdale	Florida International League	RBIs 136

Larry Doby
| 1952 | Cleveland | American League | Runs 104 |

1952	Cleveland	American League	Home runs 32
1952	Cleveland	American League	Strikeouts 111
1952	Cleveland	American League	Slugging percentage .541
1953	Cleveland	American League	Strikeouts 121
1954	Cleveland	American League	Home runs 32
1954	Cleveland	American League	RBIs 126

Samuel Drake

| 1955 | Macon | South Atlantic League | Stolen bases 24 |

Humberto (Chico) Fernandez

1954	Montreal	International League	Games 155
1954	Montreal	International League	At-bats 596
1954	Montreal	International League	Doubles 44

Silvio Garcia

1950	Sherbrooke	Provincial League	Average .365
1950	Sherbrooke	Provincial League	RBIs 116
1950	Sherbrooke	Provincial League	Home runs 21

Horace Garner

| 1951 | Eau Claire | Northern League | Average .359 |
| 1951 | Eau Claire | Northern League | Stolen bases 44 |

James (Junior) Gilliam

| 1951 | Montreal | International League | Runs 117 |
| 1953 | Brooklyn | National League | Triples 17 |

Reuben Gomez

| 1950 | St. Jean | Provincial League | Strikeouts 140 |

Orlando Gonzalez

| 1955 | Cocoa | Florida State League | Stolen bases 53 |

Jim (Mudcat) Grant

1954	Fargo-Moorhead	Northern League	Wins 21
1955	Keokuk	Indiana-Illinois-Iowa League	Wins 19
1955	Keokuk	Indiana-Illinois-Iowa League	Winning percentage .864

William Greason

1953	Oklahoma	Texas League	Starts 34
1953	Oklahoma	Texas League	Wins 16
1953	Oklahoma	Texas League	Walks 162
1953	Oklahoma	Texas League	Wild pitches 13

Samuel Hairston

| 1953 | Colorado Springs | Western League | Doubles 42 |
| 1955 | Colorado Springs | Western League | Average .350 |

Charles Byron Harmon

1950	Olean	Pony League	Games 125
1950	Olean	Pony League	At-bats 551
1950	Olean	Pony League	Hits 206
1950	Olean	Pony League	Doubles 47
1950	Olean	Pony League	RBIs 139
1951	Olean	Pony League	Doubles 37
1951	Olean	Pony League	RBIs 143
1952	Burlington	Indiana-Illinois-Iowa League	Games 124
1952	Burlington	Indiana-Illinois-Iowa League	Hits 153
1952	Burlington	Indiana-Illinois-Iowa League	Doubles 34

William Harrell

| 1953 | Reading | Eastern League | Sacrifices 14 |

Dave Hoskins

| 1952 | Dallas | Texas League | Innings pitched 280 |
| 1952 | Dallas | Texas League | Wins 22 |

Elston Howard

| 1954 | Toronto | International League | Triples 16 |

Monford (Monte) Irvin

| 1951 | New York | National League | RBIs 121 |

Sam Jethroe

1948	Montreal	International League	Stolen bases 18
1949	Montreal	International League	At-bats 635
1949	Montreal	International League	Runs 154
1949	Montreal	International League	Hits 207
1949	Montreal	International League	Triples 19
1949	Montreal	International League	Stolen bases 89
1950	Boston	National League	Stolen bases 35
1951	Boston	National League	Stolen bases 35
1953	Toledo	American Association	Runs 137
1953	Toledo	American Association	Walks 109
1955	Toronto	International League	Stolen bases 24

Clifford (Connie) Johnson

| 1951 | St. Hyacinthe | Provincial League | Strikeouts 172 |
| 1952 | Colorado Springs | Western League | Strikeouts 233 |

Sam Jones

1950	Wilkes-Barre	Eastern League	Strikeouts 160
1951	San Diego	Pacific Coast League	Innings pitched 267
1951	San Diego	Pacific Coast League	Strikeouts 246
1951	San Diego	Pacific Coast League	Walks 175
1955	Chicago	National League	Losses 20
1955	Chicago	National League	Strikeouts 198
1955	Chicago	National League	Walks 185
1955	Chicago	National League	Hit batsmen 14

Willie Kirkland

1953	Maryville	Mountain States League	RBIs 164
1953	Maryville	Mountain States League	Triples 24
1953	Maryville	Mountain States League	Games 125
1953	Maryville	Mountain States League	Strikeouts 142
1954	St. Cloud	Northern League	Average .360
1954	St. Cloud	Northern League	Triples 11
1955	Sioux City	Western League	Runs 117
1955	Sioux City	Western League	Home runs 40

Eddie Locke

| 1953 | Amarillo | West Texas-New Mexico League | Shutouts 5 |

Hector Lopez

| 1952 | St. Hyacinthe | Provincial League | Runs 115 |
| 1953 | Williamsport | Eastern League | At-bats 567 |

David Mann

| 1952 | Stockton | California League | Stolen bases 59 |

1953	Thetford Mines	Provincial League	Stolen bases 47
1953	Thetford Mines	Provincial League	Runs 114
1953	Thetford Mines	Provincial League	Triples 11
1954	York	Piedmont League	Stolen bases 88

Luis Angel Margues

| 1950 | Portland | Pacific Coast League | Triples 19 |
| 1950 | Portland | Pacific Coast League | Stolen bases 38 |

Willie Mays

1954	New York	National League	Triples 13
1954	New York	National League	Average .345
1954	New York	National League	Slugging percentage .667
1955	New York	National League	Triples 13
1955	New York	National League	Home runs 51
1955	New York	National League	Slugging percentage .659

Clinton McCord

1951	Paris	Mississippi Ohio Valley League	Games 121
1951	Paris	Mississippi Ohio Valley League	Runs 132
1951	Paris	Mississippi Ohio Valley League	Hits 173
1951	Paris	Mississippi Ohio Valley League	Total bases 283
1951	Paris	Mississippi Ohio Valley League	Home runs 16
1951	Paris	Mississippi Ohio Valley League	Average .363
1952	Paris	Mississippi Ohio Valley League	Hits 189
1952	Paris	Mississippi Ohio Valley League	Total bases 304
1952	Paris	Mississippi Ohio Valley League	Average .392

Willie McCovey

| 1955 | Sandersville | Georgia State League | RBIs 113 |

Roman Gomez Mejias

| 1954 | Waco | Big State League | Doubles 49 |

Orestes (Minnie) Minoso

1951	Cleveland-Chicago	American League	Triples 14
1951	Cleveland-Chicago	American League	Stolen bases 31
1952	Chicago	American League	Stolen bases 22
1953	Chicago	American League	Stolen bases 25
1954	Chicago	American League	Triples 18

Charlie Neal

1951	Lancaster	Inter-State League	Runs 114
1951	Lancaster	Inter-State League	Triples 24
1955	Montreal	International League	Triples 14

Dick Newberry

| 1952 | Duluth | Northern League | Stolen bases 36 |

Don Newcombe

1947	Nashua	New England League	Wins 19
1947	Nashua	New England League	Strikeouts 186
1948	Montreal	International League	Winning percentage .739
1951	Brooklyn	National League	Strikeouts 164
1955	Brooklyn	National League	Winning percentage .800

Clyde Parris

| 1954 | Elmira | Eastern League | Average .311 |
| 1954 | Elmira | Eastern League | Doubles 40 |

| 1954 | Elmira | Eastern League | RBIs 90 |

Roy Partlow
| 1946 | Three Rivers | Provincial League | Winning percentage .909 |

Charles Peete
| 1954 | Portsmouth | Piedmont League | Hits 170 |

Jim Pendleton
1950	St. Paul	American Association	Triples 19
1951	St. Paul	American Association	Runs 116
1952	Montreal	International League	At-bats 595

Arthur Pennington
1952	Keokuk	Indiana-Illinois-Iowa League	Average .349
1952	Keokuk	Indiana-Illinois-Iowa League	Total bases 246
1952	Keokuk	Indiana-Illinois-Iowa League	Runs 126

Alonso Perry
| 1955 | Mexico Reds | Mexican League | Triples 15 |
| 1955 | Mexico Reds | Mexican League | RBIs 122 |

Alfred Pinkston
1951	Farnham	Provincial League	Doubles 32
1952	St. Hyacinthe	Provincial League	Average .360
1952	St. Hyacinthe	Provincial League	Home runs 30
1952	St. Hyacinthe	Provincial League	RBIs 121
1952	St. Hyacinthe	Provincial League	Total bases 305
1954	Savannah	South Atlantic League	Average .363
1954	Savannah	South Atlantic League	Hits 180

Dave Pope
1950	Wilkes-Barre	Eastern League	Triples 18
1951	Wilkes-Barre	Eastern League	Total bases 256
1951	Wilkes-Barre	Eastern League	Triples 13
1951	Wilkes-Barre	Eastern League	Runs 113
1952	Indianapolis	American Association	Average .352
1953	Indianapolis	American Association	Triples 14

Vic Power
1950	Drummondville	Provincial League	Triples 10
1952	Kansas City	American Association	Doubles 40
1952	Kansas City	American Association	Triples 17
1952	Kansas City	American Association	Total bases 324
1953	Kansas City	American Association	At-bats 622
1953	Kansas City	American Association	Hits 217
1953	Kansas City	American Association	Average .349

Frank Robinson
| 1954 | Columbia | South Atlantic League | Runs 112 |

Humberto Robinson
1951	Farnham	Provincial League	Innings pitched 263
1951	Farnham	Provincial League	Hits 244
1954	Jacksonville	South Atlantic League	Innings pitched 276
1954	Jacksonville	South Atlantic League	Wins 23
1954	Jacksonville	South Atlantic League	Strikeouts 243
1954	Jacksonville	South Atlantic League	ERA 2.41
1955	Toledo	American Association	Winning percentage 778

Jackie Robinson

1946	Montreal	International League	Runs 113
1946	Montreal	International League	Average .349
1947	Brooklyn	National League	Stolen bases 29
1949	Brooklyn	National League	Stolen bases 37
1949	Brooklyn	National League	Average .342

Hector Rodriguez

1951	Montreal	International League	At-bats 609
1951	Montreal	International League	Stolen bases 26
1951	Montreal	International League	Hit by pitch 9

Kenneth Andre Rogers

1955	St. Cloud	Northern League	Runs 133
1955	St. Cloud	Northern League	Hits 175
1955	St. Cloud	Northern League	Average .342
1955	St. Cloud	Northern League	Total bases 301

Jose Santiago

1951	Wilkes-Barre	Eastern League	Wins 21
1953	Dallas	Texas League	Wins 21
1953	Dallas	Texas League	ERA 1.59

Pat Scantlebury

1953	Texarkana	Big State League	Wins 24
1953	Texarkana	Big State League	Starts 33
1953	Texarkana	Big State League	Complete games 28
1953	Texarkana	Big State League	Innings pitched 286
1953	Texarkana	Big State League	Hits 314
1953	Texarkana	Big State League	Strikeouts 177

Joe Scott

| 1950 | Farnham | Provincial League | Runs 89 |
| 1950 | Farnham | Provincial League | Walks 124 |

Angel Scull

1951	Wellsville	Pony League	Stolen bases 60
1952	Key West/Havana	Florida International League	Triples 14
1952	Key West/Havana	Florida International League	Stolen bases 54

Halbert Simpson

| 1955 | Tyler | Big State League | Doubles 38 |

Harry (Suitcase) Simpson

1949	Wilkes-Barre	Eastern League	Runs 125
1949	Wilkes-Barre	Eastern League	Home runs 31
1949	Wilkes-Barre	Eastern League	RBIs 120
1949	Wilkes-Barre	Eastern League	Total bases 311
1950	San Diego	Pacific Coast League	Triples 19
1950	San Diego	Pacific Coast League	RBIs 156

Antonio Sanchez (Tony Taylor)

| 1955 | St. Cloud | Northern League | Triples 10 |
| 1955 | St. Cloud | Northern League | Stolen bases 38 |

Alphonse (Al) Smith

| 1949 | Wilkes-Barre | Eastern League | Triples 17 |

Quincy Smith

| 1951 | Paris | Mississippi Ohio Valley League | At-bats 506 |

1951	Paris	Mississippi Ohio Valley League	Hit by pitch 13
1952	Paris	Mississippi Ohio Valley League	Runs 124
1953	Paris	Mississippi Ohio Valley League	Stolen bases 49

R. C. Stevens
| 1954 | Durham-Graham | Carolina League | Games played 140 |

Willie Tasby
1954	York	Piedmont League	Home runs 27
1954	York	Piedmont League	RBIs 121
1954	York	Piedmont League	Games 142

Felix Torres
1955	Douglas	Georgia State League	At-bats 446
1955	Douglas	Georgia State League	Runs 101
1955	Douglas	Georgia State League	Triples 36

Robert Lee Trice
1952	St. Hyacinthe	Provincial League	Wins 16
1952	St. Hyacinthe	Provincial League	Winning percentage .842
1953	St. Hyacinthe	Provincial League	Wins 21

James Tugerson
1953	Knoxville	Mountain States League	Games pitched 46
1953	Knoxville	Mountain States League	Starts 37
1953	Knoxville	Mountain States League	Shutouts 5
1953	Knoxville	Mountain States League	Wins 29
1953	Knoxville	Mountain States League	Innings 330
1953	Knoxville	Mountain States League	Hits 306
1953	Knoxville	Mountain States League	Runs 168
1953	Knoxville	Mountain States League	Strikeouts 286

Leon Wagner
1954	Danville	Mississippi Ohio Valley League	Hits 160
1955	St. Cloud	Northern League	Home runs 29
1955	St. Cloud	Northern League	RBIs 127

Bill White
1953	Danville	Carolina League	Stolen bases 21
1954	Sioux City	Western League	Hits 183
1954	Sioux City	Western League	Home runs 30
1954	Sioux City	Western League	Stolen bases 40
1954	Sioux City	Western League	Total bases 321

Maury Wills
1951	Hornell	Pony League	Stolen bases 54
1952	Hornell	Pony League	At-bats 533
1952	Hornell	Pony League	Runs 108
1952	Hornell	Pony League	Stolen bases 54
1952	Hornell	Pony League	Hits 160

Artie Wilson
1949	San Diego/Oakland	Pacific Coast League	Average .348
1949	San Diego/Oakland	Pacific Coast League	Stolen bases 47
1950	Oakland	Pacific Coast League	At-bats 848
1950	Oakland	Pacific Coast League	Runs 168
1950	Oakland	Pacific Coast League	Hits 264
1952	Seattle	Pacific Coast League	Hits 216
1953	Seattle	Pacific Coast League	Triples 14

| 1954 | Seattle | Pacific Coast League | At-bats 660 |
| 1954 | Seattle | Pacific Coast League | Triples 16 |

Bob Wilson

1952	St. Paul	American Association	Games 154
1955	Montreal	International League	At-bats 599
1955	Montreal	International League	Hits 190
1955	Montreal	International League	Doubles 41

Jim Zapp

| 1952 | Paris | Mississippi Ohio Valley League | Home runs 20 |
| 1952 | Paris | Mississippi Ohio Valley League | RBIs 136 |

Bibliography

The following books and newspapers were consulted in the research for this work:

Minority Newspapers:
Amsterdam News, New York, NY
California Eagle, Los Angeles, CA
Chicago Defender, Chicago, IL
Chicago Whip, Chicago, IL
Houston Observer, Houston, TX
Indianapolis Freeman, Indianapolis, IN
Kansas City Call, Kansas City, MO
New York Age, New York, NY

Omaha Bee, Omaha, NE
The People's Voice, New York, NY
Philadelphia Tribune, Philadelphia, PA
Pittsburgh Courier, Pittsburgh, PA
Rising Sun, Kansas City, MO
St. Louis Argus, St. Louis, MO
Topeka Plain Dealer, Topeka, KS

Daily and Weekly Newspapers:
Adrian Daily Times and Expositer, Adrian, MI
Baltimore Evening News, Baltimore, MD
Binghamton Daily Leader, Binghamton, NY
Chicago American, Chicago, IL
Chicago Daily Journal, Chicago, IL
Chicago Daily News, Chicago, IL
Chicago Sun Times, Chicago, IL
Chicago Tribune, Chicago, IL
Cincinnati Enquirer, Cincinnati, OH
Dubuque Daily Times, Dubuque, IA
Evening Eagle Beacon, Wichita, KS
Frankfort Evening Telegram, Frankfort, NY
Indianapolis Star, Indianapolis, IN
Kansas City Journal, Kansas City, MO
Kansas City Kansan, Kansas City, KS
Kansas City Post, Kansas City, MO
Kansas City Star, Kansas City, MO
Kansas City Times, Kansas City, MO

Little Falls Daily Transcript, Little Falls, MN
Memphis Appeal, Memphis, TN
New York Daily Mirror, New York, NY
New York Daily News, New York, NY
New York Post, New York, NY
New York Times, New York, NY
Omaha Daily Bee, Omaha, NE
St. Louis Globe Democrat, St. Louis, MO
St. Louis Post Dispatch, St. Louis, MO
Sioux City Journal, Sioux City, IA
Smith Centre County Newspaper, Smith Centre, KS
South Side Signal, Babylon, NY
Tyler Morning Telegraph, Tyler, TX
Washington Post, Washington, DC
Washington Daily News, Washington, DC
Wichita Eagle, Wichita, KS
York Gazette, York, PA

Books:

Chambers, Ted. *The History of Athletics and Physical Education at Howard University.* Vantage Press, 1986.

Daniel, Clifton, editor in chief. *Chronicle of the 20th Century.* Chronicle Publications, 1987.

———, editorial director. *Chronicle of America.* Prentice-Hall, 1989.

Durocher, Leo with Ed Linn. *Nice Guys Finish Last.* Simon and Schuster, 1975.

Grun, Bernard. *The Timetables of History.* Simon and Schuster, 1975.

Manley, Effa and Leon Hardwick. *Negro Baseball Before Integration.* Adams Press, 1976.

Marden, Charles F. and Gladys Meyer. *Minorities in American Society.* D. Van Nostrand Company, 1973.

Minoso, Orestes (Minnie) with Fernando Fernandez and Bob Kleinfelder. *Extra Innings, My Life in Baseball.* Regnery Gateway, 1983.

Paige, Satchel with David Lipman. *Maybe I'll Pitch Forever.* Doubleday & Company, Inc., 1961.

Peterson, Robert. *Only the Ball Was White.* Prentice-Hall, 1989.

Reichler, Joseph, ed. *Baseball Encyclopedia.* MacMillan Publishing Company, 1988.

Rogosin, Donn. *Invisible Men.* Atheneum, 1983.

Sowell, Thomas. *Ethnic America.* Basic Books, Inc., 1981.

Trouppe, Quincy. *Twenty Years Too Soon.* S & S Enterprises, 1977.

Veeck, Bill with Ed Linn. *Veeck As In Wreck.* G. P. Putnam, 1962.

White, Sol. *Base Ball Guide.* 1907.

Whitehead, Charles E. *A Man and His Diamonds.* Vantage Press, 1980.

Photo Credits

All photos are from the Author's Collection unless listed below.

Chapter 1

Oberlin College Archives, 12; Village of Babylon Historical & Preservation Society, 13; Oberlin College Archives, 14; Robert Brashier, 15; Mark Rucker, 16; National Baseball Library, 17; Joe Overfield, 19; National Baseball Library, 20, 21; Mark Rucker, 22; Michigan Historical Collection, 22, 23, 24, 25; National Baseball Library, 26; 27, 28; Dave Shury, 28; Woodstock Museum, 29; Martich Black History Collection, Willard Library, Battle Creek, MI, 30.

Chapter 2

R.C. Pullam, 32, 33, 34; Doris Foster, 35; Roosevelt Butler, 36; Reach Sporting Guide, 36; R.C. Pullam, 37; Mike Anderson, 38, 39; Jay Sanford, 40; Reach Sporting Guide, 41; National Baseball Library, 42, 43; Doris Foster, 44; Roosevelt Butler, 45; Doris Foster, 46, 47; Afro American Museum, 48; David Kemp, 49; Stearns County Historical Society, 50; Roosevelt Butler, 51; Mark Rucker, 53; Waseca County Historical Society, 54; Stearns County Historical Society, 55; Martich Black History Collection, 56.

Chapter 3

R.C. Pullam, 58; Smithsonian Institution, 59; *Kansas City Call,* 59; Carolyn Cassio, 60; Lloyd Thompson Estate, 60; Carolyn Cassio, 61; Donn Rogosin, 62; Larry Lester, 62; National Baseball Library, 63; Norman Johnson, 64; National Baseball Library, 64, 65; *Indianapolis Freeman,* 65; Wilbur Rogan, Jr., 66; Roger Whirworth, 67; Lloyd Thompson Estate, 67; National Baseball Library, 69, 70, 71; Doris Foster, 71, 72; Washburn University, 73; Junior Maxie, 74; Afro American Museum, 74; Wilbur Rogan, Jr., 75; *Kansas City Times,* 75; George Brace, 76; Dick Clark, 76; Pipestone County Museum, 77; National Baseball Library, 77; Afro American Museum, 78; National Baseball Library, 78, 79; University of Kansas Libraries, 80, 81; Mark Rucker, 82; Robert Brashier, 83; National Baseball Library, 83.

Chapter 4

Junior Maxie, 86, 87; Wilbur Rogan, Jr., 89; Allie Mae Ragland, 89; James Bell, 90; Minnie Martin, 91; Junior Maxie, 92; John B. Holway, 92; Lloyd Thompson Estate, 93; Larry Lester, 94, 95; Lloyd Thompson Estate, 96; Passon's Sporting Goods Store, 97; Marsha Grayson, 98; Doris Foster, 99; National Baseball Library, 101; Lloyd Thompson Estate, 102; Alberta Penn Gilmore, 103; James (Cool Papa) Bell, 103; Doris Foster, 104; National Baseball Library, 104, 105; Bertha Duncan, 105; Chet Brewer, 106; Doolittle Young, 107; Dave Shury, 107; Wilbur Rogan, Jr., 108, 109; *Pittsburgh Courier,* 110; John Holway, 110; Wilbur Rogan, Jr. 111; National Baseball Library, 112, 113; Philadelphia Afro American Museum, 113; National Baseball Library, 114; Pittsburgh State University, 116; Kansas Collection, 116; Fred Langford, 117; William Lowe, 117; *Spring Valley Gazette,* 117; National Baseball Library, 118; *Indianapolis Freeman,* 118; National Baseball Library, 119; Black Archives Mid America, 119.

Chapter 5

Jimmy Crutchfield, 122; Elsie Mitchel, 123; Robert Williams, 123; Maurice Wiggins, 124; *Kansas City Call,* 124; James Bell, 125; Bobby Conway, 126; Georgia Dwight, 126; Lloyd Thompson Estate, 126; James Bell, 127; Minnie Martin, 128; John Holway, 129, 131; Chester Brewer, 131; Dick Powell, 132; Robert Williams, 133; Smithsonian Institution, 134; National Baseball Library, 135, 136; Lilla Lewis, 138; Doris Foster, 138; National Baseball Library, 139, 140; Chester Blanchard, 140; Wilbur Rogan, Jr., 140; Sarah Brown, 141; Zonobia Wright, 142; Doris Foster, 143; Georgia Dwight, 143; Doris Foster, 144; Donafae Collins, 144; Wilbur Rogan, Jr., 145; *Kansas City Call,* 145; Beinecke Rare Book and Manuscript Library, Yale University, 146; Jay Sanford, 147; Minnie Martin, 148; Chester Blanchard, 148; Ted Chambers, 148; Normal (Tweed) Webb, 149; *Kansas City Call,* 149, 150; National Baseball Library, 150; Clara Bell, 151; Charles Zomphier Family 151.

Index